PROLEGOMENA TO FORMAL LOGIC

Prolegomena to Formal Logic

B. H. SLATER
Department of Philosophy
University of Western Australia

Avebury

Aldershot · Brookfield USA · Hong Kong · Singapore · Sydney

Published by

Avebury

Gower Publishing Company Limited,
Gower House, Croft Road, Aldershot,
Hants. GU11 3HR, England

Gower Publishing Company,
Old Post Road, Brookfield, Vermont 05036
USA

British Library Cataloguing in Publication Data
Slater, B.H. 1936-
    Prolegomena to formal logic. ----
    (Avebury series in philosophy)
    1. Language - Philosophical perspectives
    I. Title
    401

BC
7/
.S58
1988

ISBN 0 566 05693 3

Printed and bound in Great Britain by
Antony Rowe Limited, Chippenham, Wiltshire

Contents

Preface

In this book, I develop Prior's formalization of indirect speech, and demonstrate the usefulness of Hilbert's choice calculus. In chapter one I provide some of the general philosophical background, in the theory of Meaning, against which these matters gain their significance; in chapters two and six I focus on Prior, first investigating how his view of indirect speech gives us a paradox-free account of Truth, later showing how his view can be extended to locate the objects of Propositional Attitudes. Hilbert's epsilon terms, by being selection functions, turn out to clarify the theory of Conditionals, which is the topic of chapter three; but their main application comes in chapters four and five, in connection with re-modelling the traditional theory of Reference, and systematizing the more modern study of Pronouns.

There are a good number of different problems to investigate, and attack, within the literature on each of these areas, so the chapters are each collections of a variety of detailed points, as well as developments of one single theme. The theme in the first chapter is the relation of general philosophical matters to concerns in the present work: it is therefore more free ranging than the others, talking about the altered view of Semantics involved, the relevance of Aesthetics, and Wittgenstein, and also, in a specific way, about a general conclusion of the book, why thoughts must all be directed at reality.

Many of my own thoughts are directed at the extant literature, here often incorporated into the text. This not only makes the work largely self-contained, it also enables me to demonstrate many of my points exactly, and fully document and acknowledge my indebtedness to other writers. It should be very evident, however, that the book provides a highly novel treatment of most of the issues it addresses. By investigating the <u>applicability</u> of certain formal systems, the book, in the first place, adopts a style of approach which is rather uncommon, but the results obtained are also surprising in their own right. Even the literary style may be something of a shock, for it is hardly discursive or argumentative, as has become increasingly common of late: it is more factual, even snappy, making the whole something of a handbook or workbook rather than a quiet afternoon's read. I touch on some of the reasons for this change at the beginning.

One other matter is non-standard. I follow the tradition of symbolising 'and' and 'or' by means of '.' and 'v', but in place of the hook symbol, usually taken to formalise 'if', I write 'D': 'if p, q' is then 'p D q', making 'D', of course, properly a symbol not for 'if' but for 'only if' - it can be read 'determines'. I symbolise 'p if and only if q', i.e. 'p iff q', as 'p CD q'.

I am indebted to Barker House, Subiaco for their professional services during the final stages of the production of this book.

B.H.Slater,
Nedlands, W.A.,
August, 1987.

1 Meaning

SEMANTICS

If one is an Empiricist, the notion that our language might be perfect tends to be an incoherent one. Not only do such ideal objects and abstractions as God and The Self have no place in one's scheme of things, it seems they cannot have a place: isn't the natural world necessarily one without perfection? After all, supposedly man has evolved through various stages, and is in the process of improving himself even now - where 'improvement' means adapting to the human and physical context, which itself is variable and accidental. If man is an organic and growing creature in this way, how can his language be anything other than an ad hoc assembly of workable bits and pieces, with no grand design or pattern, no laws or regularities governing, and running right through the whole? Language, it seems, must be rough and ready, on an Empiricist view, for it is then a physical product, moulded by time and circumstance, and so cannot be a wonder, a marvel, or a miracle.

Such an outlook is no doubt one attitude of mind which conceives of 'Semantics' in terms of a second language, i.e. a more ideal and perfect language than the one we have been obliged to work with in our everyday interactions with men, though no doubt a second language which can be a guide to that complex and confused, more primitive one. For how can such pure and beautiful entities as

p	-p		p	q	p.q
T	F		T	T	T
F	T		T	F	F
			F	T	F
			F	F	F

in terms of which propositional logic may be defined, be in anyone's first language? If one looks from an Empiricist perspective, then, it seems, they cannot be: these tables can at best be helpful rationalisations and simplifications of any prior state of affairs.

On the other hand, how can an Empiricist rule out such neatness, such precision and completeness? On his own principles he cannot really say these cannot be, for that is to make an *a priori* judgement about the world, which is just what is ruled out on his understanding. From an Empiricist point of view there might be a high probability that the world contains no perfections, but whether or not it is perfect in any place is for experience to find out, and experience can defeat even the most highly confirmed expectations. It is true that if one hears stories of a miracle, the inherent unlikelihood of this would inevitably cast doubt on the credibility of the testimony, but, as we shall see more exactly in the next section, that still leaves marvels and wonders to be known about not through testimony, but through one's own personal experience.

Such an experience, of course, is already available to most of us in our operation with language, as Rationalists like Chomsky have urged with respect to Syntax. Our infinite capacities with this can hardly be thought to be acquired, and even if we have an innate idea of them, the same question arises, from an Empiricist point of view: how can this be? How can mankind have developed such a non-empirical skill, for instance the power to generate, endlessly, well formed sentences? Of course we do have such infinite abilities, and one doesn't think anything about it, normally, so it is the Empiricist who has got himself into the odd point of view: as Kant realised, by trying to be an external witness to something given, rather than an internal participant in something one must create. It is no accident that Freedom of Choice is equally in this 'do it yourself' category, and that Empiricists also have difficulty with that, along with God, the Self, and Mathematics. Indeed the little marvel I shall be spending most time discussing in this book, namely Hilbert's epsilon term (naturalised)

exFx,

along with its compatriots in second order logic,

ePFP,

and quantified propositional logic,

epFp,

is expressly a choice function [1], which apart from being a wonder, and perfect, and existing, thus formalises one aspect of our ability to act in the world, and not just observe it: by the end of this book we shall find it has justified a Kantian Metaphysic in considerable fine detail.

For a start, as we shall shortly see, this choice function is one agent which gives us a new view of Semantics, since it fuses its Semantics with its Syntax in a quite novel way. Syntax, traditionally, has consisted in such distinctions as that between Indicative, Exclamatory, Imperative and Interrogative forms of speech, and those between Syncategoremata, and Categoremata. Semantics, by contrast, has been thought to be concerned with the quite separate 'meaning' of such sentences and words, and in particular, therefore, with the meaning of formal symbols. But the meaning of these symbols must be given in one's first language, hence they are attempts to give abbreviated expression to natural speech. Symbols are not always thought of as such abbreviations, but only if abbreviation is its aim can 'formal logic' be evaluated, which is the major purpose of this book: the validation of a certain logical symbolization, providing a 'prolegomena' to any future formal logic. But the reverse process, it will turn out, is also involved, namely the validation and endorsement of natural speech, since Semantics itself will become modified, as a result of this understanding of symbols, so that the Semantics of a language does not stand behind the language, invisibly giving it meaning by ghostly support from a second place, but inside the language acting merely as an echo, reflection, or repetition of other parts of it. This will come about, technically, as we shall see in chapter two, through the phenomenon of Semantic Closure, which, since it was first mooted by the Positivists, has been thought to be an impossibility, only to be obtained at the expense of radical inconsistency, and illogicality. But Semantic Separation is what is an impossibility: there is no second language to be learnt to learn the meaning of English, one must merely learn to speak it, i.e. say it the right way - with the right kind of accompaniment. Intonation, breathing and stress are the sort of things one must learn, for instance, to separate Exclamatory, Indicative, Imperative and Interrogative forms of speech; order and composure help one to separate Categoremata by means of Syncategoremata. Saying words with meaning and expression is thus not at all like saying them with a translation in mind, any more than playing a piano with life and gusto is playing the piano from a score. Indeed it is often quite the reverse, since it involves knowing the music 'by heart'. The meaning and life, if they are there, are part of the speech and playing, not an additional object beyond the speech and playing.

If one doesn't use language with relish and spirit this may well be because one doesn't understand it, and, moreover, think that to understand it one must observe it, not use it. The temptation then indeed will be to try to construct a more simple 'ideal', seemingly better structured language that one can speak, and which, because it is then meaningful to one, might come to be thought of as the 'Semantics' of one's proper, natural, tongue. But this is an alienation phenomenon deriving from inattention to the original material - one doesn't learn the meaning of English by learning French, or by constructing some quite distinct symbol scheme. The meaning of English becomes manifest in this latter kind of way only if there is the possibility of incorporation of the symbols into the natural speech, so that abbreviation alone relates them. Like the proper name and pet name in 'Henry 'Bugs' Segal', we then have, in the same language, a formal, and a familiar word for the same thing - making formal and familiar names a paradigm of the true relation between language and its Semantics. But there is no way to grasp the taming effect of the right symbols, i.e. the comprehension provided by the right abstract or precis, other than to experience it: and that we shall be doing throughout this book.

Examples of such comprehension are to be found in the standard truth tables for 'and' and 'or'. It has been said against the former that it improperly does not restrict the use of '.' to cases where there is a 'rapprochement' between the sentences conjoined, while it has been said against the latter that it improperly does not restrict the use of 'v' to cases where neither disjunct is known to be true. As a result, it is common to want to cut down the 'Procrustean' formal symbols in order the fit the shorter 'natural bed'. The present approach will be the very reverse of this, for in fact the resources of natural speech are not fully exploited, unless that speech is allowed to follow, totally, the formal rules. Indeed, it is a fallacy to think that disjunctions do not follow from known disjuncts, and it is an even grosser one to think that conjunctions cannot conjoin anything whatever. Like traditional fallacies such as Affirming the Consequent, and The Conversion of O Propositions, these new fallacies may well be committed by the mass of mankind, but elementary logic teaching still seeks to eradicate the traditionally bad thought patterns, and likewise it should seek to do so with the more modern errors of the mind. Above all logic should not seek to recognise these new howlers by making them a dignified part of some 'logic of conversation', for whatever the expectations of chat, its friendly, but thereby inhibited ways prevent one from experiencing the full resources of logic, and indeed life.

It is Grice, primarily, who has tried to make formal logic compatible with natural speech by honouring this charitable, though restricted, context [2]. He has four principal dimensions of 'co-operation' which he thinks guide, or should guide, our verbal dealings with one another, but, as an overall assessment of natural language interaction, his notion of 'co-operation' already betrays a remarkable confusion between Logic and Ethics. Language use requires sharing meanings, but co-operating over little else, and an individual who doesn't do that bare minimum departs from us even before it comes to talk. Likewise, operating with money requires there to be common values for coins and other tokens, but beyond that there are no binding rules about what an individual must do with his money - even prudential rules one must obey only if one wants to be prudent. Logic does not require we 'assert neither more nor less than is appropriate for the purpose at hand', for one can say exactly what one pleases, whensoever one wishes to say it, and leave one's hearers agape at the disconnection, if it is there. Logic does not require we 'assert what is true and have adequate grounds for it', for one may make up complete fairytales, whensoever it takes one's fancy - and not just to fool people or keep them on their toes. And whether what is said is true is for the world to judge, so don't rely on a rule of logic to assure you of it. Logic does not require we shall 'only mention what is relevant to the purpose at hand', for one may wander all over the place, and be totally beside the point. And who says there is a purpose at hand? Perhaps one is speaking idly. Logic does not require we 'use linguistic means no more elaborate than what is needed to convey what we are asserting', since one could well be not asserting, for one thing, and one can be as elaborate as it is possible to be, if one likes - what else is that part of language for if it is not to be employed? Non-assertion, purposelessness, irrelevance, untruth, groundlessness are quite appropriate as far as logic is concerned: it is merely if one still wants to be empiricist that the reverse concepts come to dominate one's mind, for within that conception of language, language is not just a joy to

6

use, an aesthetic pleasure to fool around with, and make up unfounded stories of immense complexity with, with no immediate bearing on anything going on now. Language, on that view, if it is 'non-assertive' is thought merely to be exclamatory, to express feelings, imperative, to direct action, or interrogative, to seek expression, direction, or fact, but there is nothing in 'assertive' i.e. <u>indicative</u> speech which is 'non-empirical': that area, it seems, is just where the joyless conception of language applies and gets its foothold. But the non-aesthetic conception of speech is, in fact, treading water even at this point, and is almost as big an irrelevance there as it is out of place with the other three moods. That, of course, does not stop books about this conception being a good read as pieces of literature, for they merely come, as a result, to rival Science Fiction, rather than Science Fact, in their interest. Moreover the wicked can even enjoy Tom Stoppard's thought, in this connection: 'Remember, one can convince anyone of anything - so long as they are clever enough' - for many intelligent philosophers have been entranced by the Verification Principle. But the one rule philosophers should obey, if they are to be logical rather than empirical, is simply to be logical, and beyond that, what Prior dismissed as merely 'the social prerequisites of tolerable conversation' are only weakly confirmed inductive guides, which do not even have sociological generality.

Thus in one notorious case, to be discussed more fully in chapter three, it becomes essential to realise that 'If p, then I'll eat my hat/the moon is made of green cheese/I'm a dutchman' can be said, although what follows 'p', in this case, is quite arbitrary. Likewise with 'p, and ...' and 'p, or ...': the contingency of thoughts requires the former gap to be able to be filled at will; the possibility of being categorical likewise needs the latter opening to be unrestricted. Indeed the notions of arbitrariness, contingency, will and non-restriction are intimately linked with a number of central matters to be discussed throughout this book, besides the above epsilon terms. That, of course, does not mean everything is arbitrary. Indeed, as we shall see in chapter four, realising the full potential of logic requires realising the quite certain natural fact, which Empiricists doubt from the very beginning, namely that the existence of the world is necessary. Why is there something rather than nothing? Because, as Kant might have said, necessarily there are ideals, real existent ideals. Understanding the syntax of epsilon terms will show us that and how there are; understanding the syntax of 'there is something' will make us realise there is indeed something.

Wittgenstein held that philosophical confusions arose from misconceptions of syntax, and philosophical clarification conversely was producing the right conception of this. But there are still philosophers who cannot accept this seeming lowering of their status: it would be a blow to their vanity perhaps to do so. Such philosophers are not concerned, they think, with such a paltry affair as language, and in any case, how could it be that intelligent, clever men have been confused about such a basic matter? If these philosophers are concerned with language at all, it seems, it is with its 'Semantics', by which is meant its meaning in the sense not of what is part of language, but something almost beyond words. Of course the cloud of words these philosophers themselves produce in their deliberations, as a result of this incomprehension of themselves and the source of their problems, is just 'gas' in Wittgenstein's terminology, which condensation into a drop of grammar will distil the essence of.

This distillation will also end their deliberation in another sense, as well, for not only will the extended discussions of recent philosophers be shortened by a proper understanding of what meaning is, also the attempt to be always deliberate, in their method, will be abandoned. For many classical paradoxes come to be solved through the proper apprehension of our language's grammar, and with those paradoxes recognised to be solved, less pedestrian rigour, and more confidence will come back in. For while philosophers have not been scared of thinking they might have got the elementary grammar of 'something' wrong, they notoriously have been in dread, for over a hundred years, of committing other terrifying blunders. Paradoxes of analysis (in the mathematical sense), of the infinite, of set theory, and many other paradoxes elsewhere have made philosophers in this century extremely cautious, almost frightened men. If such enigmas are possible, and even clever men can be led astray, from now on, it seems, extra vigilance must be mounted to eradicate all chance of a mishap. Frege almost ended his days in misery as a result of the impasse Russell demonstrated in his set theory: heaven let that not happen to us! And, above all, let us not think that Frege's mistake was just so simple as to misunderstand 'something', or indeed was so simple as any mistake about language. Certainly Frege had trouble with 'the concept horse', but, pray to God, there is nothing seriously wrong with Frege's reified approach to sets, so we can still be academic about it. Thinkers like Frege are intelligent men, and any mistake they make is a mere slip, not a pratfall: if there is egg on an academic's face let it at least be thoughtful, amusing egg - let it at least be quiche!

But not only is it necessary that there is something, also necessary is the fact that sets are not things, and moreover that events are not things either, so let us look for a start at some clear and exact grammar, instead of misleading and restrictive guides, and voluminous if laughing gas. Davidson says that if he bought a house with four bedrooms, two fireplaces and, for some reason, a glass chandelier in the kitchen he could go on for ever adding twee details [3]. He says that the logical form of such Bourgeois sentences as those just used presents no problem, being something like

There is a house such that I bought it, it is downtown...

where the 'it' carries reference back to the original entity (for more on such pronouns see chapter five). Davidson says that the same should be said with respect to the criminal 'Brutus stabbed Caesar in the back in the Forum with a knife', so it becomes something like

There is an event such that it is a stabbing by Brutus of Caesar, it was done in the back...

and the use of 'it' here shows that events are things. But while 'it' here is indeed the stabbing by Brutus of Caesar, i.e. the event, what was in the back, i.e. the object in this case, was the place where Brutus stabbed Caesar, and a further reiteration of 'it' with 'it was done with a knife' would bring up object reference to what Brutus stabbed Caesar with, and so, again, would not carry object reference back to the event. Clearly, anyway, stabbing is not a thing, since it is representable by a lambda abstraction predicate, and so neither is the particular stabbing by Brutus of Caesar a thing: whatever the picture theory of meaning says, 'John by Brutus of Caesar' is quite malformed. To formalise events, as a result, we need not the logic of things but the logic of properties, and to say there is such an event as the stabbing by Brutus of Caesar we must say not

$$(Ex)(x=S.xbc)$$

but

$$(EP)(P=S.Pbc),$$

which is equivalent to Sbc. Moreover it is also equivalent to

$$Q=S.Qbc,$$

where $Q=eP(P=S.Pbc)$, since $(Ex)Fx$ is the same as FexFx, in Hilbert's epsilon calculus, and so likewise $(EP)FP$ is the same as FePFP. Hence there is a choice of predicate possible, to represent the event, and we could also put for 'Q', for instance, '(Ez)S'xyz', i.e. x stabbed y somewhere, or '(Ei)(Ez)S''xyzi', i.e. x stabbed y somewhere with something. But '(Ez)S'xyz' is 'S'xyezS'xyz', using the same transformation again, allowing a pronoun, 'ezS'xyz', to be formed for where x stabbed y, and showing a representation of Davidson's criminal sentence,

There is an event such that it is a stabbing by Brutus of Caesar, it was done in the back...

to be

Sbc.BezS'bcz,

or, more generally, say

$(EP)(P=S.Pbc).BQ_3$,

where the subscript '3' symbolises where the event was done, i.e. represents the 'third' in some conventional ordering of the object places in available predicates. Davidson realised that the standard symbolism for 'Brutus stabbed Caesar' did not allow for predicates with different numbers of places, and that that symbolism therefore could not accommodate the inferences, for instance, between 'John kicked Bill at 3.00 p.m. in the greenhouse', and 'John kicked Bill at 3.00 p.m.', and 'John kicked Bill'. But he must have forgotten that there is no one predicate expression for the last sentence, for an event or action may be identified in many ways, hence a choice must be made available, allowing that a quite proper symbolism for 'John kicked Bill' could be any of

Kjb, $(Et)K'jbt$, $(Ez)(Et)K''jbtz$.

In none of these is the kicking an object, though in different ones different numbers of object places occur, with the resulting possibility of pronouns being formed for the entities in the varying places. But it is an epsilon term for a property rather than an epsilon term for a thing which is required to symbolise events.

A similar point is involved in seeing that sets are not things: a set consists of things, but its abstraction from a determinate predicate merely means a set is still be given by a predicate, though an arbitrary predicate defined purely by its picking out the appropriate things. The set of A's is thus representable by

$eP(x)(Px \text{ CD } Ax)$,

and since

$(x)(Ax \text{ CD } Ax)$,

automatically

(EP)(x)(Px CD Ax)

and so, using the epsilon transformation above,

(x)(eP(y)(Py CD Aye)x CD Ax),

which is to say that the Abstraction Scheme is
provable. Clearly, however, once sets are not reified
they cannot be members of other sets, and so a
fortiori they cannot be members of themselves, hence
the Abstraction Scheme does not lead to any further
trouble, and Russell's Paradox is resolved as a
natural consequence of the correct category alignment.
Certainly there has been a good deal of work done on
reified set theory, but that this involves a simple
mistake has been suspected for some while. Both
Bernays and Quine, for instance, have produced set
theories in which the assumption that sets can be
members is held off as long as possible, and then used
only sparingly [4]. Bernays himself proves, amongst
other things, a version of Cantor's Theorem without an
assumption that the subsets of a set are things, or
that the power set of a set is a thing. Abandoning
the assumption entirely is no great loss, therefore,
the power set of the set of A's being representable as
a second order predicate. Moreover, as Bernays shows,
when using the epsilon calculus the Axiom of Choice
becomes provable.

Recently George Boolos has shown how much of our
talk about sets is in this way representable in second
order logic [5], and while he shakily holds onto a
hybrid conception, whereby set membership is still a
relation between things, he sums up:

> We need not construe second-order quantifiers as
> ranging over anything other than the objects over
> which our first-order quantifiers range, and in
> the absence of other reasons for thinking so, we
> need not think that there are collections of (say)
> Cheerios, in addition to the Cheerios.
> Ontological commitment is carried by our first-
> order quantifiers; a second-order quantifier

needn't be taken to be a kind of first-order quantifier in disguise, having terms of a special kind, collections, in its range. It is not as though there were two sorts of things in the world, individuals, and collections of them, which our first- and second-order variables, respectively, range over and which our singular and plural forms, respectively, denote. There are, rather, two (at least) different ways of referring to the same things, among which there may well be many collections.

The point also illustrates the present view of Semantics, for given the right formalisation of sets in terms of second order logic, clearly its rightness (i.e. its synthetic, if not analytic necessity) means that the 'Semantics' of this formalism is just natural speech (and vice versa), for the two are then just related by abbreviation, and expansion. But getting the right formalisation for sets, in particular, shows us also, in one area, that it is not insignificant, understanding how 'something' works, even if a misunderstanding at this level is pretty primitive; and the rightness of the formalisation, as well, shows us that ideals can be realised, not indeed in a mess of approximations, but in the perfect abbreviation or summary.

THOUGHTS

The general notion of meaning, of course, arises not just in the specific context of the semantics of formal symbols, but also in the more basic context of the sense of natural speech. When Grice first formulated his account of occasion meaning he spoke of the intention of a declarative utterance being to produce a certain effect: make the audience believe what is said [6]. Later he modified that account so that the intended effect was merely to get the audience to think the speaker believed what was said. But even that need not be the intention, indeed there need not even be the desire to produce apprehension, for someone might just be uttering a nice or nasty thought, and that thought would still have meaning.

13

Indeed it would then have the impersonal 'sentence meaning' which Grice sought to define in terms of 'utterer's meaning'. Frege distinguished

> The apprehension of a thought - thinking,
> The recognition of the truth of a thought - judgement,
> The manifestation of this judgement - assertion,

and Grice once believed that the purpose of speech was to produce the second, and, later, to produce recognition of the third. But there is also the (intentional or unintentional) production of the first to consider, which is related to the development of wonder, and also understanding.

Frege was aware that, in addition to 'assertions' which were true or false, there were also 'thoughts' which were to be assessed merely aesthetically. But he believed they could not occur <u>directly</u>. As Dummett says [7], suppositions, for Frege, were not assertoric sentences somehow occurring without assertoric force. Suppositions Frege took to only occur in fiction or drama, and certainly when an actor speaks, or a novelist writes, they would not generally be asserting their words, merely expressing thoughts with them: play-acting, supposing they are true. But that does not put those words into <u>indirect speech</u>, merely <u>unasserted speech</u>, and indeed those very same words could be asserted. Moreover what would make for assertion of the actor's and novelist's remarks, and, in an extended sense, the 'assertion' of the actor's actions, is merely that the play-acting be dropped, allowing sincerity to come in, so conversely, what would make for 'non-assertion' in direct speech and everyday life is merely that play-acting and insincerity be allowed there. And what distinguishes the two cases is not any linguistic sign for assertoric force - if only because that sign would be capable of being aped in some further facade or show. In fact there is no assertion sign in language, and Frege's original sign, though still commonly used, now means 'It is provable that', which is, of course, quite different. Certainly we can report 'It is sincerely asserted that p', but whether there is then sincerity or assertion is our judgement, which does not necessarily follow the judgement of, and hence any sign by, the supposedly sincere assertor.

Dummett is hesitant about there being assertion signs, because he does not see clearly that, in such a report as 'It is sincerely asserted that p', 'p' is no longer the whole speech; moreover he confusedly believes that, in addition to an assertion sign, there might also be a further sign, for 'dramatic force', which would do the job of negating assertions. Certainly he allows this sign might be given merely by the general context - professional acting commonly is found only in special places - but the theoretical need for such a further sign vanishes once it is realised there is no prior assertion sign for it to negate. Dummett realises that, if there were an assertion sign the actor could use it too, but comes explicitly to the conclusion that the actor, when not making assertions, is not just expressing thoughts, but rather 'acting the making of assertions'. But, against this, there is generally no pretence that an actor believes what he says. Moreover, such insincerity is not just something which arises in a special context, on a stage in a theatre at a given time, but is a general part of life - whatever an Empiricist might wish. And the fact that there is no special context means again that any judgement about the play-acting/sincerity is expressed in an attitude taken towards the proposition/behaviour, and is not something for which there could be a certain sign in that proposition/behaviour.

Now Frege's doctrine required that subordinate clauses in indirect speech invariably were merely sources of aesthetic delight because they expressed thoughts rather than assertions, and contrariwise that complete sentences in direct speech were capable of scientific assessment because they invariably expressed assertions rather than thoughts, so now we become free to see that Frege's contrast is invalid on both sides of the divide, for one can have assertions in certain indirect speech contexts, viz 'It is known that p', and contrariwise thoughts can be voiced in direct speech - just as Davidson's theory of indirect speech requires, since there 'It is believed that p' involves a 'p' which may be expressed as a separate

sentence, and which, therefore, is in direct speech
unasserted, i.e. which is not itself an expression of
a belief.

The point enables us to see why thoughts are
independent of any Gricean speaker's intention. For
they are not voiced in the person of the speaker, any
more than the actor speaking some lines is endorsing,
or even the reverse, lying with them. Both utterers
are merely enunciating the words, in an appropriate
context, so that the words are distinct, and can be
understood. The words clearly have, therefore, in the
theatrical case, their public meaning, and nothing
else. The indirect speech case is only slightly
different from this, for the speaker of 'It is
believed that p' is the author, i.e. chooser, of 'p'
and not merely its proclaimer. Even with reported
speech this selection occurs, for reporting speech is
not quoting that speech, but putting it into one's own
words. The meaning-giving form

    s means that p

is an intermediary in this spectrum. It is not a
report on speech, nor is it a judgement about a
personal attitude, but it is giving, in one's own
words, an expression publicly understandable by one's
audience, and involves not the assertion of 'p' but
merely its appropriate enunciation.

Thoughts, therefore, are certain non-committal ways
of using certain signs, and they should not be
hypostatised, any more than sets or events. For
Frege not only held that there were thoughts which
were made into assertions by the addition of a certain
sign, he also held a certain ontological doctrine
regarding them, i.e regarding their place in the Third
World. One world was the internal world of private
Idealist ideas, a second world was the external world
where Realist sentences and other objects lived, but
there was also a third world inhabited by thoughts,
and, no doubt, other human creations. Thoughts were
timeless, and hence were not objects of sense, but
they also lacked bearers, so they were not internal
ideas. We shall have much more to say about this
threefold type of scheme later, but we need not

investigate Frege's Ontology, here, to appreciate his distinctions another way: thoughts are not objects, but a special use for certain objects linked with understanding. Thoughts are symbols: we select certain signs to put personal ideas into publicly available language.

What are symbols? Poetic symbols are the most easy to grasp; indeed recent Aesthetic Theory has more thoroughly studied the options in this area than recent Meaning Theory [8]. There was a comparable shift in Aesthetic Theory to Grice's shift in Meaning Theory, for instance, way back at the beginning of this century: the 'communication' theories of Tolstoi, and Bell/Fry, then turned into the 'self-expression' theory of Collingwood. Thinking in terms of the transmission of emotion, the former writers conceived of art-works as media permitting the feelings of the artist or creator to be reproduced within the spectators or listeners: to make the hearer not just believe something but have a full affective response. Collingwood argued against the arousal of emotion being the point of the aesthetic exercise, saying that it was merely the presentation, for cognition, of the artist's feelings which was involved: getting others to know how one felt. The great virtue in art, for Collingwood, as for Leavis, was sincerity, and therefore getting that passion and conviction recognised. But Collingwood's view was itself questioned, by Langer, for instance, who held that an art-work was not to be seen as a 'symptom' of some feeling, merely a 'symbol' for it; the same distinction has been made, more recently, by Scruton. Scruton's account starts as follows [9]:

> Relying on these broad distinctions, we might say that there is such a thing as entertaining the proposition that p unasserted, and we might describe this as a mental act analogous to the overt act of saying 'p' unasserted in the way that Geach has argued that judging that p is a mental act analogous to the overt act of asserting 'p'...Clearly there are modes of thought that involve not the assertion of 'p', but the more elusive ability simply to hold the proposition that p before one's mind, to entertain p as a

17

possibility, or as a supposition. Indeed much of our more complex thought processes - imagination, for one - are of this kind, and we know exactly what it is to say 'p' unasserted. Moreover, it is a celebrated conclusion of Frege's that assertedness cannot be part of the meaning of a sentence.

This is clearly phrased in Fregean language, but it eventually enables Scruton to distinguish 'asserted' symptoms from 'unasserted' symbols as follows:

> For when I say that a funerary monument expresses grief I may mean one of two things: (a) it was intended to be expressive of a man's grief, (b) it succeeds in being expressive of grief. The first of these is descriptive, while the second is (perhaps) affective: and yet the connection of sense between them is entirely straightforward. Moreover, feature (b) is clearly a mark of success, and has more than an analogy with expression in art. It is also a feature that is at least partly independent of intention, and can, therefore, be attributed to the monument, whether or not the monument was ever intended to be expressive, and whether or not the grief it purports to express was real.

Symbols 'embody' feelings, as Bouwsma and Hospers have explained: they therefore, as such, neither present the artist's views, nor engender those views in the audience. Language, generally, is symbolic in this sense, though it is 'thoughts', rather than 'emotions' that are expressed by it. Moreover it is only because symbols are involved that it can be choice, i.e. convention which settles meaning, not any causal process. The meaning of 'gavagai', for instance, could not be the class of occasions which would cause its affirmative, i.e. assertive use, because what might prompt the thought would not necessarily cause the belief, although the thought would have the same public meaning as the belief.

Quine's trouble with 'gavagai' in fact points to the central crisis in Empiricism: there aren't necessarily any common sense data which can provide objective truth conditions for protocol beliefs. But does that mean we must retreat into Idealism, and concentrate instead on the variety of ways a stimulus may be read, by a variety of viewers? A third alternative, in the Aesthetics area, has been elaborated by Scruton: non-descriptive meaning.

> So far we have contrasted belief (and the associated act of judgement) with only one other kind of thought – the entertaining of a proposition unasserted. This is as yet an insufficient basis for a theory of aesthetic description that will meet the requirements of the preceding chapter. For we need an account of some mode of thought that is directed at, and aroused in response to, its object, in the manner of aesthetic experience. And the mere entertaining of a proposition about an object is scarcely yet a genuine response to it. However we find that we are also in a position to describe other species of thought in terms of the idea of entertaining a proposition...If I say that I think of the Chairman as an elephant, say, then clearly I am saying something about a mental disposition of mine: it is not sufficient for the truth of this pronouncement that I should entertain the proposition 'The Chairman is an elephant' on one occasion...The idea must strike me as in some way right or appropriate if it is really to be a description of the way I think of the Chairman. This is not to say that the thought has an 'asserted' character: for clearly it would be a total misrepresentation of my thought process to say that I am under the impression that the Chairman is (literally) an elephant.

Hence Scruton, following Hare, defends a general account of 'truth conditions' in terms of 'acceptance conditions'. Now the classic Empiricist sense of 'truth condition' was not the purely formal one which applies even to notions of value. With 'beautiful', or 'good', for example, we can certainly say that something is beautiful or good if and only if it is true, respectively, that it is beautiful or good, but the Empiricists wanted more. They wanted a specification of conditions under which a sentence would be verified, so that giving the truth conditions for a sentence involved giving a definition of its words which was 'epistemological'. The definition of the words, as a result, had to include at some stage ostensive definition, and moreover ostensive definition in contexts where there was public experiential definition, i.e. unanimity. Indeed it was believed that the whole epistemological edifice rested upon elementary experiential sentences which were intersubjectively verifiable without doubt, by observation, in this way. But the trouble with this notion of experience is that it is too like pure thought, i.e. the pure 'entertaining of a proposition unasserted'. For knowledge of it is taken to be immediate and so it can be based on nothing, that is, it can rest on no features which must be previously recognised to make the protocol judgement. Hence there is no control over what protocol judgement is made, and while it might happen that there is unanimity of judgement, there is no forcing this, which is enough to defeat the Empiricist enterprise. Now certainly once it is realised that people need not experience X as X, it is soon realised that there is still some control over what Y they may <u>experience</u> X as, for Scruton shows that experience of X is limited if not by accuracy, then at least by appropriateness: one cannot imagine just anything of a known Chairman, as one maybe can of an unknown one. However, fantasy is more widely ranging than the imagination which Scruton thereby restricts himself to, and the pure non-experiential 'thinking of X as Y', i.e. the pure 'entertaining of 'X is Y' unasserted', from which Scruton starts, is really quite unbounded.

Strangely, in the light of his experiential restriction, Scruton realises that the extreme of the non-Empiricist conception of language is illustrated in such remarks as Wittgenstein's

Tuesday is lean, Wednesday is fat,

and not just synaesthetic comparisons like 'the colour is warm', 'the style is heavy'. But there is no way that any features of Tuesday or Wednesday are attended to to make the former aesthetic judgements, even if some, though by no means a conclusive some, may be brought in with respect to the colour and the style. Hence there is no degree of appropriateness in the first sort of case, even if there is, to some limited extent, in the second. But the fact that there is never any more than appropriateness, so long as there is choice, means that no aesthetic 'description' is purely descriptive: it is expressive of a thought which might or might not also be present in an experience. So while, as a result, thought is now fundamental, that thought is no longer a basis for belief, since that thought is now recognised to be choice based, and so to be, less or more, subjective. The fact that aesthetic descriptions are choice based means that, if they have a function, this is merely to get the hearer to 'see the point' (a symbol is involved, not a symptom) and so, to the extent that such descriptions are settlable this is a matter of agreement (of Hare's acceptance rather than Ayer's verification.) Scruton thinks there is no real conflict with Grice's account of the meaning of utterances, in this, so long as that is extended to allow for non-descriptive elements, and for the non-assertion which characterises their use, but, as we saw above, the publicity and impersonality of pure thoughts defeats any Gricean intentional analysis.

The need for non-assertion, moreover, bears proof, in the general case. For while there certainly may seem to be something odd about 'p, but I don't believe it', i.e. Moore's paradox, Hintikka argued that this was not inconsistent, being merely 'doxastically indefensible', since it was $Bx(p.-Bxp)$ that was inconsistent [10]. Hence statements need not be sincere, although, according to Hintikka, the fact that truths were unbelieved could not be self-recognised. Prior would have accepted the former result but rejected the latter, since its proof rested on questionable (and indeed, by Hintikka, later questioned) principles [11]. Moreover Prior allowed that someone can be sincere when saying he believes falsely that p. We shall arbitrate on these two accounts of propositional attitudes in a moment - settling the matter in Prior's favour - but what we already have is that it is a clear fact that utterances do not require they be taken to be believed, as Grice's theory of meaning requires.

This means that, if one says 'p, but I don't believe it' and finds it odd, then one is not alive to one's possible insincerity, i.e. to the fact that one may be just playing along, without belief in, or commitment to, what one is saying. The detail of Prior's analysis is best at exposing the levels of self-deception which may be involved. Let us write,

x believes correctly that p   as Bxp.p
x says truly that p   as Sxp.p
x says sincerely that p   as Sxp.Bxp.

Now if we had

(1) Bx(p.q) D (Bxp.Bxq)

i.e. whoever believes a conjunction believes each of its parts, and

(2) BxBxp CD Bxp

i.e. someone believes something just so long as he believes that he believes it, and vice versa, and also

(3) Bxp D -Bx-p,

i.e. no one both believes that p and believes that not-p, then the above 'doxastically indefensible' point of Hintikka's would go through. For from Bx(p.-Bxp) we could get Bxp and Bx-Bxp, using (1), and hence BxBxp using (2), giving the result, because of (3). But the difficulty with this is that it does not allow for sincere assertion of an expression equivalent to 'p.-Bxp', namely

I find it incredible that p,

that is, it does not allow for beliefs in miraculous experiences. For one certainly may not believe one's eyes, and yet not to credit them requires recognising what they tell you, and this process may be self-recognised even when it is also recognised that one's eyes are good. Hence there is definitely something wrong with Hintikka's result, and the above axioms, as a consequence.

Equally the axioms would entail

   -Bx(Bxp.-p)

i.e. that no one believes he believes falsely that p.
This follows because Bx(Bxp.-p) would entail BxBxp and
Bx-p, using (1), again, and hence Bxp using (2),
giving a contradiction again, using (3). But, as
Prior shows, there is no need to make such an extreme
judgement, based on such unstable foundations, to see
what is wrong with someone's saying that he believes
falsely that p. Using simply propositional
quantification it follows not that it is impossible
for the speaker to believe this, but merely that the
speaker is either mistaken in what he believes, or
insincere in what he says. For

   Sx(Bxq.-q)

entails

   (Ep)(Bxp.-p) v (Ep)(Sxp.-Bxp),

since if not then it is possible that

   Sx(Bxq.-q).(p)(Bxp D p).(p)(Sxp D Bxp),

but substituting 'Bxq.-q' for 'p' in the right-hand
conjunct here gives

   Sx(Bxq.-q) D Bx(Bxq.-q),

and so

   Bx(Bxq.-q),

but the same substitution in the middle conjunct gives

   Bx(Bxq.-q) D (Bxq.-q),

and so

   Bxq.-q.

But we must also have, from this conjunct

Bxq D q,

hence also we get q, which is impossible.

Prior finds fault with principles (2) and (3) by saying that (2) (or, at least, half of it) contradicts the fact that we often find we did not believe what we thought we did (equally we sometimes do not believe we believe what we do believe), also that (3) contradicts the fact that men's beliefs are often inconsistent. Prior finds (1) alone 'plausible', but, as we shall see later, this principle is suspect as well, leaving Prior's propositional quantification as the only logic in the area. There will then be the laws of this logic, which are just those of quantification theory, but, because people might not apply those laws correctly, there will then be no laws of thought.

USE

Explicit promising is a good case where sincerity is not required - though in a different sense from the general one. If someone says 'You will get a present' he may or may not be sincere, and you may or may not get a present, but if someone says 'I promise you will get a present', whether or not he is sincere, and whether or not you get a present, if conditions are right, he does promise. This means, as well, that, despite Austin's denial, explicit performatives may be true, although their truth conditions are then non-empirical. For, given the conditions are right, such a statement is true by mere say-so. The case is no different from explicit stating [12]: if someone says 'It will rain tomorrow' he may or may not be sincere, and it may or may not rain, but if he says 'I (hereby) state that it will rain tomorrow', whether or not he is sincere he undoubtedly states something - so long as he means what he says.

But how does language gain meaning? Surely it cannot just be by being pronounced in an appropriate context? When people speak of Wittgenstein's doctrine of meaning as use, they do not simply mean the opposite of mention, i.e. the uttering of the words without quotes, and so thinking with them, not just about them. Wittgenstein's doctrine of meaning as use included a whole host of different uses - to command, to express, as well as to state and to promise, so it can hardly be taken to be merely proclamation. Or, rather, it can hardly be taken to be that all the time. For there was a set of cases Wittgenstein drew our attention to, very similar to Austin's performatives, in which the appropriate enunciation was enough to make the words true, and where, therefore, the only meaning could be in the conditions of utterance: in fact there are at least two sets of cases Wittgenstein brought up, paradigm cases for the application of a word, and propositions which belong to our 'frame of reference' or 'form of life'.

The former paradigms themselves fall into two groups, those relating to names and identifying descriptions (referring phrases), and those relating to non-identifying descriptions and predicates (descriptive phrases). Austin himself was concerned with both types, for

I name this ship, Endeavour

was performative in his strict sense, while his notorious

That is a pig

was 'performative' in a rather broader sense. The form of the first case is important, in that it includes the word 'Endeavour' without quotes: the speaker is not recording a name but giving one. Likewise with introductions to people: 'This is John', for instance, is quite unlike 'He is called 'John'' - although an introduction is still different from a baptism. The location of the pig is important in the second case: it must be in full view; and equally the social context is important, for the sentence to be true by mere say-so: this must be a teaching situation in which instructions in the use of language are being given, making its proper expression:

That's what I call a pig.

25

Austin was not too clear about this, since he saw his role against the Empiricists, and notably Ayer, as finding a definitely true empirical judgement: he subscribed thereby to a form of Direct Realism [13]. Thus while he contrasts cases where evidence like smell, pig-food, grunts and so on is present, with the case where the pig is in full view, on his account 'no evidence' is involved in the latter case, since when the pig was in full view one could 'just see' it was there, and to speak of 'the evidence of one's senses' was just a trope. But 'the evidence of one's senses' is not a trope, for one might not have good eyes, and hence rightly not believe what they told one. Hence Ayer had a proper reply to Austin there: one has evidence for the pig even when it is in full view, so the empirical judgement about it might have been mistaken, even if it isn't. But Austin would still have been right if instead he had spoken about 'no justification' being involved in teaching situations, i.e. where the meaning of a word was being given, so all he had to do was shift the case to one where a concept was being defined rather than applied. His correct line would then have been that when there are smells, grunts, pig-food etc. he says it is probably a pig, while if the pig is before us he says it is certainly a pig. These remarks then introduce the learner to the whole language game of doubt, ignorance, knowledge and certainty, with the central aim of getting him to use the entire spectrum of expressions properly. But there would then have been no ultimate justification for Austin saying without doubt the object in front of him was a pig, any more than there would have been justification for Moore saying the objects in front of him were hands. This would have been just what they <u>chose</u> to do. However, that would not make its being a pig, or their being hands, a linguistic matter, for saying that something is P is not just saying 'It is P': it also involves, for instance, taking the object as a standard of comparison, or paradigm, for other things one will call P. Hence while the 'foundation' of knowledge is mere linguistic say-so, properly confirmable facts may result.

Likewise with understanding the addition of 2.

Wittgenstein's point here was not that there is no fact about what adding 2 results in, but merely that it is our chosen, unjustified paradigms for 'adding' and '2' which enable us to recognise this fact, supposing we use that process of comparison with paradigms involved in what is called 'thinking'. He says, [14],in Remarks on the Foundations of Mathematics (I-116), that while everybody could continue the series as he likes, that would not mean we could infer anyhow, since we shan't call it 'continuing the series' or 'inference' in every case. The laws of inference do not compel a person to say or write what he does like rails compelling a locomotive. And even if we say that, while everyone may say what they like, still they can't think what they like, that only makes it an essential part of 'thinking' that we make certain sorts of transition.

Other remarks illustrate more precisely how it is a performative linguistic choice in a paradigm case which is the basis for mathematical compulsion, certainty, and fact. Considering an elementary proof that 5 consists of 3 and 2, viz.

III II,

Wittgenstein says (I-53) that he will admit this is a proof if that is only to admit that he wants to use this picture. So (I-61) the above is a demonstration only for those who acknowledge it as a demonstration, and if anyone doesn't acknowledge it, then he has parted company with us even before it comes to talk. Hence (I-62) while we have something that looks inexorable it is nothing but a pattern, which has a certain 'action at a distance'. The action at a distance consists in our taking the pattern as an ideal case, i.e. a model in terms of which to see other facts; and any certainty in those facts then consists merely in their actually arising in the case of the paradigm. Again, (I-42) considering a certain puzzle which consists in making a rectangle out of given pieces, Wittgenstein asks what we discover when we succeed in forming it. We find that the pieces can be arranged in a certain way, but 'the pieces' are not just the actual ones in the rectangle illustrated, they are also pieces elsewhere which have yet to be

27

arranged in the discovered way.

Empiricists have had great difficulty with Mathematics, since all objects are physical objects and so, seemingly, the ideal objects of Arithmetic and Geometry cannot exist, except in approximation. Hence the appeal, to Empiricists, of a linguistic account of mathematical necessity: if there are no extra-linguistic objects for such matters to be about, it becomes plausible to think mathematical truths are about the words used to describe ordinary objects, or indeed words used to describe no objects at all. Wittgenstein's later thought on Mathematics is notable because he showed there is an alternative to this linguistic account: he pointed out that there are physical objects which are not 'empirical' in the classic sense. The standard metre in Paris was a stock example of his, with regard to which he said, for instance, that it cannot be said either to be or to not be a metre long, because it is the paradigm in terms of which all metre lengths are ultimately measured. Now the standard metre in Paris is indeed the ideal metre, and this is a physical object, for it is

the object whose length is 1 metre

i.e.

exLx1

where 'Lx1' is 'the length of x is 1 metre'. But, against Wittgenstein, it is not the case that this object cannot be said to be, or to not be, a metre long. Indeed the whole point is that it is said to be a metre long, although this is just a matter of choice, and so not an empirical matter. Moreover this decision is not just a mere fact about the one object, since that object is thereby the source of a concept. In fact the standard metre is a metre long just so long as there are things a metre long

L(exLx1)1 CD (Ex)Lx1,

meaning that if the standard metre is not a metre long there are no metre long things

-L(exLx1)1 CD (x)-Lx1.

Of course these are the Hilbertian definitions of the quantifiers, showing that epsilon terms, quite generally, symbolise paradigm objects. But exFx is what is F _if anything is_, allowing it might not be F, so Hilbertian paradigm objects are not the 'paradigm cases' of Linguistic Philosophy, which were thought to be guaranteed to have their character. What is guaranteed with Hilbertian ideals is not that they have their inscribed character, but merely that they exist, i.e. that there are such paradigm objects, for every predicate in our language.

   Irving Copi [15] explains this fact, in classical terms, by considering four unique quantificational tautologies

   1. (y)[(x)Fx D Fy]
   2. (y)[Fy D (Ex)Fx]
   3. (Ey)[Fy D (x)Fx]
   4. (Ey)[(Ex)Fx D Fy].

These correspond to the four classic quantification rules Universal Instantiation, Existential Generalisation, Universal Generalisation, and Existential Instantiation, the first two being unpuzzling, the latter two rather strange. How can it be necessary that there is something such that, if it is F, everything is F? How can it be necessary that there is something such that, so long as there is something which is F, _it_ is F? Copi removes the oddity of these theses with reference to Aristedes, often called 'the just'. Supposedly there was a saying to that effect, namely

   If anyone is just, Aristedes is just,

which is an instantiation of (4); contrariwise we can say

   If Aristedes is corruptible, everyone is corruptible,

which is an instantiation of (3). Of course the given

principles are quite general ones, for any predicate 'F', and are easily demonstrated, in that case, by means of <u>Reductio</u>. For given, for instance,

$$-(Ey)(Fy \supset (x)Fx)$$

then

$$(y)(Fy.(Ex)-Fx)$$

i.e.

$$(y)Fy.(Ex)-Fx,$$

which is impossible. Classical logic therefore was aware of such paradigms, but it is only in the epsilon calculus that we can go on to identify them, and, moreover, realise that their identification is a matter of choice. For only then can we say

$$(Ex)Fx \supset FexFx,$$

and realise that only if there was just one F would exFx be totally determined.

Wittgenstein saw all this intuitively, but he did not just point out the existence and place of such paradigms in connection with understanding the functioning of general terms in language. He also used this insight, as above, to give an account of arithmetical and geometrical truths, and eventually to generate a quite new theory of knowledge. Roger Shiner has explained Wittgenstein's 'Activist' theory of knowledge, contrasting it usefully with traditional 'Foundationalist' and 'Coherentist' alternatives [16]. But it is important to note that the whole thrust to find a third alternative to classical Empiricism and Idealism is very much a united twentieth-century enterprise. Existentialism also based its theory of knowledge, as well as theory of value, on action, and so there is much to be learned from continental writers like Sartre and Heidegger, even if their focus was not just on doing things with words.

In Heidegger's case, for instance, he makes an important distinction between things 'ready to hand'

and those merely 'present' [17]. Things ready to hand are tools and utensils, which we can use to operate in the world; things which are merely present are distant or unusable in some way, so we can only spectate them. What is ready to hand is meaningful, what is merely present is meaningless. We become a spectator when we are 'out of action', but the resulting waiting and seeing is an abnormal state, in which a consequently contingent 'empirical' world is made to seem real. This contingency was the basis of Roquentin's experience of disgust in Sartre's novel _Nausea_, and elsewhere occurs as a sense of absurdity, disengagement or alienation. But since it is indeed an absurd state, the Existentialists reverse the traditional Empiricist difficulty about getting in touch with the 'External' World. An accident could certainly put us out of action, and make us mere spectators, but the world we live in is only external, and hence absurd, at moments of such breakdown and crisis, and we get in touch with our world (which is the objective world, but now owned and understood) merely by acting in it. The fundamental premise of Skepticism is therefore wrong: a skeptic about the world starts from the presumption that we have no access to the world except through our senses, and then proceeds to undermine our trust in these organs; but the reply to him is not, like the Direct Realist, to accept his premise, and, by talking say about skills, build up our confidence in our spectatorial capacities; the reply to the skeptic consists in denying him his premise, and pointing out that we have access to the world through action - even going for a walk, for instance, is one way of becoming part of it - and the world is then not external to us, but depends upon us for its existence as much as we are dependent on it. The Activist, as a result has no trouble with human freedom, since this is the very starting point of his philosophy: one's world is what one makes it, and it is only to the extent that things are not determined by one that things seem to be determined for one.

Wittgenstein says in On Certainty (148) that he does not first of all satisfy himself that he has two feet when he gets up from a chair. He does not reason about the matter: simply getting up is how he acts.

He says (110) that giving grounds comes to an end, but the end is not an ungrounded presupposition, it is merely a way of acting. So it is not (204) a kind of seeing on our part; it is our acting which lies at the bottom of our language game. He also says on Truth (374), that we teach children 'that is your hand' not 'that is perhaps (or 'probably') your hand'. So an investigation or question 'whether this is really a hand' never occurs to him, and (630), it is simply the normal case, not to be capable of mistake about the names of certain things in one's first language. As a result Wittgenstein held (83) that the truth of certain empirical propositions belongs to our 'frame of reference'.

But they are not then 'empirical' propositions, since not only is an investigation something which never occurs, and a mistake about names beyond our capacities, it is also nonsense to suppose an investigation or mistake is relevant or possible. Names are given by choice, and nothing could reveal that the ship was Endeavour, before it was so named, or that it was not Endeavour after that ceremony.

Austin was puzzled about the difference between Performatives and Constatives, recognising that 'I state that...' was performative in his sense. But all use of language is 'performative' in a general sense, so the only real distinction for this word to mark is that between 'explicit' performatives and other forms of speech. The way language-use is performative, in general, is then best described by talking of 'Speech Acts', and the rest of Wittgenstein's senses of 'use', besides proclamation, are then also covered by this term. Austin distinguished the Perlocutionary Effects of utterances, from their Illocutionary Force or Purposes, and both from Locutionary Acts of straight uttering. The first of these is what meaning-theorists like Grice, have fastened on. The second has been the main interest of Speech-Act theorists like Searle. The third, however, is the proper locus of meaning, as Strawson, amongst others, has realised. The meaning of a word is a speech act, but it is not saying the word with a certain effect, nor saying the word with a certain force, merely saying the word with a certain referent, or definition. Meaning a sentence is saying it with its public entailments.

Hence it is not just saying, for instance, 'a is P', since that is only a matter of elocution, but it is still saying 'a is P' a certain way - with the appropriate referent for 'a' and the appropriate definition for 'P'. Conviction is not involved, since the expression of a belief is not necessary; being convincing is not involved, since the generation of a belief is not necessary either. The latter would be a perlocutionary effect, the former an illocutionary force, whereas meaning is a locutionary act. Meaning is a form of doing. So the meaning of a word is not its referent, for in the first place not every word has a referent, and even for those that do, the meaning of them is the using of them with those referents, not the referents themselves. Likewise the meaning of a word is not its definition, since, again, only some words have a definition, and even for those that do, the meaning of them is instead the act of using of them with those definitions. Certainly there is a public meaning form

$$s \text{ means that } p$$

which statically summarises the entailments we create or abide by when using public language, but the meaning of the sentence is still found in personal acts of use, since what the form abbreviates is

$$(x)((x \text{ says and means } s) \ D \ (x \text{ says that } p)),$$

showing that the words need to be used, to give them life.

Saying something and meaning it certainly starts with elocution, i.e. saying what one intended to say, so that the utterance is not an accident, and corrected by a subsequent remark like 'what I meant to say was...' But to say that somebody meant what they said is to say more than that they meant to say it: it also means that they thought it, so saying without thinking is its opposite, not saying without conviction, any more than saying without truth. But thinking it does not mean, for instance, uttering it subvocally in some imagined, internal, way; quite the reverse: it involves directing what is said outwards, towards the world, respecting the language conventions of one's linguistic community.

CONTEXT

There are certain elements in language, variously called 'indexicals', 'egocentric particulars', which serve to link language-use to the world. At one time it was thought that this phenomenon of deixis should be erased from a logically perfect language: fictional propositions, which were taken not to refer to the world, were customarily excised, but the propositions which remained were almost made 'fictional' in their place. Quine's 'eternal sentences', for instance, were designed, amongst other things, to eliminate the temporal location of the speaker and give a timeless expression to human thoughts, also his 'elimination of singular terms' in favour of quantificational statements was designed to give a referenceless expression to those human thoughts. But it is a general result of the Hilbertian analysis that all quantified statements are representable as straight subject-predicate expressions, not just as generalizations, universal or existential. Moreover, as we shall see, temporal location is not eliminable, and even fictional propositions refer.

Thus

All S is P

is

-(Ex)(Sx.-Px)

and hence is

-(Sa.-Pa),

where a=ex(Sx.-Px). Also 'Some S is P' is 'Sb.Pb', where b=ex(Sx.Px), by the same process, and

Any S is P,

by which I mean

$(Ex)Sx$ D $PexSx$

is

Sc D Pc

where $c=exSx$. Hence none of these expressions escapes from the burden of reference just because they are otherwise formulable so as to hide it. Equally, as we shall see more fully in chapter six,

Ralph believes there are spies

is

$BrSexSx$

because it is '$Br(Ex)Sx$', and

There is someone Ralph believes is a spy

is

$BrSexBrSx$

because it is '$(Ex)BrSx$'. Hence, again, both of these propositional attitude expressions involve a specific object of thought, and are not intrinsically general. Indeed, were it not for such specific objects of thought, all the associated language use would be irreducibly '_de dicto_', whereas, in fact, none of it is and all of it is formulable '_de re_', showing that all of it relates, in one way or another, to a part of the world which it is about.

The rediscovery of the traditional subject, however, is only the beginning of an interpretation of such results. Temporal location, as we shall shortly see, is also ineliminable, indeed the epsilon calculus helps us first of all to see that there is a certain temporal context, including, amongst other things, a single day, tomorrow, and why, as a result, there is no branching time [18]. For suppose the possibility that

35

Socrates will run tomorrow

were

$$(Et)(FOt.d(0,t)=1.Rst)$$

i.e. there is a time in the future, one measure from now, and Socrates runs then. It would follow that we could specify this time as obeying a certain description

$$FOt_1.d(0,t_1)=1.Rst_1,$$

where $t_1 = et(FOt.d(0,t)=1.Rst)$, indeed the time would then be <u>defined</u> as one where Socrates runs. So while with this mode of expression branching time would become possible, and we could express the chance that

Socrates will not run tomorrow

by using

$$(Et)(FOt.d(0,t)=1.-Rst),$$

i.e.

$$FOt_2.d(0,t_2)=1.-Rst_2$$

where $t_2 = et(FOt.d(0,t)=1.-Rst)$, the interlocking of time and event would mean that $-(t_1 = t_2)$, because Rst_1, but $-Rst_2$. Hence there would be two 'tomorrows', one on each branch, with logical determinism along each branch. However, the formalisation is clearly wrong, since it conflates

$$-(Et)(FOt.d(0,t)=1.Rst)$$

with

$$(Et)(FOt.d(0,t)=1.-Rst),$$

and that error would still be present if we added a uniqueness clause, making 'Socrates will run tomorrow' state 'There is just one time in the future one measure from now, and Socrates runs then'.

By contrast, the material contingency of events requires 'Socrates will run tomorrow' to be the straight contradictory of 'Socrates will not run tomorrow', and so not only is it the case that there cannot be two tomorrows, one where Socrates runs and one where Socrates does not run, it is also the case that there must be reference to tomorrow, not a statement that there is just one. Clearly the proper expression for a metric temporal statement is not a quantified one, but one which drops the quantifier and the variable it binds in the above, reducing 'Socrates will run tomorrow' to the temporal operator form,

F1Rs

i.e. 'In the future, one measure from now, Socrates runs', and showing thereby that tomorrow will be the same day, in identity if not character, whether F1Rs or F1-Rs is true.

Now the contradiction between 'Socrates will run tomorrow' and 'Socrates will not run tomorrow', which prevents an escape from Determinism by means of branching time, still allows a proper escape from this, as Prior has shown, by means of the introduction into Tense Logic of a further modality 'It is preventable now that p', supposing this is understood to concern and vary with human potential, and not some abstract space-time structure independent of man. But the fact that times are not defined in terms of the events which may or may not happen then also means that McTaggart's tensed A-series forms are indeed, as he said, primitive, and cannot be defined in terms of his before/after B-series forms. Russell, for instance, argued against McTaggart that the A-series expression

The battle of Waterloo is in the past

is formulable as

The battle of Waterloo is earlier than this judgement,

but the present is not defined in terms of there being

such a judgement, indeed there might be no such judgement. And if we replace 'this judgement' with 'now', only too clearly 'is' in that judgement must then be replaced by 'was', returning us to an A-series expression, again. Equally with dates: these require an origin for the dating to be given, but if this is in terms of an event at 0 A.D., for instance, this does not define 0 A.D., and if it is in terms of the number of years ago that origin occurred, we are back to tensed expressions again.

There is no way, therefore, that the temporal element in deixis can be eliminated, supposing it is present. For if there is reference to time, then no timeless expression for the thought is possible, and hence there is no corresponding 'timeless' truth: there are merely other corresponding timed truths. Thus it might seem that we could replace

(A):There was a revolution seventy years ago

with some 'atemporal' expression like

(B):There is a revolution in 1917,

in which not only is the date taken to provide a non-indexical reference to the year, but also the temporal 'was' is excised in favour of the 'historical present'. But the historical present is just the present tense used of another time, for that tense is not only properly used of the now present: historians, futurologists, and tense logicians use it to think themselves to be not now present. So while, no doubt, a historian might like to think he was back in 1917, and say to himself merely

(C):There is a revolution going on now,

there is really no temptation to say that this thought is an atemporal one: it expresses the imagined cotemporaneity of the historian and the event. Certainly (C) and (B), actually said in 1917, in some sense say the same thing as (A) said in 1987, but the availability of a present tense expression for use to say the same thing, at some time, does not show that such an expression is available to say that thing now, somehow 'timelessly'. What could in fact be said in place of (A) now is

(D):There was a revolution in 1917

and as a result its equivalent

(E):It was true that there is a revolution in 1917,

in which the 'is' is the historical present, but this expressly shows that the temporal verb in the original does not get excised in the reformulation of it, and so does not produce a 'timeless' truth. With 'O' = 'now'

$$(En)(Pn \ v \ Fn)((Ex)Rx.O=1917 \ A.D.)$$

has an invariable truth value, unlike (D) i.e.

$$(En)Pn((Ex)Rx.O=1917 \ A.D.)$$

but the former has the quite different expression 'It either is, was, or will be that there is a revolution in 1917 A.D.'.

The point shows that not all statements are eternal ones, and so clarifies Lemmon's distinction [19] between statements and propositions. For Lemmon was inclined to take statements to be what only eternal sentences might be used to utter. When there was a tense in the sentence, and when the sentence was temporally indefinite, Lemmon was inclined to speak of 'propositions'. Propositions were then the constant senses of non-eternal sentences, and it was only in terms of them that one could explain such idioms as

It used to be true that the population of London was under 4 million, but this is no longer true today.

But while the non-eternal proposition, say

$$P200(p < 4,000,000)$$

might be true while the non-eternal proposition

P0(p < 4,000,000)

was not, the statement made by the former today is not thereby excluded from variability, since, again, even its present, dated, equivalent

The population of London was under 4 million in 1787 A.D.

involves a temporal verb, being

(En)Pn(p < 4,000,000.0=1787 A.D.),

which was false before 1787 A.D.. This makes it unlike the eternal statement

(En)(Pn v Fn)(p < 4,000,000.0=1787 A.D.),

but it also shows the statement about 200 years ago is not this eternal statement even though it implies it. The eternal statement is what is timelessly true, but it is in no sense equivalent to the tensed statement. Moreover, there seems no reason to deny there is a proposition, i.e. a 'constant sense', in connection with it.

So how are we to distinguish statements from propositions? Well, the two tensed propositions just given are different, but make the same statement, so how are the two tensed expressions equivalent? The one is

P200(p < 4,000,000)

the other is

(En)Pn(p < 4,000,000.0=1787 A.D.),

so supposing 200 years ago was 1787 A.D. i.e.

P200(0=1787 A.D.)

the two would be materially equivalent, but not logically equivalent. The distinction is usually put, as above, by saying they may make the same statement, though not the same proposition, but, for a start, one must not be misled by the grammar of 'make' here, since there is no <u>thing</u> made in making a statement or proposition: there are merely classes of expressions which are, in various ways, equivalent to one another, and making the statement or proposition means making a certain verbal action, involving selection from one of those materially, or logically equivalent sets. Thus Lemmon considers 'The driver of the van had no hair' and 'Tom Jones was bald', and suggests first that they make the same statement if the referents of the individual terms and the implications of the general terms are materially the same, then second that they make the same statement if these things are the same analytically. The latter, as we shall see more fully in the next chapter, isolates what makes the same proposition, in such cases, but clearly neither identifies any <u>thing</u> as 'the statement', or 'the proposition', merely a certain set of materially, or logically equivalent expressions to make one's choice of spoken or written words between.

The point gives us an independent reason for saying that when a fiction is spoken about still something may be stated, only then something which may not be stated by means of another proposition - fictional statements are thereby just one sort of eternal statement. A statement can still be made when a fiction is the subject, and our later treatment of fictions will show exactly how fictional terms still have a reference - merely an indeterminate one. But already we can see that a fictional statement of the form of the above is simply about something which cannot be identified any other merely material way, for, taking such a statement to be given by a class of materially equivalent expressions, and the corresponding proposition to be given by a class of logically equivalent expressions, only those latter expressions will be available in the fictional case, allowing that a statement can still be made, although one which can only be made by the one proposition.

But let us first have a model for the situation in mind. As Lemmon realises, even a definite description, like 'the king of France', is indexical to some extent, and when used on one occasion may

41

refer to one king, on another occasion to another
king. Its use on different occasions, say in 'The
king of France is bald' would then be said to make a
different statement. Now, as we shall see in more
detail in chapter four, definite descriptions are
formalised by means of epsilon terms, so the correct
expression for the varying indexical references of
'the king of France' are different temporal identities
for the epsilon term representing it in the
proposition, and the different statements are then
made by means of choices from different sets of
material equivalents contingent upon those different
temporal identities. As a result, the fictional case,
when there is no king of France, is merely when there
is no other materially given identity for the epsilon
term in the proposition, i.e. no materially given
choice of another term to refer to the same thing,
which allows that fictional propositions can still
refer, and hence still talk about something.

For what is the general form of the proposition in
this case? Well the general form is 'The king of
France is bald', i.e. 'BexK'x' in which 'K'x' is
'Kx.(y)(Ky D y=x)', or, more properly, since a present
tense verb is involved

POBexK'x.

But different statements are made when this is said of
different times, and we can now see what this amounts
to. For suppose we are talking about a sole king of
France n years ago (say n=200, or n=300, given now is
1987 A.D.) then we are saying,

PnPOBexK'x,

which is

PnBexK'x.

But also, we know

Pn(Ex)K'x

i.e.

PnK'exK'x,

and hence

(Ex)PnK'x

and

PnK'exPnK'x.

The uniqueness clause in 'K'' then gives us the temporal identity

Pn(exK'x=exPnK'x),

i.e. that n years ago the king of France was the king of France n years ago, and so in addition to PnBexK'x, we can also say

PnBexPnK'x,

showing we can often produce a conditional material equivalence between the temporally indefinite

The king of France was then bald,

involving an 'eternal' subject, and the temporally definite

The king of France n years ago was then bald,

involving a 'temporal' subject, supposing the former was said of n years ago.

But the fact that statements can then be made about a non-fictional object is crucially a matter of the material equivalence being available, on that supposition, a material equivalence which is derivable from the temporal identity also available then. For the material equivalence depends upon there being a sole king of France at the given time, and if we assume there was no king of France at the time in question, (say n=100), then we cannot get a corresponding temporal identity: Pn-(Ex)K'x does not entail Pn(exK'x=exPnK'x). As before, this does not mean we cannot make either of the two propositions PnBexK'x, PnBexPnK'x, it only means that they are not guaranteed to be materially equivalent by the bare fact that they both involve 'n'. For the referent of 'exK'x' is not now limited to being the same as the referent of 'exPnK'x', since, <u>ex hypothesi</u>, neither of them satisfy PnK'x, which was what previously ensured that the referents were the same. But if making the same statement involves being materially equivalent in the given conditions, making the same statement by means of a different proposition requires having an otherwise materially identifiable subject, hence, lacking that material identification, the two propositions in this case do not now necessarily make the same statement. But every proposition makes a statement, since logical equivalents are just a subclass of material equivalents; statements can thus still be made in the fictional case, and that in the full sense that something with a reference can still be said then. Certainly 'making a statement' has been used so that it excluded 'talking about fictions', but once it is appreciated that the proper analysis of statements and propositions is in terms of equivalences between different expressions, we realise we can distinguish, amongst cases where something is said, a number of cases where what is said is equivalent (in some sense) to something else, and as a result the criteria for 'making a statement' start to bifurcate: 'talking about non-fictions' was one aspect of this, which now gets a narrower application.

There is something else, also, which now gets a narrower application: talking about sentences and words. For discussion of the differences between making statements and making propositions is now all formulable in object-language terms - using, if necessary, tense-logical constructions. The temptation, when talking about truth and truth-bearers, has been to talk about the sentence

'The king of France is bald',

and its statement at different times, also its eternal, i.e. constant sense. But a statement of 'The king of France is bald' is:

The king of France is bald,

and in a like manner, as we shall see more fully in the next chapter, we can drop all mention of linguistic items in the present Semantics. The need for this was realised by Lemmon, since at least he appreciated that sentences could not take the place of statements or propositions. The former belong to a language in a way that the latter do not, he said, making, for instance,

'The population of London is under 4 million' used to be true, but is no longer true today,

a sentence about a language in a way that the previous, similar sentence is not. But now we do not even have that previous sentence; we have the statement which was isolated before, and the sentence which was then used to make it is left to linguists to study. Likewise with temporal statements: we do not now speak of

'The king of France is bald'

being true or false at different times, but simply use the expression

PnBexK'x,

for different values of 'n'. This says it was true n years ago the king of France is bald, and so it places reference to the other time entirely into the tense operator, keeping the historical present of the given sentence within the subordinate clause. But it is not a sentence which is spoken of in that subordinate clause, and so the whole is not a 'meta-logical' remark, in the previously understood sense, in which Semantics was thought to be about 'object languages'. That conception of Semantics involved forgetting one last, but by no means least, element in the world to which statements and propositions must relate, namely their maker: an inescapable part of the context of any proposition is the agent who puts the associated sentence into use.

A commentator on Wittgenstein's Tractatus, James Griffin, says [20]:

The picture theory is supposed to have been suggested to Wittgenstein by a courtroom model of an automobile accident:

> In the proposition a world is as it were put together experimentally. (As when in the law-court in Paris a motor-car accident is represented by means of dolls, etc.)

A doll and a little automobile can be put in a number of relations to one another, but all of them will also be possible for the real things. Even this characteristic a propositional sign has. Because even though, when we write or speak of an automobile accident, the elements we are using are not little automobiles and dolls, pictorial form guarantees that they will behave as if they were. It is this last feature in particular, I believe, which leads Wittgenstein to conclude that a propositional sign is little short of a _tableau vivant_.

But while a propositional sign (i.e. a sentence) is such a picture, a proposition or statement is not a picture, for it is not a thing one can watch, but a deed one can do, starting with a choice one can make. As we saw before, an accident could certainly put us out of action and make us mere spectators, but what we would then experience would necessarily lack the joy and meaning of a _tableau vivant_ brought to life.

NOTES

[1] For a full account of the epsilon calculus see A.C. Leisenring's _Mathematical Logic and Hilbert's Epsilon Symbol_, Macdonald, London, 1969, see also, for instance, G.T.Kneebone's _Mathematical Logic and the Foundations of Mathematics_, Van Nostrand, London, 1963, Ch. 4, and R.Routley's 'A Simple Natural Deduction System', _Logique et Analyse_, 12, 1969.

[2] H.P.Grice's work is to be found in 'Logic and Conversation', see P.Cole and J.L.Morgan, eds _Speech Acts_, Academic Press, New York 1975.

[3] D.Davidson's theory of events is in _Essays on Actions and Events_, Clarendon Press, Oxford 1980.

[4] W.V.O.Quine's set theory is in <u>Set Theory and its Logic</u>, Harvard, 1963; P.Bernays' set theory is in <u>Axiomatic Set Theory</u>, North Holland, Amsterdam, 1958, see in particular p117 for his proof of Cantor's theorem, and p197 for the relation between the epsilon calculus and the Axiom of Choice.

[5] For G.Boolos' work see, for instance 'To be is to be a value of a variable, or to be some values of some variables' <u>Journal of Philosophy</u> LXXXII, 1984, the quote given is from p449.

[6] For Grice's work on Meaning see 'Meaning' <u>Philosophical Review</u>, 66, 1957, 'Utterer's Meaning and Intentions' <u>Philosophical Review</u>, 78, 1969, 'Utterer's Meaning, Sentence Meaning, and Word-Meaning' <u>Foundations of Language</u>, 4, 1968.

[7] For M.Dummett's work on Frege see <u>Frege: Philosophy of Language</u> Duckworth, London, 1981; relevant passages are on pp310,311.

[8] For a summary and assessment of various theories of expression see J.Hospers' 'The Concept of Artistic Expression' <u>Proceedings of the Aristotelian Society</u>, LV, 1954/5.

[9] Roger Scruton's views are to be found in <u>Art and Imagination</u>, Methuen, London, 1974, the three quotes here being from pp88,216, and 89-90, respectively.

[10] J.Hintikka's original theory of Belief was given in <u>Knowledge and Belief</u>, Cornell U.P., Ithaca, 1962.

[11] A.N.Prior's account is in <u>Objects of Thought</u> Clarendon Press, Oxford, 1971, see especially Ch.6.

[12] J.L.Austin's attempted distinction between Promising and Stating is in 'Performative-Constative', see J.R.Searle ed. <u>Philosophy of Language</u>, Oxford U.P. 1971; Austin's general work on Speech Acts is in <u>How To do Things With Words</u> Oxford U.P., 1962.

[13] For Austin's debate with A.J.Ayer, see the former's <u>Sense and Sensibilia</u> Oxford U.P. 1962, and the latter's contributions to K.T.Fann ed. <u>Symposium on J.L.Austin</u>, Routledge, London, 1969.

[14] Wittgenstein's <u>On Certainty</u>, which I shall discuss later, was published by Blackwell at Oxford in 1969, his <u>Remarks on the Foundations of</u>

Mathematics by Blackwell in 1956.

[15] For I.Copi's point about paradigms, see his _Symbolic Logic_, 4th ed., Macmillan, New York, 1973, p109.

[16] Roger Shiner's article 'Wittgenstein and the Foundations of Knowledge' is in _Proceedings of the Aristotelian Society_, LXXVIII, 1977/8.

[17] For M.Heidegger's distinction amongst things see _Being and Time_ translated by J.Macquarrie and E.Robinson, Blackwell, Oxford, 1973, pp99-107; also, for instance, W.Biemel's _Martin Heidegger_, Routledge, London, 1977, pp39-44.

[18] For the formulation of tense logic expressions, also their relation to Determinism, see Prior's _Past, Present and Future_ Clarendon Press, Oxford 1967 Chs I,VI, and VII, see also my 'Hilbertian Tense Logic' in _Philosophia_ 1987.

[19] On the general problem here see, for instance, E.J.Lemmon's 'Sentences, Statements and Propositions' in _British Analytical Philosophy_ eds B.Williams and A.Montefiore, Routledge and Kegan Paul, London, 1966, see in particular p102.

[20] J.Griffin's _Wittgenstein's Logical Atomism_ was published by the Clarendon Press at Oxford in 1964, for the quote see p99.

2 Truth

BEARERS

I want to look, first, in this chapter, at three views of what is true, and start to defend one of those views against the two others. As we shall see in more detail in the next section, and as we noted before with Lemmon, on some accounts of Semantics the prime elements involved are sentences. That would be a Realist view, and was adopted by Carnap, amongst others. On more Idealist conceptions, however, a different kind of object is taken to be involved, namely that object referred to by the nominalization of a sentence, an 'objective' as Meinong called it [1]. There is a third position which is neither Realist nor Idealist in these senses: Arthur Prior explained it, first in 'Oratio Obliqua' [2], then in his book Objects of Thought. There has been a return to more Idealist conceptions recently, as we shall see at the very end of this book. It has been more common, over recent decades, however, to approach these matters from a Realist point of view, and Quine in this period has been noted for his defense of this [3]. Certainly the position may be articulated in some detail.

Thus despite the fact that language use is often slack, ignorant and confused, Quine still wants to speak of synonymy and analyticity broadly in terms of dispositions towards certain kinds of verbal behaviour, synonymy being related to a supposed equal inclination to utter two words or sets of words in certain sorts of situation, and analyticity being related to an imagined strict adherence to certain sets of words. In place of saying that the general mass of sentences, with all their irregularities, are truth carriers, Quine then says it is his 'eternal sentences' which are, and he carries through this 'extensional' analysis to attributes and relations, hoping he can reduce both to reified sets of one sort or another, i.e. with sets being thought of as a kind of thing. Of course he would not accept that reduction in the context of propositional attitudes, since it would render them transparent, so a verbal reduction he takes to be preferable there, along with a verbal analysis of the subordinate clauses.

It is this latter fact which renders the approach inoperable, since it prevents the giving of meaning. For on a verbal account,

s means that p

must be analysed like

s means the same as 'p',

and the question what either s or 'p' then means is left unanswered, indeed we have been sent in a circle, or off on an infinite regress. Meaning is given by using some words, in a certain context, not just mentioning them, so while the proper expression is 'verbal' in the sense that only words can be used to give expression to articulated thought, it cannot be 'verbal' in the full sense, so that it merely refers the hearer to some piece of language, i.e. an object. Quine himself comes to realise the possible virtue of this 'use' account, and Prior, who is notable for having developed it, quotes him approvingly to that effect [4]:

This method of dispensing with 'propositions' in belief contexts has been advocated, a little hesitantly, by W.V.O.Quine. After toying with the use of square brackets to transform sentences into 'that' clauses, which name the 'objects' of 'propositional attitudes', Quine decides that we can do without these after all. 'We can continue to formulate the propositional attitudes with help of the notations of intensional abstraction...but just cease to view these notations as singular terms referring to objects. This means viewing 'Tom believes [Cicero denounced Catiline]' no longer as of the form 'Fab' with a=Tom and b=[Cicero denounced Catiline], but rather as of the form 'Fa' with a=Tom and complex 'F'. The verb 'believes' here ceases to be a term and becomes part of an operator 'believes that', or 'believes [ ]', which, applied to a sentence, produces a composite absolute general term whereof the sentence is counted an immediate constituent'. This is precisely my own proposal; it is one of the two points in the philosophy of logic on which Quine seems to me to be dead right.

But Prior does not show in detail the applicability of his approach to problems of meaning, saying merely two things. First he says that, while, for example, fearing that p amounts to doing something with, or standing in some relation to a sentence which means that p, clearly it does not amount to fearing that sentence. And Quine, on his linguistic account, had a ready answer to that, since he did not analyse

Tom believes that Cicero denounced Catiline

quite as

Tom believes 'Cicero denounced Catiline'

but as

Tom believes-true 'Cicero denounced Catiline',

where 'believes-true' and the like were introduced to 'alleviate the sense of oddity'. Prior's objection to this Quine also thought he could turn, since it

involved distinguishing fearing that p from the
acknowledged associated relation to a sentence which
meant that p: the point is quite general, since, as
Prior says, 'I have broken my leg' does not have the
same meaning as 'I have broken what would normally be
called in English 'my leg'', it being contingent that
such a phrase as 'my leg' exists, and that its use in
English is what it is. This was the substance of
Church's objection to Carnap's analysis of assertion
and belief, and Quine replied to that that it was of
dubious worth, since it involved the notion of
synonymy. But Quine was none too consistent on this
point, for he thought there was a further difficulty
with the supposed equivalence: it involves the notion
of a language, whereas it is the speaker who is giving
the words their meaning, making his final analysis of
the above

Tom believes-true 'Cicero denounced Catiline' in
my sense.

Hence Quine, even if this 'analysis' is not really an
analysis, but merely 'serves any purposes of the
original that seem worth serving', is on what he
himself must regard as shaky ground here, for he has
introduced the notion of sense, and that means he
cannot really object to the use of the notion of
synonymy - moreover it is as crucial to an
understanding of intensional constructions to give an
analysis of synonymy as it is to give an analysis of
belief.

Indeed the whole difficulty lies in construing the
entirety of such contexts as 's means that p', 'He
thought that p', 'He believed that p' etc. If we take
'that p' to be a noun phrase, and even if we qualify
that description by saying it is an 'abstract' noun
phrase, we shall end up thinking that belief, thought
and meaning are relations: relations between the
world, or some people, and some object. When it is
not taken to be an 'extensional' sentence, or class of
sentences, this object is usually called an
'intension', and it is thus a further sign of the
failure of extensional analyses that the study of this
part of language is commonly called 'intensional
logic', or 'non-truth functional' logic. The latter

label indicates one further reason for taking 'abstract noun phrases' to denote objects, for with truth functions we can substitute and save truth purely on the basis of material equivalence, but substitution of material equivalents in the above contexts does not necessarily preserve truth, and so it might look as if the 'p' in such contexts did not occur as it occurs in 'q and p', indeed it might seem that a sentence does not properly occur in them at all, but rather some other form of words, i.e., as above, a 'that' clause.

Now the abstract Intensional analysis suffers as grave a defect as the concrete Extensional one before. For if

> s means that p

is analysed as

> s means x

where 'x' refers to some entity, but now a non-linguistic entity, then, while we have escaped the obvious circularity of the previous approach we have still the potential for an infinite regress, for we can ask what x means, since 'x', being a term, can again be substituted for 's' in the form, requiring that a similar statement

> x means y

makes sense. And so on. Thus while, for instance, an Intensional account can give a similar definition of synonymy to Prior, viz.

> (Ex)(s means x.t means x)

there is also produced the possible expression

> (Ex)(s means x.x means t).

which is nonsense. Certainly if the variables and constants here were propositional variables and constants we could give something like this a sense, with these propositions describing the occurrence of

certain events, and 'means' being strictly 'causes' or
'induces' - but this is 'natural meaning' not 'non-
natural' meaning, and so it is a probabilistic rather
than conventional relation.

Hence it is crucial to the proper meaning form

s means that p

that what s means be not a further object, whether
extensional or intensional, otherwise no meaning will
be given by this form, only something which in one way
or another passes us on. So we must fully appreciate
Prior's strictures about the substitutional nature of
propositional quantification, for it is expressly by
taking it to be objectual that we would get into the
above difficulties.

If we start from an open sentence such as 'x is
red haired' and ask what the variable 'x' stands
for here, the answer depends on what we mean by
'stands for'. The variable may be said, in the
first place, to stand for a name (or to keep a
place for a name) in the sense that we obtain an
ordinary closed sentence by replacing it by a
name, i.e. by any genuine name of an individual
object or person, say 'Peter'. The name 'Peter'
itself 'stands for' a person, viz. the man Peter,
in the sense of referring to or designating this
man; and the variable 'x' may be said, in a
secondary sense, to 'stand for' individual objects
or persons such as Peter. It 'stands for' any
such object or person in the sense that it stands
for (keeps a place for) any name that stands for
(refers to) an object or person.
If we now consider the open sentence 'Peter F's
Paul', it is equally easy to say what
'F'...'stands for' in the first sense - it keeps a
place for any transitive verb, i.e. for any
expression which forms a sentence from a pair of
names. The question what it 'stands for' in the
second sense, i.e. what would be designated by an
expression of the sort for which it keeps a place
is senseless, since the sort of expression for
which it keeps a place is one which just hasn't
the job of designating objects. Similarly with

the two variables in 'If p then q', or the one in 'James believes that p'. The variables here stand for, i.e. keep places for sentences; but since it is not the job of sentences to designate objects, there is just no question what objects these variables 'stand for' in the second sense.

Propositional quantification is needed to explicate, for instance:

Cohen and I always believe the same things

as

(p)(Bcp CD Bip)

and elaborations of this kind of quantification are needed to explicate, for instance

What Percy says is believed by Pauline

as

BuepSrp,

where 'epSrp' is a descriptive form for a proposition, i.e. an expression for 'what Percy says'. But as far as these purposes are concerned, this quantification could be referential, yet it must not be if we are to explicate meaning, belief, propositions, synonymy, and analyticity properly: 'He thought that p' must end with a sentence, not a name.

Prior rejects the name view, in both its forms, making out that 'He thought that p' is really quite like 'q and p', and arguing, as a consequence, that the idea that the 'truth-functional' thesis applies universally is what must be dropped. For Prior the proper parsing of 'He thought that p' links the 'that' with the 'thought' not the 'p'. And what does preserve truth is still something but something more like logical equivalence, what Prior simply called 'propositional identity' [5]. We can support Prior on the first point by remembering that the 'that' needn't, in fact, occur in such contexts at all, so _a fortiori_ it needn't go with the 'p'. We can get some idea of what propositional identity involves if we remember, for instance, that for us to say what Peter says, when he says 'I love Mary', we must not say 'I love Mary, too': we must say 'He loves Mary' or 'He loves her' or 'Peter loves Mary' etc. In fact we must say something which is logically equivalent to the content of Peter's remark, though the proof of this will not emerge until the next section.

Prior is rather cagey about what propositional identity consists in. In <u>Objects of Thought</u> he says

> If the proposition that p really is the very same proposition as the proposition that q, then certainly any function of the proposition that p is the very same proposition as that function of the proposition that q. For example, if the proposition that <u>all bachelors are unmarried</u> really is the very same proposition as the proposition that <u>all unmarried men are unmarried</u>, then the proposition that <u>Jones wonders whether all bachelors are unmarried</u> is the very same proposition as the proposition that <u>Jones wonders whether all unmarried men are unmarried</u>.

But he does not make a categorical judgement of the form 'The proposition that p is the very same proposition as the proposition that q'. In 'Oratio Obliqua' he, of course, denies that propositional identity is material equivalence, but he also denies that it is strict equivalence or mutual entailment. And there are certainly difficulties with strict equivalence, since in some modal logics not even, for instance,

L(p CD q) D L(Lp CD Lq)

is a thesis, so the left hand side cannot guarantee general intersubstitutability. Moreover, there are considerable difficulties with mutual entailment, supposing this is defined in terms of the stronger conception of what is provable, for while

It is provable that (p CD q)

might ensure the general intersubstitutivity of 'p'

and 'q', it would require that belief/wonder etc. about one necessary truth was _ipso facto_ belief/wonder etc. about all of them, since they are all provably equivalent. Now Wittgenstein, in line with this, denied one can properly be said to believe necessary truths, and Prior generally accepts that substantive beliefs in this area are beliefs about words, so his hesitancy about provable equivalence as a criterion of propositional identity is something of a mystery, but is possibly due to the following non-linguistic thought he had in 'Is The Concept Of Referential Opacity Really Necessary?' [6]:

> ...when what is in question is the law CIpqCfpfq, apparent exceptions arise when we take the 'I' to stand for material or strict equivalence. For example, 2+2=4 if and only if 573+982=1555..., but it by no means follows that if anyone can see without calculation that 2+2=4 he can see without calculation that 573+982=1555.

Moreover, even if we did settle on provable equivalence as the criterion of propositional identity, further questions would still remain, for while it is generally considered provable, for example, that all bachelors are unmarried men, so that 'x is a bachelor' might well make the same proposition as 'x is an unmarried man', the corresponding point involving co-referential individual terms is not generally thought to be available, based on provable identities like, say, 'Tully is Cicero'. So just what provable equivalence is in general, is not entirely clear. Indeed Stalnaker, who does take provable equivalence as the criterion for propositional identity [7], holds that term identities are necessary only in certain cases, although he gives no clear delimitation of those cases. However, he gets around the general difficulty in much the same way as Prior, by shifting, when discussing beliefs about necessary truths, to beliefs about what certain forms of words express. Thus Prior says:

> There is here, I suspect, a confusion between wondering whether all bachelors are unmarried, and wondering whether what is expressed by the sentence 'All bachelors are unmarried' is true.

And by 'wondering whether what is expressed by the
sentence 'All bachelors are unmarried' is true' I
do not mean wondering, with respect to what is
expressed by the sentence 'All bachelors are
unmarried', whether it is true; for this is indeed
the very same thing as wondering whether all
bachelors are unmarried. What I mean by it is not
this but wondering, with respect to the sentence
'All bachelors are unmarried', whether what it
expresses is true. And a man might well wonder
about this without wondering, with respect to the
sentence 'All unmarried men are unmarried',
whether what it expresses is true. For a man
might well not know that what the sentence 'All
bachelors are unmarried' means is simply that all
unmarried men are unmarried.

Hence Prior distinguishes, in the case where 'p' is
'All bachelors are unmarried'

(Eq)(M'p'q. He wonders whether q)

from

He wonders whether (Eq)(M'p'q.q),

for it is contingent whether any, and what truth is
expressed by 'p', even while it is necessary that p.
This same distinction would also have helped him with
what can be seen without calculation, for one might
well not be able to see without calculation that
'573+982=1555' expresses a truth while being quite
capable of seeing without calculation that '2+2=4'
does so.

We will meet distinctions like this again, towards
the end of this book, along with a non-linguistic way
of distinguishing certain beliefs, wonderings and
calculations in the general area of necessary truths.
But we shall shortly see that propositional identity
is indeed just logical equivalence, even if seeing, in
opposition to Stalnaker, that term identities are all
logically necessary is something we shall again only
get to much later on. Stalnaker, however, realises
something else we have already started to glimpse:
that because of his criterion for propositional

identity there is an inevitable gap between propositions and their expressions, indeed a proposition is quite unlike a sentence, or any object, since it has no structure:

> When a person believes that P but fails to realise that the sentence P is logically equivalent to the sentence Q, he may fail to realise that he believes that Q. That is, he may fail to realise that one of the propositions he believes is expressed by that sentence. In this case, he will still believe that Q, but will not himself express it that way.
> Because items of belief and doubt lack grammatical structure, while the formulations asserted and assented to by an agent in expressing his beliefs and doubts have such a structure, there is an inevitable gap between propositions and their expressions.

PRIOR

Although few would follow Carnap's account of Semantics today, one Realist theory of that vintage which has held philosophers' imaginations right up to the present time is Tarski's account of truth. Certainly there have been Idealist philosophers who took truth to be a predicate of intensional objects; but by far the most common account, these days, would hold that truth was a predicate, though a straightforward predicate of extensional objects of the most basic kind, namely sentences.

Thus Anil Gupta, for instance [8], simply, but explicitly assumes that the objects of truth are sentences, having previously assumed that truth is expressed by a predicate - or, rather, that he 'preferred to work under that assumption', having found that, although the sentence operator theory can give an analysis, for instance, of

Everything Jones believes is true

as

$$(p)((\text{Jones believes that } p) \supset p),$$

and he had no wish to argue against intensional operators or propositional quantifiers, still this analysis conflicted with his primary assumption, that the language he was concerned with, while it had a concept of truth, had no 'complicating factor' such as indexicals, vagueness, ambiguity, intensional constructions, or truth-value gaps. Clearly, however, if truth itself is an intensional construction such a language would be impossible, and all the wishes, preferences and assumptions made in connection with it would be to no avail. William and Martha Kneale, who are more sympathetic to indexicals, for one thing, put the anxiety of logicians who insist that truth is an affair of sentences down merely to a phobia about abstract entities, arguing that the blanks in

....expresses....

must both be filled by designators, and so it is quite proper to designate supersensible objects, so long as one does not take that to mean they must be observed by a kind of super-sense. But it is not a phobia which motivates this flight from intension; instead it is a very rational apprehension of a grammatical fact. For in the construction

It is true, p

the 'p' is to be replaced by a sentence, not a designator, and hence, as we saw with Prior before, no object, whether sensible or supersensible, is involved. That does not mean that, since the 'p' is to be replaced by a sentence, we can say

It is true, 'p'

for that, as much as the intensional object account, is nonsense. Clearly 'p' is to be replaced by a sentence which is used, not one merely mentioned, so our language, while 'extensional', must allow not just for its own study, but for its own action. The trouble with both Realism and Idealism, one might say, was that they thought that truth, if not value, could simply be contemplated.

Hence we get Tarski's truth-schema much debated: a simple version of which would be

'p' is true iff p.

But there are difficulties with this formulation, and not just because it improperly suggests there are two occurrences of 'p' involved: the name of a sentence, although sometimes given by putting quotation marks around it, does not necessarily include the sentence, any more than beating someone necessarily includes eating them. But in the oft repeated bi-conditional

'Snow is white' is true iff snow is white,

there is also a conflict with Tarski's requirement that Truth be a meta-concept. For the 'is true', and the 'snow is white' on the right hand side, since they are in the same compound, are in the same language, and a language containing its own truth predicate Tarski thought impossible, on account of his investigations of The Liar. Hence a name for the sentence on the right hand side should not occur on the left hand side. Tarski could try to get round this by turning his bi-conditional into an interderivability result, for that would allow that translation between two separate languages, one on the left and the other on the right, was involved in the case. But it is more common to ignore this matter, and simply shift to a different case and say instead

s is true iff p,

where 's' names a sentence in the object language whose translation is 'p' in the meta language, i.e. where s is a sentence which means that p, in other words Msp.

But this definition still does not allow for indexicality, nor for senselessness, vagueness or ambiguity. The difficulty with ambiguity is perhaps most acute, for if s were allowed to be ambiguous, say 'It's a bank', there would be several determinate, but different, values for epMsp, and while

61

'It's a bank' is true iff epMsp

would give determinate truth conditions for each choice, the need for choice would leave the sentence itself without objective truth conditions. Hence, to save the T-scheme, ambiguity must be excised. And likewise with vagueness and senselessness, for if there is continuous or unrestricted choice about what the sentence means then all we can say is

'It's a democracy' is true iff epMrp,

'Wednesday is fat' is true iff epMtp,

where r and t are the given sentences, and the epsilon term in each case chooses from a whole host of propositions, making the truth conditions of the sentences quite indeterminate. Hence, to defend Tarski, vagueness and senselessness must be excised. Yet how is that to be done? We might try to formulate an existence and uniqueness precondition for truth to be predicable of sentences, namely

(E!p)Msp D (s is true CD epMsp),

for, on that precondition, there is no choice left in the epsilon terms, but that is to abandon the absoluteness of the T-scheme, and bring in intensional constructions. There is no escaping such difficulties, however, for even if we try to allow for indexicality, they must also be catered for. Thus we do not get any nearer the truth if we say, for instance,

s potentially uttered by u at t in w is true in L iff p,

where s is replaced by a canonical description of a sentence of the language, and 'p' is replaced by a translation of it, since this translation qualification should properly be expressed as a precondition, bringing in an intensional construction, and conditionalising the T-scheme, again. We can relativise the meaning form to occasions, so that one might say something like

62

$$(E!p)Msop \ D \ (s \ is \ true \ at \ o \ CD \ epMsop)$$

but this is no longer the extensional bi-conditional from which we started.

Naturally Prior does not follow Tarski's account, however formulated [9]. On Prior's view Truth is primarily expressed by means of an adverb, and occurs in contexts like 'He said truly that p', which would be formalised 'Shp.p'. On this account 'It is true that p' would be

$$(x)(Sxp \ D \ (Sxp.p))$$

and, in a somewhat similar manner, Truth would be analysed away in other contexts - for instance, 'Something Cohen believes is true' would be '(Ep)(Bcp.p)'. Prior's view therefore has a quite different starting point from Tarski's:

> The basic form which Tarski defines is 'The sentence S is a true one'; the form which we define is not this, but rather 'x says truly (thinks correctly, fears with justification) that p'. And we define this quite simply as 'x says (thinks, fears) that p; and it is the case that p', or more briefly 'x says (thinks, fears) that p; and p'. (Put 'It is not the case that p' for the second 'p', or 'It is the case that p', and we have our definition of 'says falsely', or 'thinks mistakenly', or 'fears without justification'.) From these definitions and ordinary logic we may deduce all such statements as that
> (A) If anyone says that snow is white, then he says so truly if and only if snow is white.
> From Tarski's definitions and ordinary logic, we may deduce the truth of all such statements as
> (B) The sentence 'Snow is white' is true if and only if snow is white,
> and indeed for him the deducibility of all such statements is a criterion of satisfactoriness for a definition of truth.

However, this means, of course, that there is not just a difference, but a categorical difference between the two accounts:

In the first place, there are quotation-marks in (B) but not in (A). These in fact belong to Tarski's informal exposition rather than his rigorous theory; but it is essential to his theory that in sentences of his type (B) the sentence which is used in the second clause should be mentioned (by name - however the name be formed) in the first. In (A), on the other hand, the sentence 'Snow is white', which is used more than once, is not mentioned at all (it nowhere goes into quotation marks, or is spelt, or given a 'Goedel number', or named or designated in any way). (B) is about the sentence 'Snow is white', (A) is from beginning to end not about this but about snow.

Hence on Prior's view Truth is an operator on sentences, not a predicate of them: an operator modifies its sentence (in the case of Truth vacuously), it does not comment on it. Prior's theory, on which 'It is true that p' could be abbreviated to the modal form 'Tp', therefore has no difficulty with the person, place and time indexicality in

It is true that I am here now iff I am here now,

any more than it has difficulty with the non-indexicality in

It is true that u is in w at t iff u is in w at t.

The use of the same expression, both times, rigidly ensures that the same person, place and time are spoken of, and the same sense of the words is involved. Hence, likewise, the ambiguity of

It is true that it is a bank iff it is a bank,

and the vagueness of such things as

It is true that it is a democracy iff it is a democracy,

is carried through the entirety of the biconditional,

and so does not affect just one part, and so does not bring into question the truth of the whole.

That does not mean that Prior abandons the use of 'true' as a predicate, although an account of this he only sketches:

> In any case, this informal metalogic in which 'x means that p' is a fundamental form ought some time to be formalised. And we might be able, in such a metalogic, to define 'x is a true sentence' as 'x is a sentence, and for all p, if x means that p, then p'. Whether truth thus defined would turn out to be Tarskian I don't know.

So Prior had in mind a relationship like

Vx CD (p)(Mxp D p),

although he couldn't quite see how it could be applied to paradoxes like The Liar:

> We could then say that if x means that x is false, it will have two contradictory meanings - that it is false and that it is true - and will be simply and non-paradoxically false. But we have to be careful here. We can't, for example, distinguish in such a case between the <u>principal</u> meaning of x and its other meaning or meanings; for then we could use 'x principally means that' for the [delta] of our theorems, and prove such things as that x cannot principally mean that something that x principally means is false unless it principally means something else as well, and then we are back where we started. So on the whole the prospects of a language containing its own semantics still don't look too bright.

But the prospects of a language containing its own semantics are undimmed, and Prior himself was not being too bright at this point. For the notion of principal meaning in such a case is indeed just incoherent, while 'where we started' was a previous tangle, about the paradox of The Preface, which the theorem about principal meaning had brought to his mind, and that previous tangle involved a quite unrelated confusion - between sentences and propositions. On the first score, it is likewise the case that nothing can uniquely mean that something it means is false, i.e.

$$Msp.(q)(Msq \supset q=p).p=(Er)(Msr.-r)$$

is inconsistent. For then, if p, we would have

$$(Er)(Msr.-r),$$

giving, say,

$$Msw.-w,$$

but then also w=p, and so p.-p. But if on the other hand -p then

$$(r)(Msr \supset r),$$

giving p, and hence a contradiction again. But the paradox of The Preface is resolvable in quite a different way. For what Prior had previously said was

> We cannot assert in a book that something asserted in the book is not the case, unless something other than this is asserted in the book and is not the case. No doubt in a book in which nothing else is asserted but truths, or indeed in which nothing else is asserted at all, anyone can inscribe, or have inscribed, the sentence 'Something asserted in this book is false', but he cannot then say by this inscription, or by any inscription, what would normally be said by this one, namely that something asserted in the book is not the case. He, or somebody else, could say this very thing elsewhere, and would then of course be saying it falsely, but he cannot (under those conditions) say it there.

But there is no difficulty about the sentence having its customary meaning when alone in the book, since the 'something other' then asserted in the book would be a second proposition expressed by the sentence. There need not be two sentences in the book, but in the given case at least two propositions would be made

66

there. Moreover, that would not provide a difficulty for the truth predicate, since that sole sentence, on the above definition, would simply not be true, even though something it meant would be true. Formally, we have

Ms(Et)(At.-Vt)

when

As.(r)(Ar D r=s).

But

Vs CD (p)(Msp D p),

therefore

Vs D (Et)(At.-Vt),

therefore

Vs D -Vs,

therefore

-Vs.

But As, hence

(Et)(At.-Vt),

therefore

(Ep)(Msp.p).

Now

-Vs CD (Ep)(Msp.-p),

so

Msq.-q,

say. But if

$$q=(Et)(At.-Vt)$$

then

$$(t)(At \ D \ Vt),$$

which is false. Hence

$$Msq.-(q=(Et)(At.-Vt)),$$

which shows s is ambiguous.

We therefore gain a much richer theory of truth, on Prior's account, then even he realised, for not only can Truth now be an operator as well as a predicate, the prospects of a language containing its own Semantics start to become real. But more is gained even than that, for we now have a quite general argument for the substitutivity of logical equivalents in intensional constructions. For if 'x says truly that p' is 'Sxp.p', and x says that p, what is it that must be true for his saying to be true, but p? If 'Something Cohen believes is true' is '(Ep)(Bcp.p)', then what has to be true for that thing, which Cohen believes, to be true, is ep(Bcp.p); for then, not only Bcep(Bcp.p), but also ep(Bcp.p). But outside of any intensional construction there is no doubt that the truth conditions of any proposition are given by logical equivalence, therefore, by generalisation of these two cases, inside of any intensional construction there should equally be no doubt that the identity of any proposition is given by logical equivalence. For if what must be true for x's saying to be true is p, and p is true just when q is true, then what must be true for x's saying to be true is q, making what x is saying as much q as p. Moreover a proposition will be as transparent or opaque inside an intensional construction as it is outside it.

C.J.F.Williams does not quite see this last point [10], in the first place because he naturally thinks of opacity/transparency as relating to the referential terms in expressions, and so, since he recognises that a sentence is not a referential term, he does not see any relation between Prior's theory of Truth and the common doctrine of the opacity of intensional constructions:

> If 'Percy says that...' is taken as an opaque
> context this is because certain positions in what
> follows it, e.g. the position marked by 'x' in
> 'Percy says that x is a fast driver', are not
> regarded as purely referential. What is forbidden
> is for a quantifier outside the context to bind a
> variable in such a position. The discussion is
> held in terms of positions occupiable by singular
> terms. But it is not a position of this sort
> which is occupied by the variable 'p' in
> (1) [For some p, both Percy says that p and p.]
> Expressions capable of standing in the position
> marked by 'p' are not 'referential' expressions at
> all but sentences...It is not clear what sense
> could be attached to the question whether the
> position marked here by 'p' was or was not 'purely
> referential', and it may accordingly be doubted
> whether the views of these theorists on
> quantification and opacity have any relevance to
> quantification of propositional variables of the
> sort exemplified by (1).

But this misses the point that the transparency of 'p'
cannot now depend upon whether it occurs inside or
outside an intensional construction. However,
Williams realises there is still the broader question
of substitution of identicals with propositional
quantification, even though, following Prior, he is
uncertain of the criterion of propositional identity:

> Can identicals be substituted <u>salva veritate</u> for
> identicals in the position occupied by 'p' in
> 'Percy says that p'? It is not entirely clear
> what are to count as identicals in this case - the
> absence of a clear criterion of identity for
> propositions is frequently lamented. But whoever
> claims that there is failure of substitutivity in
> the position occupied by 'p' will have to bear the
> onus of providing us with the relevant criterion
> of identity. Whatever it is, it will not, I
> think, serve to substantiate his claim about
> failure of substitutivity. Let us suppose that
> changing 'Percy says that Mary is Paul's half-
> sister' to 'Percy says that Mary and Paul have

just one parent in common' changes its truth
value. In that case, what Percy is said to say in
the two cases cannot be regarded as identical, and
we do not have failure of substitutivity because
identicals have not been substituted for
identicals. The fact is that a necessary
condition for regarding 'Mary is Paul's half-
sister' as the same proposition as 'Mary and Paul
have just one parent in common' is that we can
substitute one for the other salva veritate in
such a context.

But while substitutivity in such contexts is indeed a
necessary condition for propositional identity, a
sufficient condition for this is just logical
equivalence, making

Percy says that Mary is Paul's half sister

definitely equivalent to

Percy says that Mary and Paul have just one parent
in common,

because what would have to be true for the former
saying to be true is

Mary is Paul's half-sister,

which is what would have to be true for the latter
saying to be true, i.e.

Mary and Paul have just one parent in common.

Prior's theory of Truth thus requires that
propositional identity is logical equivalence, and we
shall see in detail in later chapters how this means
that there is as much opacity in intensional
constructions as there is outside them, i.e. that
there is also extensional opacity. In the remainder
of this chapter we shall find there are several more
virtues in Prior's account of truth; but already it is
evident that it gives us a more satisfactory view of
what facts are. These are not correspondences between
sentences and the world: they are no more than states
of the world, for if the fact is that p then simply it

70

is true that p, i.e. p. Certainly this state of the world is somehow related to the sentence 'p', but that is an accident, and not what defines the fact: moreover the truth of sentences is a secondary matter, since they are not, fundamentally, what is true. The Correspondence Theory of Truth, of course, is a Realist theory, and its antithesis is the Idealist Coherence theory. The Idealist theory, we may say, eliminates correspondence by eliminating one of the terms in the Realist correspondence, namely the objective world: the Activist theory eliminates correspondence the other way, by eliminating any thing which is true. On the Realist theory there are two things, the world and what is true (a sentence); on the Idealist there is only one thing, namely what is true (an intension); on the Activist theory there is again only one thing, but this time the world. For what is (operationally) true on the Activist theory is not a further thing, but what is a fact, i.e. a non-reified proposition. It is no accident, on account of this, that propositional attitudes become as referentially transparent as the propositions then subject to the attitude: language cannot be used to talk about unworldly 'images/senses/intensions', but must be used to talk about the world, since there is nothing else to talk about other than the world. Hence even in 'intensional constructions' any referential terms cannot be used to talk about other things.

As a result, as well, of course, there are no longer two levels of language, its Syntax and its Semantics. Semantics is not 'about' language, as Linguistics, for instance is: the Semantics of a language is merely a re-expression, in mnemonic or surveyable terms, of other portions of the same language. Thus the truth table for material implication does not validate, in the sense of give a foundation for, say, the inference from q to p D q:

p	q	p D q
T	T	T
T	F	F
F	T	T
F	F	T

it merely endorses that inference, amongst others, by displaying its equivalent, i.e. that Tq entails T(p D q), using the vacuous modal operator, for which (p)(Tp CD p). The truth table might be better presented with no separate heading, to show this, viz

$$
\begin{array}{lll}
Tp & Tq & T(p \ D \ q) \\
Tp & Fq & F(p \ D \ q) \\
Fp & Tq & T(p \ D \ q) \\
Fp & Fq & T(p \ D \ q).
\end{array}
$$

DAVIDSON

One of the appeals of Tarski's T-scheme has recently seemed to be that it can be transformed to give us an account of Meaning. There is a great similarity between

s is true iff p,

and

s means that p,

and this has inspired Davidson to equate the two expressions [11]. Or, at least, that is what he has been prepared to do in many of his writings. For there are difficulties with the extensionality of the bi-conditional form, since, as a matter of fact, we have not only

'Snow is white' is true iff snow is white

but also

'Snow is white' is true iff grass is green.

Foster puts the point thus [12]:

The right starting point is to note again something which has already come up, namely the disparity between the weakness of what T-sentences state and the constraints on their construction. Any sentence of the form 'x is true if and only if p' is true just in case the sentence designated by what we substitute for 'x' has the same truth value as the sentence we substitute for 'p'. But for this biconditional to qualify as a T-sentence, as a theorem of a theory meeting Convention T, it is necessary in addition that the sentence substituted for 'p' be a translation of the sentence designated by what we substitute for 'x'. But if so, it seems that a T-theory can, in some sense, serve as a theory of meaning. For although a T-theory is not itself a theory of meaning – since the facts it states do not suffice for mastery – if one knows a T-theory and knows that it is a T-theory, one knows enough to interpret the language.

Prior, of course, has a different account of the meaning giving form, taking 'x means that p', as we have seen, to be 'Mxp', on a par with 'He believes that p' being 'Bhp'. Using Prior's symbolism we can formulate the first Davidsonian view as

(x)(p)(M'xp CD (Vx CD p)))

and a revised Davidsonian view as

(x)(p)(M'xp CD (M'xp.(Vx CD p))),

where 'M'xp' is 'Mxp.(q)(Mxq D q=p)', and its incorporation on the right hand side, in the revised view, is intended to express Foster's translation restriction on the T-scheme. Clearly, however, the resulting expression cannot be a definition of the meaning giving form, since this now occurs on both sides of the equivalence. So it seems more appropriate in the end to consider

(x)(p)(M'xp CD L(t D (Vx CD p)))

where t is a T-theory which entails just those instances of the T-scheme in which a translation is involved.

Now there is a lot to be said for this view of Meaning, for it would enable us to prove some of the theses about propositional identity enunciated before, and also, as a bonus, mount an account of the nature of truth-value gaps. The thesis about propositional identity derives from the fact that if, for any p_1 and q_1, we can prove

$$p_1 \text{ CD } q_1$$

then with the above as a theorem we can prove

$$M'xp_1 \text{ CD } L(t \text{ D } (Vx \text{ CD } q_1))$$

but also

$$M'xq_1 \text{ CD } L(t \text{ D } (Vx \text{ CD } q_1)),$$

hence

$$M'xp_1 \text{ CD } M'xq_1.$$

Substitution of logical equivalents in such contexts would therefore be partially secured, and also Stalnaker's view about the structureless nature of propositions. For since, amongst other things,

Cicero is a bachelor CD (Cicero is unmarried. Cicero is male),

is provable then

x (unambiguously) means Cicero is a bachelor

if and only if

x (unambiguously) means Cicero is unmarried and male,

showing that what x means cannot depend on the structure of any verbal expression with that meaning, i.e. be of either a conjunctive, or atomic form. Such a result would be important, for instance, in undermining thesis (3) in section two of chapter one. For while it may seem plausible that Bx(p.q) entails Bxp, given the structure of the former, the fact that the former could be exactly equivalent to, say, Bxr, where 'r' lacks a conjunctive form shows there can be no formal reason for the supposed belief entailment.

The further point about truth-value gaps would depend upon noticing the difference between the truth operator

It is true that p   i.e. Tp

and the truth predicate

x is true   i.e. Vx.

For while, if (Ep)M'xp, there is little difference between these forms, in the contrary case, i.e. if -(Ep)M'xp, we can force a separation and consider things the Tarskian tradition has tried to suppress. On the T-theory view, if (Ep)M'xp, since we presumably have, if x" is the negative of x, that

(p)(M'xp CD M'x"-p),

there is a single p_1 for which

Vx   CD p_1,
Vx" CD $-p_1$,

which matches very well the

Tp   CD   p,
T-p CD   -p,

derivable from the vacuous operator truth scheme, '(p)(Tp CD p)'. But if -(Ep)M'xp, i.e. if x is senseless or ambiguous, then there is no one p_1 for which the first two relations hold, and a divergence between the two types of truth relation starts to emerge. Prior was inclined to take a sentence to be false simply if it was not true, i.e. if (Ep)(Mxp.-p), but this ignores the possible ambiguity of x", and sentence falsity is distinguishable from non-truth if, instead, we take falsity to be the truth of the negative, i.e. (p)(Mx"p D p). Then, since the above operator relations still hold, but the predicate relations may not, predicative truth-value gaps (and gluts) would seem to be not only forced, but also explained.

The point, however, shows that the T-theory equivalence is far too strong, since if x has no unique meaning what is established is

-(Ep)L(t D (Vx CD p)),

and that is nonsensical, since it entails

(p)M(Vx CD -p),

when we must, at least, have

Vx CD Vx.

In fact the appropriate relation cannot be a biconditional, and must be reduced to

(x)(p)(M'xp D (Vx CD p)),

for given Prior's definition

Vx CD (q)(Mxq D q)

then if M'xp, since then

(q)(Mxq D q) CD p

we get

Vx CD p.

In fact this result is hardly new, because

(x)(p)(M'xp D (Vx CD p))

is equivalent to the first alternative we drew from Foster, namely

(x)(p)(M'xp CD (M'xp.(Vx CD p))),

since 'X CD (X.Y)' is the same as 'X D Y'. Also, a consideration of the Epimenides paradox has recently produced this conclusion [13]: taking (a) to be '(a) is not true' Charles Sayward says with regard to the principle of application of the T-scheme

That principle says schema (T)

    x is true iff y

holds where x is a designation of sentence y. But it does not hold for sentence designation '(a)' and sentence (a).

This calls for a simple, obvious emendation. The principle should say (T) holds where x is a designation of a sentence y which expresses one proposition. The paradoxical sentence (a) does not express one proposition. Either it is ambiguous or, more plausibly, nonsense, expressing no proposition at all. For the supposition that it does express one proposition leads to a contradiction.

It is interesting to speculate, as a result, whether a 'T-theory' of the kind much debated, though with much abstraction, in recent years, does not have the simple form

$$(x)(Ep)M'xp.$$

Certainly this entails all the desired instances of the Tarskian T-scheme, although it is not a 'theory' for a language, merely a Gupta-type presumption that all the language's sentences are univocal. The desire for this univocality has clearly been evident, in the Tarskian tradition, but its formal expression has been suppressed, no doubt for fear of realising that without univocality the subject in Semantics could not be words and sentences, and would have to be their use.

Now the restricted T-scheme we have approved still allows the truth predicate its truth-value gaps, since predicative bivalence, unlike operator bivalence, will again only be assured in the case of meaningful and unambiguous sentences. Moreover the approved scheme does not jeopardise the account of propositional identity we drew from Prior, since, for one thing, that was a general result about all indirect speech forms, and not just the meaning giving one, but, more importantly, it depended on expressions such as

Cohen believes that q, and that is true

involving a proform for a proposition, not a demonstrative to a sentence, so that the substitution produces not

Bcq.V'q',

but

Bcq.Tq.

This enables Prior to produce theorems about Meaning entirely parallel to those about other propositional attitudes, but, of course, it also gives him an advantage over Davidson in at least two, and indeed, as we shall see more fully in the next section, three ways. For Prior is far better equipped to handle the two main cases which give the Davidsonian meaning formulae trouble: senselessness, and ambiguity. Moreover, like Sayward, he realises there is the third thing which forces the other two on one's attention, namely paradoxes like the Epimenides, and the Liar. He says [14]:

Now it would generally be held that in a well-organised language each correctly formed sentence would have precisely one meaning...Either, therefore, we must admit that our language is not as well organised as this; or we must deduce...that nothing can mean that something it means is false, i.e. that for no x can x mean that something that it means is false, or in other words, whatever inscribed sentence x might be, x does not mean that something that x means is false.
Suppose, however, that we arbitrarily assign the proper name 'Baf' to a certain series of black marks on white paper, namely the series of marks which constitute the last six words in the second sentence of this paragraph. Baf does not mean that something that Baf means is false. But if those last six words, i.e. the inscription Baf, do not mean...that something that Baf means is false, they do not mean anything. But in any well-organised language, if a subsentence of a complex sentence has no meaning, neither has the sentence as a whole. From this it would follow that the

78

second sentence in this paragraph, which appears to mean that Baf does not mean that something that Baf means is false, itself has no meaning.
...so it may be worth looking again at the alternative we first put aside - that sentences of this language have more than one meaning at once.

In other words, there is indeed something that means that something that it means is false, hence our language is not organised as was presumed, i.e. it is not completely univocal. However, it is still well-organised, for if there is no clear thought that a sentence expresses we can write, in Priorian terms, -(Ep)Mxp; while if there are, say, two meanings for a sentence we can say (Ep)(Eq)(Mxp.Mxq.-(p=q)). But how could an extensional account of Meaning, like Davidson's original one without the introduction of translations or T-theories, even think up, let alone handle these things? Even to think of them would be to expose the blunder. In the former case, since '-(Ep)Mxp' is the same as '(p)-Mxp', an extensional account must say '(p)-(x is true iff p)', which is '(p)(x is true iff -p)', which in particular means, say that x is true iff q, and x is true iff -q, which entails that q iff -q. Hence the account would be led into logical absurdity. In the other case, if the sentence had two meanings, p and q, then since an extensional account must say both that x is true iff p and that x is true iff q, it must say something which might be false, for it need not be the case that p iff q. Hence there is no way, given a reduction of 'x means that p' to 'x is true iff p', one can even consider ambiguity or senselessness: a custard pie in the face could be the only result.

There is also a consistency argument against this account of 'that' which is worth considering. For in Davidson's theory of indirect speech, 'Galileo said that p' is analysed as 'Something Galileo uttered has the same content as 'p'', and hence, on that account of 'that', ''p' means that p' would have to be ''p' has the same content as 'p''. But that is not to say 'p' has any content, and so it makes the meaning form tautologous. Also, analysing 'M'p'p' as '(q)(M'p'q CD M'p'q)' is defining the form in terms of itself. But it is not just Davidson's inconsistent treatment of

'that' which is removed once we shift to Prior's
parallel accounts of 'x means that p' and 'Galileo
said that p'. Davidson's 'what 'the earth moves'
means', in his theory of indirect speech, becomes
analysable, and his basic notion of samesaying in that
theory also comes to be better expressed. For
Davidson's full re-wording of 'Galileo said that p'
was 'Galileo uttered a sentence that meant in his
mouth what 'the earth moves' means now in mine', and
he denied that 'what 'the earth moves' means' involved
a reference to a meaning, or was otherwise to be
treated as a singular term. There is, for one thing,
another inconsistency here, now with Davidson's
objectual treatment of the predicative 'what Jones
did' in his theory of events, for he was happy with
that referring to an object, indeed he made a point of
insisting that it did. But with Davidson's hestitancy
over substitutional quantification, he would clearly
be reluctant to follow even Williams when he says
[15]:

> But before we look at differences between 'What
> the postman brought' and 'What Percy says', we can
> at least note that both are properly called
> incomplete symbols. The reasons for calling 'What
> Percy says' an incomplete symbol, in so far as
> they differ from those for calling 'What the
> postman brought' an incomplete symbol, are more
> rather than less reasons for so calling it. And
> so all the Russellian reasons for rejecting the
> question 'What is it that the phrase 'What the
> postman brought' refers to, names or denotes?' are
> at least as good reasons for rejecting the
> question 'What is it that the phrase 'What Percy
> says' refers to, names or denotes?' Battles over
> whether 'What Percy says' refers to a Proposition,
> a sentence type, a sentence-token or an utterance
> are thus mere shadow-boxing. We should not be
> arguing for one answer to the question rather than
> another: we should recognise the question is
> inappropriate. Since it is an incomplete symbol,
> 'What Percy says' is not a name; and so, like
> 'What the postman brought' and, for that matter,
> 'Something', it is not the name of something.

But Prior's analysis of Truth and Meaning can do

better than this, for we can use

epMsp

for 'what 'the earth moves' means', where s is 'the earth moves', and by allowing for ambiguity and senselessness, this epsilon term account is an improvement upon Williams' iota term account. For on an iota term account the natural expression could only approximate to a subject expression if appropriate uniqueness and existence conditions held, but not only does

FexFx CD (Ex)Fx

define the quantifiers, it also gives the only restriction on exFx. Hence, even if (Ep)Msp, there might be a choice about what epMsp is - accommodating ambiguity; and if -(Ep)Msp then epMsp is anyone's guess - accommodating senselessness; and all this while accommodating the natural expression exactly as a subject expression.

The notion of synonymy, on an epsilon term account, also gets a finer analysis, and turns out to be ambiguous, as a result. This can be

epMsp = epMs'p

i.e. 'what s means is what s' means', which does not require either sentence to mean anything, and it can be

MsepMs'p

i.e. 's means what s' means', which requires that s mean something. An iota term account would identify more closely the corresponding pair of forms.

Hence the Priorian approach analyses and distinguishes a number of locutions in the area, as well as avoiding both the reification of meaning and the abandonment of it. But the value of Prior's meaning calculus over Davidson's informal account lies not just in its greater formality and comprehension: as before, it is part of a theory applying to all indirect speech, for if Davidson had symbolised as 'Msp' his alternatively understood ''the earth moves' means that p', he would not only have been able to analyse his basic idea of samesaying, and extract what 'the earth moves' means, he would also have been able to abandon his paratactic analysis of 'Galileo said that the earth moves' since he would then have seen, with Prior, that it was equally elementary. Davidson's proposal about Meaning, of course, is centrally in the Fregean tradition attempting to show how the meaning of sentences relates to their truth conditions, and thereby the meaning of their parts. But the structure of sentences does not settle truth conditions: ambiguous and vague sentences, for instance, have standard structures, but no truth conditions, so the whole programme is fundamentally misconceived. This programme, of course, derives ultimately from Frege's view that the referents of sentences were constituted by the referents of their parts, and gained its prime expression in Wittgenstein's early Picture Theory of Meaning. The idea was that the structure of sentences was to be mirrored in their meaning, i.e that the relation was to be like that in

'p' means that p.

But, as we saw before, such a form as this is logically equivalent to

'p' means that q

so long as p is logically equivalent to q, so to give the meaning of a sentence is not to give something with the same structure as the sentence, indeed it is not to give anything with a determinate structure. The idea that meaning derives from structure is as fallacious as the idea that ambiguity or senselessness derives from structure.

Moreover, not only is the notion of a structured meaning incoherent, and the associated notion of the truth conditions of sentences not universally applicable, the non-choice origin for Meaning and Truth these views engender is boring. For it is not only that only for sentences with a single determinate meaning can a truth-value-gap-less truth predicate be defined, it is also only for such sentences that there is no choice about their operational truth. Philosophers have been too wedded to the reply Euthyphro gave to Socrates' question 'Do the gods love piety because it is pious, or is it pious because the gods love it?' Euthyphro opted for the former answer, preferring to think that piety was not dependent upon the gods' pleasure, but that this pleasure was drawn from them in response to some objective quality inherent in moral acts. Only then, indeed, would piety be definable in terms of truth conditions, and have a substantive nature, with any pleasure the gods took in it an accidental mark. But not all concepts have truth conditions in this sense, as we saw with Scruton in chapter one, and so it may well be that the other arm of Socrates' disjunction should be chosen. On that view piety is constituted by the gods' pleasure, and so is not an independent quality to which they simply respond. The notion of 'pleasure' in this case is best glossed as 'favour' or 'choice', for no appetite, or sensation, is involved, indeed no causal process at all, since to think so would diminish the gods' stature. Of course Wittgenstein's later notion of 'game' was intended to capture this paradigm of language use: one without rules, but merely arbitrary similarities. It is no accident, therefore, that Hilbert's choice calculus is the mechanism which symbolises these things.

THE LIAR

There is one further, and notorious difficulty with Tarski's account of truth - it leads to the Liar Paradox. For it is certainly possible to have sentences which refer to themselves, e.g.

    s: This very sentence is not true,

or pairs of sentences which refer to each other, e.g.

    r: The sentence immediately below is not true,
    t: The sentence immediately above is true.

If one applies the T-scheme to such sentences one straight away gets a contradiction, as more deviously, with Davidson, by way of the meaning-formula. For instance, s is true iff s is not true, since 'this very sentence' is just s.

Now there is a universal panacea which, it might seem, will solve all such problems at a stroke. Moreover it is derivable merely by taking the Tarskian view of Semantics to its logical conclusion: for if truth is a meta-concept, then likewise such notions as entailment and equivalence must be. In particular, as we saw before, the separation between object and meta-languages must mean that instances of the Tarskian bi-conditional, at least in the form

'p' is true iff p

are malformed, unless this is re-expressed to become itself a meta-remark, linking ''p' is true' with 'p', for the truth predicate has to be in a different language to 'p'. Hence in place of the traditional expression for the truth scheme it might seem we really should have that ''p' is true' is equivalent to 'p', and that ''p' is not true' is equivalent to '-p', where these remarks give translations of meta-statements into object statements, in a meta-meta-language, and are not reducible to any same-level bi-conditionals. With respect to the puzzling s above we should then have merely

's is true' is equivalent to 's is not true',

and the move from bi-conditional to interderivability result enables us to avoid the contradiction. For now all we are committed to, if we say 's is true', is that we must also say 's is not true', and vice versa, and the way out of this impasse is clear: we just stay silent. By refusing to confront the Liar we take derivability of a contradiction to require not denial of the premise, merely non-assertion of that premise. Likewise with r and t: we do not have the contradictory bi-conditionals

r is true iff t is not true
t is true iff r is true

but merely the corresponding pair of meta-equivalences which prevent consistent assertion of anything. And, again, that does not give the sentences a third truth value - neither-true-nor-false - for, since we are not using Reductio we do not go on to derive 'r is not true' from the fact that 'r is true' entails 'r is not true', nor do we derive 'r is not not true' from the fact that 'r is not true' entails 'r is true'. We do not say r is neither true nor not true, we simply do not say either that it is true, or that it is not true. We deliberately ignore the matter.

Leo Simons has constructed a logic fulfilling the above requirements, and allowing such willful ignorance [16]. It has all the classical rules of inference save Reductio, and Conditional Proof, but that leaves all such rules as meta-remarks which are not reducible to object level ones. But the rejection of Reductio, and the separation of meta-equivalences and entailments from object-level bi-conditionals and conditionals, also means we do not ever say 'either p or -p', indeed we have no tautologies, so with regard to his system Simons says:

> The foregoing results may be of philosophical interest. It is conceivable that a philosopher, chary of certainties, may want a canon of inference which does not allow the demonstration of any sentence as 'true no matter what'. At the same time, he may wish to be able to infer conclusions from premises if the premises tautologically imply the conclusions, so long as the conclusions are not themselves 'certain' but at best 'contingent'...It is therefore pertinent to observe this logic might be expected to be of interest to whomever wants to avoid confrontation with what are supposed to be paradoxes entailed by the acceptance of the law of the excluded middle.

Indeed it is common in this context to construct logics which make the Law of the Excluded Middle contingent, even if few are so thoroughgoing as Simons' in rejecting all tautologies. But that extreme is required, it would seem, and not only if we are to take to heart Tarski's notions about semantical concepts being meta-concepts, and the consequent radical separation of meta-language from object-language. For Conventionalism with respect to logical necessity can only get its proper expression in such a logic: according to that doctrine it is more correct to say, for example, ''bachelor' means the same as 'unmarried man'', and ''contrary' means the same as 'cannot be together true'', than 'bachelors are unmarried men' and 'contraries cannot be together true', and hence there are very general, philosophical grounds for thinking that contingent rules of linguistic replacement are the proper expression for logical truths.

It is therefore possible to be drawn into Tarski's ideas to the extent that they seem to generate a quite new, purely inferential logic. But even if one ignores Tarski's difficulty with

'p' is true iff p,

a new, if less radical logic might seem to be called for. Thus the fact that a contradiction has been arrived at, in connection with the Liar, and therefore, by <u>Reductio</u>, some assumption must be incorrect, may lead to the view not that Tarski's account of Truth is in error, but that the specific rules which would suggest it might be are not applicable, or at least not universally applicable [17]. Not just <u>Reductio</u> is brought into question by this process, since there are other rules commonly used to obtain paradoxical conclusions, for instance in the derivation of Curry's Paradox, which considers the sentence

(1): V(1) D q.

This gives, by Tarski's bi-conditional truth scheme, that

V(1) CD (V(1) D q),

whence, by Absorption, we get

V(1) D q,

and by <u>Modus Ponens</u> twice, V(1) and then q, and all this for arbitrary 'q'. So the conclusion now might seem to be that either <u>Modus Ponens</u> or Absorption must be given up, and not Tarski's truth scheme, and certainly that it was Classical Logic that was at fault, somewhere, not that truth scheme.

The fallacy in all this reasoning is, of course, the thought that such rules as <u>Reductio</u>, Absorption, and <u>Modus Ponens</u> are valid just in a certain place, 'Classical Logic', perhaps the further and equally fallacious thought being that the laws of logic are like Political Laws or Moral Laws, which certainly do vary from place to place. But while some formal systematisation of propositional logic might allow or prohibit the transition from one set of signs to another set of signs, and allow or prohibit the categorical assertion of certain sets of signs, there is nothing formal or systematic which allows or prohibits any inference between, or judgement about, the propositions those signs mean. It is one thing to recognise that, given 'P' and 'Q if P' one may move to 'Q', in a certain verbal game, but, as Lewis Carroll pointed out many years ago in his story about Achilles and the Tortoise, it is quite another thing to recognise that necessarily if P, and Q if P, then Q [18]. Likewise, in connection with Conventionalism, there is a world of difference between,

> In English 'bachelor' means the same as 'unmarried man'

and

> Bachelors are unmarried men.

The latter employs the English language to make a necessary remark, whereas the former is part of a contingent study of the language. Moreover a person would or would not have been a bachelor whether or not there had been an English language, or the word 'bachelor' in it, for whether he is a bachelor is settled by quite extra-linguistic facts. Hence whether or not it is that if P, and Q if P, then Q, is not a matter of linguistic licences but extra-linguistic necessity, the source of such necessity being definition - though that definition is not verbal definition, i.e. rules for the use of words: some way of using '-', for instance, might enable us to say 'for certain propositions it is true that p.-p', but that would not show it was possible for contraries to be both true, merely that '-' did not then form contraries. By definition not of '-', or of 'contraries' but of <u>contraries</u> these cannot be both true, and so that fact is not a contingent one about the expected use of some sign - after all such expectations might not be met.

Now Tarski was aware of the contradictory consequences of his Conventionalist ideas, when faced with The Liar, and, of course, a similar consequence arises if we pursue the Idealist reification of propositions. For if we consider

The proposition expressed by this very sentence is not true,

and take 'the proposition' here to refer to some non-linguistic entity, which may have the truth property, then there is again a conflict with the T-scheme, now in the form 'Tx CD x' where 'x' is a kind of name. For the above would then also satisfy '-Tx CD x'. Clearly, therefore, it is the fact that propositions are not entities of any kind, and hence cannot be referred to, or involved in self-reference, which makes the Priorian approach so effective. So it is specifically the <u>reification</u> of propositions, whether as sentences or intensional entities, which is the primary thing which must be abandoned. But, faced with the absurdity The Liar seemed to generate, Tarski did not retract his Conventionalist reification of propositions, nor some or all of classical logic, as above: he took the even more radical step of restricting the applicability of classical logic, his conclusion being that natural languages were simply inconsistent, and so one had better keep to a hierarchy of formalised ones, in which the possibility of self-reference was not incorporated, i.e. which were not (in one sense) 'semantically closed'. This was linked with other ideas at the time, notably Russell's hierarchical way out of his, self-referential, paradox, and views about the inferiority of natural language, as it was then understood. Nevertheless, it was a remarkable turn in the history of logic, for it required that no consistent logic could have a use abbreviating natural language, and hence dramatically undercut all notions of validating one formal logic as opposed to another, by the procedures adopted here.

Strangely, there was a mathematical result about the limitations of formal systems, which surfaced at much the same time as Tarski's work, and which shows the way out of Tarski's impasse. That was, of course, Goedel's result about the incompleteness of formal systems, although its significance for the theory of logic is sometimes thought to lie elsewhere [19]. Thus it is commonly thought that Goedel's result showed there were expressions provable in natural language which were not provable in certain formal systems, schematically such a set of signs as

'this very sentence is not provable in P.M.'.

But what is provable 'in natural language' is not this set of signs, but instead that that very sentence is not provable in P.M., i.e. the fact, indeed the necessity which the given signs may be used to state. So the distinction between natural language and the formal system of <u>Principia Mathematica</u> is not that, say, the former is a system with far more powerful proof procedures, but simply the fact that what is provable there are propositions, not sentences, i.e. interpreted sets of signs, not sets of signs - which makes provability there an operator, not a predicate. A comparable difference was noted by Goedel himself in his identification of Intuitionistic Logic with the Modal Logic S4 [20]. A transformation of Intuitionistic Logic shows it is a logic of provability, with rules following the Modal Logic, but there is a fact about the natural provability operator which expressly shows that that modality is not a formal provability predicate, namely

Prov((Prov p) D p).

For if that were the case in a standard formal system, that system would be inconsistent.

In fact it is possible to point up Goedel's second result using the first, and his first using Hilbert's epsilon calculus. For standardly, using 'B$_Z$' for 'It is provable in Z', we may say things like [21]:

$$(Ex)Pr(x,'p') \; CD \; (B_Z \; p) \qquad\qquad (L)$$
$$(B_Z \; p) \; D \; p \qquad\qquad\qquad\qquad (M)$$
$$B_Z \; (g \; CD \; -(Ex)Pr(x,'g')) \qquad (N)$$

so if $(Ex)Pr(x,'g')$, we would have g, by (L) and (M), but also -g, by (M) and (N). Hence $-(Ex)Pr(x,'g')$, by Reductio, and so g, by (M) and (N). This is, in effect Goedel's heuristic proof of his theorem, and it shows that 'g', though unprovable in Z, is true in the standard model. However the above is not a proof in Z, since, for instance, (M) is not provable there, because it entails Z's consistency. Hence we cannot go on 'B$_Z$ g', and get a further contradiction, with '-$(Ex)Pr(x,'g')$'. However, the fact that we have proved g here can make it seem that in natural language we are in danger of inconsistency, for if we removed the subscript from 'B$_Z$' above, and took 'B' to mean provability simpliciter, then, all other things being the same, we could go on 'B g', and derive a contradiction with '-$(Ex)Pr(x,'g')$'. But such a thought rests upon the new (L),(M) and (N) still being secure, and the second use of Reductio which would then arise brings that into question. Certainly the new (M) is guaranteed, since provability does entail truth, and we could code up natural language to get the needed self-reference to establish the new (N), for any predicate '-$(Ex)Pr(x,y)$'. So it is the new (L) which must be insecure. What the new (L) says is that provability, in natural language, as in formal languages, is a predicate of sentences, so that is what must be denied: what was proved above, for instance, was not 'g' but that g, making provability, in natural language, again, not a predicate of sentences but a modality of (non-reified) propositions.

But this point can be further supported by considering not Goedel's heuristic proof but his formalised one, transposed into the Hilbertian calculus. For, as Goedel showed, we have, for a certain relation 'R':

$$-Pr(n,'(y)Ry') \supset (Ez)Pr(z,'Rn') \qquad (J)$$
$$Pr(n,'(y)Ry') \supset (Ez)Pr(z,'-Rn') \qquad (K)$$

and so if $Pr(n,'(y)Ry')$ then, from (K), $(Ez)Pr(z,'-Rn')$, while $(Ez)Pr(z,'Rn')$, since '(y)Ry' entails 'Rn'. Hence, if Z is consistent, which it is, we have $(n)-Pr(n,'(y)Ry')$, but also, as a result, from (J), $(n)(Ez)Pr(z,'Rn')$.

Now this might seem to show that it is not provable in Z that (y)Ry, while it is provable in Z that Rn, for all n; and the impossibility of this reading is clearly demonstrated, not just by this expression in natural speech, but also given a transcription into the epsilon calculus, since '(y)Ry' is there just 'Rey-Ry'. Hence Goedel's theorem, as before, shows merely that certain signs '(y)Ry' are not derivable, while other signs, like 'Rn', are derivable, in Z. Certainly there would also be derivable '(En)(n=ey-Ry)', but not 'n=ey-Ry', for any numeral 'n', by the nature of epsilon terms, hence we would not have

$$(En)((Ez)Pr(z,'Rn').(Ez)Pr(z,'n=ey-Ry')),$$

and while we would have

$$(En)((Ez)Pr(z,'Rn').n=ey-Ry),$$

it is precisely the fact that the first part of this is about signs which prevents the transparent substitution of the second part, and so prevents the universal expression, which states the facts, being derivable.

But showing how the use of natural language can be consistent, and classical logic unimpugned, requires more than recognising that provability, like truth, is not a predicate, but an operator, and that, as a consequence, logic is not about sentences but propositions. It requires, as well, setting out the resulting detailed solution of The Liar, if not other paradoxes. It is therefore doubly important that we find a way out of this Paradox, not only for its own sake, but also for the general methodology of this book. Fortunately a way out is readily to hand, once we follow Prior's account of Truth, although Prior's own exposition was somewhat incomplete, and inconclusive [22]. The point rests on the possible ambiguity of Liar sentences, for when we take truth to be an operator on non-reified propositions rather than a predicate of sentences we must consider, e.g. s:

What this sentence means is not true

and while we might now say

Ms(Ep)(Msp.-p),

that doesn't prevent us consistently saying

(Ep)(Msp.-p),

since together we only get

(Eq)(Msq.q),

and the expression is shown to be ambiguous. The point is of sufficient importance to be proved twice more. Thus granted

Ms(Ep)(Msp.-p),

we may ask whether (Ep)(Msp.-p) or -(Ep)(Msp.-p). But the latter entails

(p)(Msp D p)

giving, by instantiation

Ms(Ep)(Msp.-p) D (Ep)(Msp.-p)

and so

(Ep)(Msp.-p),

hence definitely (Ep)(Msp.-p). So suppose

Msq.-q

(e.g. use the abbreviation q=ep(Msp.-p)), then if

        q=(Ep)(Msp.-p)

then

        -(Ep)(Msp.-p)

so

        -(q=(Ep)(Msp.-p))

i.e. s is ambiguous. Again, consider

        Ms-epMsp,

from which there follows

        (Ep)Msp

and hence

        MsepMsp.

Now

        -(epMsp=-epMsp)

hence

        (Ep)(Eq)(Msp.Msq.-(p=q)),

and so the Liar expression is proved ambiguous yet a
third way. Note, as well, that we get the same result
if we consider

        What this sentence unambiguously means is false,

i.e. s where

        Ms(Ep)(Msp.(q)(Msq D q=p).-p).

The options here are that

        -(Ep)(Msp.(q)(Msq D q=p).-p)

or

                            93

(Ep)(Msp.(q)(Msq D q=p).-p),

so, in the latter case, say

    Msr.(q)(Msq D q=r).-r

making

    r=(Ep)(Msp.(q)(Msq D q=p).-p),

and hence

    -(Ep)(Msp.(q)(Msq D q=p).-p),

and so this is definitely the case. But as a result

    (p)((Msp.-p) D -(q)(Msq D q=p)),

and so

    (Msr.-r) D (Eq)(Msq.-(q=r)),

using 'r' as above, and hence getting again

    (Eq)(Msq.-(q=r)),

so one cannot even believe this 'Liar' when it says it is unambiguous.

   The solution to Curry's Paradox we can formulate remembering

    (p)(M'sp D (Vs CD p)),

for then if

    V(1) CD (V(1) D q)

leads to q, when -q, we must say

    -M'(1)(V(1) D q),

i.e.

    -M'sp,

with s=(1) and p=(V(1) D q). Hence while, in this
case,

   (1): V(1) D q

defines a sentence, it does not produce a distinct
proposition, and by not doing that it provides yet
another crucial test showing that Tarski's account of
truth is quite wrong.

   Charles Parsons [23] realises that Tarski's account
of truth is wrong, and reformulates it, complexly, as

   (x)((x is a proposition.'p' expresses x) D (x is
   true CD p)).

He then considers, in effect, a sentence (1) which
says

   (1) expresses a false proposition

and argues that if x is a proposition, and (1)
expresses x then

   x is true CD (1) expresses a false proposition.

Supposing x is not true he gets by Existential
Generalisation

   (Ez)(z is a proposition.-(z is true).(1) expresses
   z)

i.e.

   (1) expresses a false proposition,

giving him that x is true. But since x is arbitrary
it follows categorically that

   -(Ex)(x is a proposition.-(x is true).(1)
   expresses x)

i.e. there is no false proposition expressed by (1).
But if y is a proposition that (1) expresses we get
again that

95

y is true CD (1) expresses a false proposition

and that y is true, hence there is no proposition at all expressed by (1).

Parsons realises, however, that there is a difficulty with this solution:

> A difficulty that arises immediately is the following: (1) says of a certain sentence which turns out to be (1) itself, that it expresses a false proposition. We have shown that (1) expresses no proposition. But then (1) seems to say something false. Are we not forced to say that (1) expresses a false proposition after all?

He goes on to offer a way out:

> A simple observation that would avoid this is as follows: the quantifiers in our object language could be interpreted as ranging over a certain universe of discourse U. Then a sentence such as
> (Ex)(x is a proposition.A expresses x)
> is true just in case U contains a proposition expressed by A, i.e. by (1). But what reason do we have to conclude from the fact that we have made sense of (1) and even determined its truth-value that it expresses a proposition which lies in the universe U?

But the difficulty with this way out is that in 'the universe' in which Parsons has 'made sense' of (1) it would still be provable that

-(Ex)(x is a proposition.(1) expresses x)

since there was no mention of 'universes' in the above proof. Clearly the only solution to Parsons' dilemma is to realise that (1) may be ambiguous, and that a comparable argument starting from, say,

(p)((s only expresses p) D (s is true CD p))

would show there was no one proposition (1) expresses, allowing there might be some proposition that it expresses which is false.

This means that on Prior's account natural language is consistent and can contain its own Semantics, though it is not semantically closed, in at least one sense, since the non-availability of reified propositions as objects of reference means there can be no self-reference in connection with them. Prior's account also means we can go ahead with our 'prolegomena' to formal logic; and there is also a further consequence, about Semantics not being distinct from Proof Theory, which we shall come to in the next chapter. As we have seen, if truth is redundant then truth tables are not a defense of Tautologies, they are a repetition of them, and likewise some elements in Classical Modal Semantics will come to have an 'object-level' use.

NOTES

[1]   For Idealist conceptions of Intensions see, for instance, W.& M.Kneale's The Development of Logic, Clarendon Press, Oxford 1962, Ch.X.
[2]   Prior's 'Oratio Obliqua' was published in the roceedings of the Aristotelian Society supplementary volume, 1963, see also Prior's Papers on Logic and Ethics, Duckworth, London, 1976.
[3]   Quine's discussion of Intensions is in Word and Object, M.I.T.Press, Cambridge Mass., 1960, Ch.VI, see, in particular pp212-216.
[4]   Prior's discussion of Quine, and the non-intensional account of propositions is in Ch 2 of Objects of Thought, see p20 for the immediate quote, and p35 for the later quote about the related substitutional account of quantification. For details of further quotes see notes 5, 9, 14, and 22. © Oxford University Press 1971. Reprinted from Objects of Thought, edited by P.T.Geach and A.J.P.Kenny (1971) by permission of Oxford University Press.
[5]   Prior's discussion of truth-functionality and propositional identity is in op.'cit. note 4, Ch.4; for the following quote see p53, for the later one about wondering, see p55.
[6]   Prior's 'Is the Concept of Referential Opacity

really Necessary?' is in <u>Acta Philosophica Fennica</u>, 16, 1963, see p190 for the quote. Secondary discussion of Prior's system includes C.J.F.Williams' <u>What is Truth?</u>, Cambridge U.P. 1976.

[7] R.Stalnaker's discussion is in 'Propositions' in <u>Issues in the Philosophy of Language</u> eds A.F.MacKay and D.D.Merrill, Yale U.P., New Haven, 1976, see p87 for the final quote of this section; see also his <u>Inquiry</u> M.I.T.Press, Cambridge Mass.,1984.

[8] A.Gupta's remarks are in his article 'Truth and Paradox' in <u>Recent Essays on Truth and the Liar Paradox</u> ed. R.L.Martin, Clarendon Press, Oxford 1984.

[9] Prior's views are in Ch.7 of op. cit note 4, see pp98,99,104,106, and p86, respectively, for the following five quotes.

[10] For the views of Williams see op. cit. note 6, pp5-6; see also, for instance, G.Pitcher's Truth, Prentice-Hall, New Jersey, 1984, for more on facts and classical theories of truth.

[11] For Davidson's views on Meaning, also those on Indirect Speech, see 'Truth and Meaning', 'In Defence of Convention T', 'On Saying That' and 'Reply to Foster' in <u>Inquiries into Truth and Interpretation</u>, Clarendon Press, Oxford 1985.

[12] J.A.Foster's 'Meaning and Truth Theory' is in G.Evans and J.McDowell eds <u>Truth and Meaning</u>, Oxford U.P., 1976, for the quote see p17. The book as a whole also illustrates a point made later, about the abstraction in this tradition.

[13] See C.Sayward's 'Prior's Theory of Truth' in <u>Analysis</u> 47.2, 1987, for the Tarskian difficulty with ambiguity and senselessness; see, in particular p86 for the given quote.

[14] Prior, op. cit. note 4, pp105-6.

[15] For Williams' views on propositional reification see op. cit. note 6, p40.

[16] For L.Simons' work see 'Logic Without Tautologies' in <u>Notre Dame Journal of Formal Logic</u>, XV, 1974, for the quote, see p429.

[17] For a derivation of a non-classical logic directly from Tarski's truth-scheme, see, for instance, G.G.Priest's 'The Logic of Paradox' <u>Journal of Philosophical Logic</u>, 8, 1979.

[18] Lewis Carroll's story about Achilles and the Tortoise is in <u>Mind</u>, IV, 1895, p278.

[19] See Priest, op. cit. note 17, for a discussion of the relation between Goedel's Theorem and natural language.

[20] K.Goedel's comparison of Intuitionistic Logic and S4 is in 'An Interpretation of the Intuitionistic Sentential Logic' in <u>The Philosophy of Mathematics</u> ed J.Hintikka, Oxford U.P., 1969.

[21] For details of Goedel's heuristic and formal proofs, see, for instance, G.T.Kneebone's <u>Mathematical Logic and the Foundations of Mathematics</u> Van Nostrand, London, 1963, pp231,237.

[22] See Prior op.cit. note 4, Chs 6 and 7, and my 'Prior's Analytic' in <u>Analysis</u>, 46.2, 1986.

[23] C.Parsons' 'The Liar Paradox' is in R.L.Martin op. cit. note 8; for the quotes see p17.

3 Conditionals

HOOKS

My ultimate aim in this chapter is to give a unified
account of 'if' in terms of the material connective
hook, i.e. what is here written 'ɔ'. There are a good
number of points to be made on the way to that
objective: about how it has come to seem that 'if' is
not univocal, about how standard modal logic has
failed to see it needs an expression for 'It would be
the case that', about conditionals whose probability
is a conditional probability, and about the classic
paradoxes of material and strict implication, the
validity of disjunctive syllogism, and the
impossibility of true contradictions. I end with a
survey and assessment of some recent theories of
subjunctive conditionals, giving a formulation of them
in terms of the modality 'It would be the case that';
I start by showing how hook is a more adequate
symbolisation of 'if' than it has recently seemed.

Those seeking to deny the truth-functional
definition of 'if' have a hard job on their hands.
Either they must deny the standard link with
disjunction, or deny the truth-functional definition
of 'or'; and likewise for conjunction and 'and'. Most

commonly the line would be that 'if' has many uses, and that, while hook captures the most basic of these, other senses of the term require different formulations.

Let us take the conjunctive case, as an illustration. Someone wishing to deny the standard truth-functional definition of 'if' must find fault either with

p	q	p.q
T	T	T
T	F	F
F	T	F
F	F	F

as a representation of 'and', or with

p	-p
T	F
F	T

as a representation of 'not', or with

if p, q = not(p and not-q)

as the correct propositional relation between 'if', 'not' and 'and'. The fact that a propositional relation is in question rules out of order Strawsonian objections in terms of the usability of 'and' to couple nouns (Peter and Paul were gentiles), adjectives (It was bright and beautiful) or adverbs (He spoke clearly and distinctly), also the usability of 'non' etc. to form such nouns, adjectives, adverbs (non-gentile, unbeautiful, indistinctly) [1]. Such forms are definable in terms of propositional relations, in any case. More to the point are questions about whether there are restrictions on propositions which may be conjoined with one another, about whether 'and' commutes, and about whether negatives are contradictory, i.e. of opposite truth value.

There certainly are restrictions on what may be conjoined with one another consistently, but that does not prevent any pair of propositions making a proper conjunction of the form 'p.q', any more than does the fact that there are restrictions on what may be conjoined with one another truly. There are less well defined bizarenesses to do with what are not on the same topic, but that again leaves 'Sodium is a metal, and Henry VIII had six wives' and the like as weird conjunctions not as non-conjunctions, and positing a suitable context will, in any case, erode the strangeness (a quiz show, for instance). Getting the right context is perhaps one way of seeing that 'They got married and bought a house' does commute, unlike, say 'They got married and then bought a house', but clearly, also, being careful to distinguish 'and' from 'and then' is another and more direct way of seeing this. We considered, in the last chapter, putative examples where negatives were not contradictory, and saw in detail what confusions there were in seeing them that way.

That leaves the propositional relation between 'and', 'not' and 'if' as the only feasible point at which to try to break the above argument for the standard definition of 'if'. But it can hardly be doubted that at least one sense of 'if' is covered by this definition, so the argument against it must be that it does not capture all senses of 'if'. Indeed, it is sometimes said that another sense of 'if' is given by the definition of fish-hook rather than plain hook. For we may define

Necessarily if p then q,

as

L(p D q),

where necessity is defined in terms of 'truth in all possible worlds', i.e. 'in every possible world it would be the case', and such an expression is commonly symbolised in a conditional fish-hook form [2]. But this does not itself show that 'if' is ambiguous. For the truth in all possible worlds of a conditional would be symbolised

$(i)(V(p,w_i)=1 \ D \ V(q,w_i)=1)$

102

or, as I shall often write it,

(i)(Wip D Wiq),

and this does not have a direct reading in a straight
'if X then Y' form. That is not to deny that there
are necessitated conditionals, or that they have
properties different from indicative conditionals; but
it is crucial that we should resist them being
straightaway called 'conditionals' - otherwise we
shall lose sight of 'if', and might even be moved to
cook up other 'conditional' forms.

The situation with necessitated conditionals,
however, is even more subtle, for, using Hilbert's
epsilon calculus, it turns out that there is a
formulation for quantified conditionals as plain
unquantified conditionals, while that reformulation
gives even less support to the thesis that a different
sense of 'if' is involved, since the 'if' in the
reformulation is yet again the standard material hook.
Thus in Hilbert's predicate calculus, not only is

(Ex)Fx CD FexFx

but as a result

(x)-Fx CD -FexFx,

and so

(x)Fx CD Fex-Fx.

Hence the above quantified conditional

(i) (Wip D Wiq)

may also be written

Whp D Whq,

where h=ei-(Wip D Wiq), making the necessitated
conditional equivalent to a plain material one. So
not only are necessitated conditionals quantified
conditionals, and not straightaway expressible as
conditionals, there is also a means of reducing them

to plain conditionals which shows the relationship in them is still material. For two, independently conclusive, reasons, therefore, there is no need for the introduction of a new symbol, fish hook, in this area. Nor, clearly, would the case for such a symbol be any more plausible if we tried, in opposition to the above, to use the relativised notion of necessity more common in standard treatments of Modal Logic. Thus it is common to define necessity not in the above way but in this sort of way:

[VL]. For any wff, o, and for any wi belonging to W, $V(Lo,w_i)=1$ iff for every w_j belonging to W such that w_iRw_j, $V(o,w_j)=1$,

i.e.

WiLo CD (j)(Rij D Wjo)

where R is some possibly reflexive, transitive, or equivalence relation. But if so then

WiL(p D q)

i.e.

(j)(Rij D Wj(p D q))

is even less a conditional connecting p and q than the previous necessitated conditional, while its representation as a plain conditional would again be a representation as a material conditional.

I do not follow this relativised account of modality and necessity, however, for a number of reasons. First because there is commonly written into it, with mention of the 'w's, the Idealist ontology of 'possible worlds', i.e. the idea that there are other worlds besides this one, those worlds being often spoken of as kinds of object. What there are, instead, are a range of views, accounts, theories, stories etc. about this world, which might be idealised as consistent and complete, but which must not be reified as consistent and complete worlds. Moreover, what goes on in those views, accounts, theories and stories is not something which is actually going on, and so should not be put in the indicative. It is an imaginative exercise, akin to the use of the 'historical present', to say, for instance, that on Stalnaker's account of Conditionals a conditional *is* true in the actual world when its consequent *is* true in the selected world, for the actual facts about conditionals are not relative, or dependent on theories about them (not even the true theory about them). Properly speaking, it is merely that, on Stalnaker's account a conditional <u>would be true</u> in the actual world if its consequent <u>were</u> true in the selected world - and that is a grammatical remark, about what mood of the verb should follow story credits. Indeed we could not distinguish the truth from pure stories otherwise: certainly if Stalnaker's account is correct we can make the given indicative statement (unprefaced with 'On Stalnaker's account'), but even if that account is correct what follows 'On Stalnaker's account' should be, linguistically, what 'would be' the case. It is necessary, therefore, to speak of 'possible world description' or 'actual world description' in connection with the residual 'i' of 'w_i', to avoid charges of 'Modal Realism': reading 'Wip' as 'It would be the case, on view (account/theory/story) i, that p', rather than 'It is the case, on view (account/theory/story) i that p', avoids the other aspect of this ungrammatical thesis.

Now the consequent fact that possible world stories are possibly true world stories means that the above relativised account of necessity cannot be correct. For while relativised necessities of a kind are available in the present symbolism, viz

WiLo CD Wi(j)Wjo,

it is now also the case that there is an 'a' for which

(A): (p)(Wap CD p)

i.e. that there is a possible world description which is the actual world description, and that

(i)(Wip D Mp),

i.e. that even if it is not the actual world description, any possible world description possibly describes the actual world. But on the relativised account of necessity

Mo CD WaMo

giving

Mo CD (Ej)(Raj.Wjo),

and that does not allow Wio to entail Mo without a further premise. Clearly if

WaLo CD (j)(Raj D Wjo)

then

Lo CD (j)(Raj D Wjo)

and the right hand side does not define necessity, unless

(Ej)(-Raj.Wj-o)

is ruled out. But, since 'R' has to be defined independently of 'o', ruling this out involves ruling out

(Ej)-Raj

which gives us

Lo CD (j)Wjo,

and hence

WiLo CD Wi(j)Wjo,

again. There is thus no escaping the unconditional nature of necessity, and we must reformulate the standard account, giving it a closure condition

Lo CD (j)Wjo

in place of [VL] above.

The other rules for the manipulation of the quasi-modal operator 'It would be the case, on account i, that', however, merely derive from translating the standard account into the present symbolism. Thus, standardly, we have

(1). For any propositional variable, p_j, and for any w_i belonging to W, either $V(p_j,w_i)=1$ or $V(p_j,w_i)=0$, but not both.

(2). For any wff, o, and for any w_i belonging to W, $V(-o,w_i)=1$ iff $V(o,w_i)=0$.

(3). For any wffs o and o', and for any w_i belonging to W, $V((o \lor o',w_i)=1$ iff either $V(o,w_i)=1$ or $V(o',w_i)=1$.

So if we take

(B): (i)(-Wio CD Wi-o)

we allow for (1) and (2), while if we take

(C): (i)(Wi(o v o') CD (Wio v Wio'))

we allow for (3). This means the Rule of Necessitation is provable, at least in the form: for any tautology t, and any theory i, Wit - since, for instance, Wi(o v -o) is (Wio v Wi-o) by (C), and hence (Wio v -Wio) by (B). Also, from (A) we can get that Lo D o, since (i)Wio D Wao, while from (C) we can get

(Wi-o v Wio') CD Wi(-o v o')

and so, from (B) again

(Wio D Wio') CD Wi(o D o')

and hence

L(o D o') D (Lo D Lo'),

by generalisation. Hence the present modal system based on principles (A), (B) and (C) is very much like

the classic system T even although its contained
definition of necessity is far more like that in S5.
There is no way, moreover, that further axioms may be
added to it as truths about necessity, since
consistent stories have been constructed (within
classical modal logic, no less) in which the
characteristic axioms of other systems are not valid:
for instance, the characteristic axiom of B, i.e.

o D LMo (i.e., 'o D (i)Wi(Ej)Wjo')

is not valid in S4 (the logic of provability, see
before.)

But while the present system is a recognisable modal
logic, there are more expressions symbolised in it
than in any classical system, for we now have a
representation of the modality 'It would be the case
that', using our indirect speech, operator expression
'Wi', and that gives us a representation of
subjunctive expressions generally, including
subjunctive conditionals. But these turn out to be
material conditionals connecting modal parts, rather
than, as classically symbolised, non-material
conditionals connecting non-modal parts. For, as with
necessitated conditionals (which are, strictly
necessitated subjunctive conditionals, saying that
necessarily if p were true, q would be true) it has
been common, of late, to try to represent subjunctive
conditionals by means of some non-hook, but hook-type
expression. As a result of this it has come to seem
that 'if it were the case that p it would be the case
that q', is not of the hook-form 'X D Y', since it is
not of the indicative form 'if p then q'. But,
indeed, it is of the form 'X D Y', and the 'if' in it
is the straight material connective. The difficulty
in the formalisation of subjunctives has been in
getting hold of a formalisation of the 'it would be
the case that', not in getting hold of a new
formalisation of the 'if'. I write the elementary
subjunctive 'on account i it would be the case that p'
as above as 'Wip', where 'i' is some possible world
description, and the previous conditional subjunctive
'On Stalnaker's account, a conditional would be true
in the actual world if its consequent were true in the
selected world' is then of the form

Wi(p D q),

which is the same as the conditional

Wip D Wiq.

As was stated at the beginning, we shall look in more detail, later in this chapter, at the extant general theory of subjunctive conditionals, and in particular distinguish there, more fully, necessitated subjunctives from ones of this sort about mere possibilities, but one clarification of the extant theory already becomes apparent, for we now have a better understanding of how the various subjunctives relate to the indicative conditional, and to actual states of affairs, generally [3]. On Stalnaker's theory, 'the' conditional would entail the 'corresponding' material expression, where this is to be symbolised

$(p > q)$ D $(p D q)$.

Stalnaker presumes, therefore, that the two expressions do have the same antecedent and consequent, trying, as above, to incorporate the difference into the connective, instead of, as it naturally lies, in the connected. Now the material expression (which is the straight indicative conditional) can certainly be presented in the general form of a subjunctive, for using the completely true story, i.e. realised possibility a, we can say

$((p D q) CD Wa(p D q)).(Wa(p D q) CD (Wap D Waq))$.

But that makes the non-necessitated subjunctive conditional 'Wip D Wiq' quite distinct from the indicative, unless i=a, and shows there is certainly no entailment between them. D.K.Lewis' difficulty in this area is illustrated with his derivation of the 'counterfactual' from 'p.q', i.e. 'Wap.Waq'. Clearly, however, only 'Wap D Waq' follows from this, not 'Wip D Wiq' for arbitrary 'i'.

But the general fact that, since 'i' in the above is arbitrary, at least one type of subjunctive conditional has only a definite truth value given a certain authorial credit, or the like (supposing we don't have $(j)Wjp.(j)Wj-q$, or $(j)(Wjp \supset Wjq)$, which would rule the particular form out or in, on general grounds) also divorces the present account from Lewis' and Stalnaker's, since with those accounts various 'closeness' conditions are incorporated into the definition of the 'counterfactual' or 'conditional', to try to make its truth value objectively determinate. But no question about the closeness of Stalnaker's account to the actual facts is involved in evaluating the conditional 'On Stalnaker's account, a conditional would be true in the actual world if its consequent were true in the selected world'. This conditional is evaluated simply by reading Stalnaker's account, and so is not true or false according with the truth value, or even near truth value, of that account: it is an indirect speech form, and has an epistemological basis accordingly. Stalnaker is himself puzzled about the epistemological question regarding subjunctive conditionals. He realises that many such conditionals are contingent statements about possibilities not necessary statements about impossibilities, and he also realises that contingent statements must be capable of confirmation empirically; so he wants to argue that one sometimes has evidence about 'non-actual situations'. But the evidence for at least one contrary-to-fact conditional is found just by reading a certain story - in the above case, one of Stalnaker's own stories. This is indeed about an unrealised possibility rather than a necessity, but there is no difficulty about getting 'empirical' confirmation of it, unless there is some difficulty in getting close to that story. There might be some difficulty about adjudicating between, say

> If Bizet and Verdi had been compatriots, they would have been French

and

> If Bizet and Verdi had been compatriots, they would not have been French

in some incomplete story. For taking up its writing

ourselves and arbitrarily completing it to include detailed comments on the matter would merely give us something of the form

WjWi(p D q)

not categorically

Wi(p D q).

But while 'Conditional Excluded Middle' does not hold for necessitated conditionals, i.e. we do not have

(i)Wi(p D q) v (i)Wi(p D -q),

undoubtedly the law holds for the non-necessitated sort of conditional, for we have

(i)Wi(p D (q v -q)),

and this is

(i)(Wi(p D q) v Wi(p D -q)).

Hence all <u>complete</u> stories settle the truth value of all propositions.

IFS

A great number of points have been made, in the literature on conditionals, regarding their 'non-truth-functional' features. Points, in particular, have been made about even-if conditionals and general conditionals not being truth-functional conditionals, and also about what happens when the antecedent of a conditional is false, and about the need for a connection or relevance between the parts.

With regard to even-if conditionals there is surely no difficulty in formalising 'q, even if p' as 'q, and q if p', i.e. 'q.(p D q)'. Indeed, it is just 'even if's expression of irrelevance which hook is singularly adapted to symbolise. Thus Hodges' 'I won't sing, even if you pay me 1,000 pounds' is true in just the same circumstances as 'I won't sing' is true, and a similar analysis must be given of 'The choir was sensitive, even if at times a little strained' [4]. There is, of course, with such expressions, always the possibility of asserting just their entailed conditionals, i.e. we can say 'If he felt embarrassed, he showed no signs of it', as well as 'Even if he felt embarrassed, he showed no signs of it'; but if the former is indeed what is meant then 'he showed no signs of it' is no more entailed than 'he did not feel embarrassed'. Sometimes, however, such non-even-if conditionals are definitely not what is meant, since 'If you want to wash your hands, the bathroom is first on your left', for instance, does not entail, but is simply entailed by 'The bathroom is on your left'.

With regard to general conditionals I make a somewhat similar point to the one I made with respect to necessitation conditionals: these are quantified conditionals, as commonly understood, i.e. are to be symbolised '(x)(Px D Qx)', and so are not directly of the conditional form. But they may be put into a conditional form, using the Hilbertian calculus, as before, since the instanced one is also 'Pb D Qb' where b=ex(Px.-Qx). What also confuses here is the fact that, in addition to universal statements, which are properly symbolised in this quantified and unquantified way, there are conditionals in the area which cannot be symbolised without some new features within formal logic, to handle pronouns. As we shall see more fully in chapter five, 'All P is Q' is to be distinguished from 'If anything is a P, it is a Q' – the latter being directly a conditional of the form '(Ex)Px D QexPx'. The point also applies to subjunctive conditionals like 'If ever it were that p, it would then be that q': this is not a conditional expression for the necessitated conditional

(i)(Wip D Wiq)

i.e.

Wcp D Wcq

where c=ei(Wip.Wi-q), but a special particular

subjunctive

$$(Ei)Wip \ D \ W(eiWip)q,$$

i.e.

$$Wdp \ D \ Wdq,$$

where $d=eiWip$.

Now Strawson says [5]:

> Throughout this section I have spoken of a 'primary or standard' use of 'if...then...' or 'if', of which the main characteristics were: that for each hypothetical statement made by the use of 'if', there could be made just <u>one</u> statement which would be the antecedent of the hypothetical and just <u>one</u> statement which would be its consequent...Not all uses of 'if', however, exhibit all these characteristics. In particular, there is a use which has an equal claim to rank as standard and which is closely connected with the use described, but which does not exhibit the first characteristic...I have in mind what are sometimes called 'variable' or 'general' hypotheticals: e.*g*., 'If ice is left in the sun, it melts'...To a statement made by the use of a sentence such as these there corresponds no single pair of statements which are, respectively, its antecedent and consequent. On the other hand, for every such statement there is an indefinite number of non-general hypothetical statements which might be called exemplifications, applications, of the variable hypothetical; e.*g*. a statement made by the use of the sentence 'If this piece of ice is left in the sun, it will melt'.

But it will not do to say that with conditionals like 'If ice is left in the sun it melts', we have conditionals in which there is no single antecedent and consequent. In these conditionals, while we do not have such antecedents as 'this piece of ice is left in the sun', (LexIx), we do have antecedents like 'some ice is left in the sun', ((Ex)(Ix.Lx)), allowing a consequent 'that ice left in the sun melts',

(Mex(Ix.Lx)), of much the same form as the consequent in the other case, namely 'that piece of ice melts', (MexIx). Combined with 'if..then..' we therefore get, in the 'variable' case, conditionals of the straightforward material form 'if anything is P, then it is Q'. On the other hand, with a universal statement like "All ice left in the sun melts', which Strawson would identify with such a conditional, we certainly can locate no separate statements which are the antecedent and consequent, in the natural language form given, but that is for the eminently satisfactory reason that no conditional expression is directly involved, merely a subject-predicate one.

A partly similar point may be made about the antecedent and consequent in unquantified subjunctive conditionals, i.e. ones of the form 'Wjp D Wjq', when -(j=ei(Wip.Wi-q)). Thus Strawson says

...a statement of the form 'if p then q' does entail the corresponding statement of the form 'p D q'.
The force of the word 'corresponding' in the above paragraph needs elucidation. Consider the...following very ordinary specimens of hypothetical sentences:
   (1) If the Germans had invaded England in 1940, they would have won the war
...The sentences which could be used to make statements corresponding in the required sense to the subordinate clauses can be ascertained by considering what it is that the speaker of each hypothetical sentence must (in general) be assumed either to be in doubt about or to believe is not the case. Thus...the corresponding pairs of sentences are:
   (1a) The Germans invaded England in 1940; they won the war
...Sentences which could be used to make statements of material implication corresponding to the hypothetical statements made [before] can now be framed from these pairs of sentences as follows:
   (M1) The Germans invaded England in 1940 D they won the war
...The very fact that these verbal modifications

114

are necessary, in order to obtain from the clauses of the hypothetical sentence the clauses of the corresponding material implication sentence is itself a symptom of the radical difference between hypothetical statements and truth-functional statements.

There is thus a tendency to say that one cannot assert the antecedent and consequent of

If the Germans had invaded England in 1940, they would have won the war,

and this is now taken to be one further reason for believing such a form is not a material conditional, since it certainly is not an indicative conditional like

If the Germans invaded England in 1940, they won the war.

But when allowance is made for the fact that such subjunctive conditionals - when they are not universalised, as with '(i)(Wip D Wiq)' - are theory relative, so that there is an implicit reference in them to some story, view or account, then there is no difficulty in finding their antecedents and consequents amongst assertible statements. For if the whole is properly

On account i, if the Germans had invaded England in 1940, they would have won the war,

then we can form from this compound the two elementary subjunctives

On account i, the Germans had invaded England in 1940,

and

On account i, the Germans would have won the war,

and even drop explicit reference to any account. Note that elementary subjunctive claims are not necessarily guesses as to the actual facts, i.e. of the form

'Wap', i.e. 'On the true account, it would be that p', nor are they necessarily counter the facts, i.e. of the form 'Wip' when 'Wa-p'. Indeed, there may be counterfactual indicatives, as in the German invasion case above.

Now it is these overlooked elementary subjunctives which theorists in the area quite possibly have had unconsciously in mind when making remarks about the impossibility of false antecedents, and the resulting incompatibility of 'if p, q' and 'if p, -q'. Certainly elementary subjunctives like 'Wiq' presume that the story i is consistent, and that means 'Wiq' rules out 'Wi-q'. But that does not make the elementary subjunctives themselves conditionals, and so it does not make the comparable results for conditionals hold. Certainly there are links between such elementary subjunctives and conditionals: for instance, we can say

Wip D (i=a D p)

since given Wip and i=a we can get Wap, and hence p. But there is no way to reverse this relationship, since 'If i=a, then p' is consistent with 'Wi-p': the conditional is 'If i=a, then Wap', which is equivalent to 'If i=a, then Wip', and so, together with 'Wi-p', we only get '-(i=a)'. The fact that there is no incompatibility between 'If p, q' and 'If p, -q', when p is contingent, was, in any case, proved many years ago by Lewis Carroll, using a story concerning three barbers [6]. Always one of A, B and C is in, but A never goes out without B, hence we can say

If C is out, then if A is out, B is in

but also

If A is out, B is out,

and so in the case where C is out get two true conditionals with the same antecedent but contradictory consequents.

With regard to what happens when the antecedent is inconsistent, it is sometimes also said then that one cannot have both 'if p then q' and 'if p then -q', as on the truth-functional account. But <u>Reductio</u> would be impossible, if one could not draw a contradiction from an assumption. It is also sometimes said that such conditionals, being always merely 'conditional assertions' cannot be evaluated as true or false, in either of the 'false antecedent' cases, and the need for <u>Reductio</u> again disproves this. Certainly, if the antecedent is not impossible, then one cannot, in general, determine the truth of either subjunctive expression, 'if Wip then Wiq', 'if Wip then Wi-q', without a specification of 'i', but if these have then any 'non-assertibility' that is only because, unlike indicatives, they are not truth functionally related to 'p' and 'q', but 'Wip' and 'Wiq', and so need a story to be written. The 'conditional assertion' position, moreover, is confused in another way. Thus Mitchell says [7]:

> Now instead of saying 'If it rains the match will be cancelled', it is certainly possible for us to say, with no change of meaning, 'Either it will not rain or the match will be cancelled' or 'It will not rain without the match being cancelled'. And those two variants seem to be accurately analysed as exemplifying the forms '-p v q' and '-(p.-q)'. This conclusion is puzzling since, while on the one hand, we have seen good reason to reject the equivalence of 'p D q' with 'if p, q', it seems to be perfectly correct to substitute '-p v q' and '-(p.-q)' for <u>either</u> 'p D q' or 'if p, q'. How can this inconsistency, or apparent inconsistency, be resolved?
> We remove it when we recognise that the proposition which we assert when we say 'Either it will not rain or the match will be cancelled' does not, in spite of appearances, exemplify the form '-p v q'. '-p v q' is verified if either of the disjuncts is true; thus it is verified if '-p' is true. But 'Either it will not rain or the match will be cancelled' does <u>not</u> express a proposition that is true if it does not rain, but one that is verified if it does rain and ·the match is cancelled, and falsified if it rains and the match is not cancelled. Thus its truth conditions are identical with those of 'if p, q' but not ·with

117

those of 'p ⊃ q' (or '-p v q' or '-(p.-q)').

But this would mean that 'or' and 'and' did not commute, yet what is the distinctive sense, for instance, of Mitchell's last sentence reversed, i.e. 'Its truth conditions are identical not with those of 'p ⊃ q' (or '-p v q' or '-(p.-q)'), but with those of 'if p, q''? Of course, there is none.

There is another confusion about assertibility which may be at work in obscuring the compatibility of 'if p, q' and 'if p, -q'. For if someone says the former then one might not want to contradict it, by saying 'p and -q', but still not want to agree to it, and say 'if p, -q' instead. So if one is not keenly aware of the difference between denying a statement and not asserting it, then it might come to seem that when saying 'if p, -q' one was saying something contrary to 'if p, q'. Not wanting to say 'It is either in the cupboard or the wardrobe'. but not wanting to say 'It is neither in the cupboard nor the wardrobe' either, one might want to say 'It is either in the cupboard or the garden shed'. But that does not make 'It is either in the cupboard or the garden shed' contrary to, or otherwise inconsistent with 'It is either in the cupboard, or the wardrobe'. These two disjunctions are compatible, for clearly both would be true if the object in question was in the cupboard.

The point may be reversed to clarify the denials of conditionals. For it might well be thought that

It is not the case that if it rains the exercises will be held indoors, therefore it will rain,

was not a valid argument, if the premise was confused with

If it rains, it is not the case that the exercises will be held indoors,

or was otherwise thought to be entailed by it. But, again, non-assertion is to be distinguished from denial: certainly 'Either it does not rain, or the exercises will not be held indoors' may be asserted when 'Either it does not rain, or the exercises will be held indoors' is not asserted, but they may be asserted together, making them, and the two conditionals in the above, compatible, so the second of those conditionals does not entail the denial of the first.

Adams believes that 'If it rains, the game will be postponed' and 'If it rains, the game won't be postponed' are inconsistent, and gives a probabilistic, though clearly inconclusive, argument for this [8]:

> A plausible explanation of the intuitive inconsistency of the propositions in the examples consists in observing that it would be irrational to <u>accept</u> all propositions in an inconsistent set at once, because in fact it is not possible for all propositions of the set to be simultaneously probable. Our probabilistic analysis supports this intuition since it follows from the conditional probability representation that the two propositions 'if it rains the game will be postponed' and 'if it rains the game won't be postponed' cannot simultaneously be more than 50 per cent probable...It is true that this ignores problems having to do with the possibility that the antecedent 'it will rain' might have probability 0, which will be considered briefly below, but at least we can say that the propositions in question cannot be simultaneously probable if there is a non-zero probability of rain.

In connection with probability conditionals there are, therefore, further, more particular, reasons for taking 'Probably if it were that p, it would be that q' as contrary to 'Probably if it were that p, it would be that -q'. For it is common to give a conditional probability analysis of such probability conditionals, but it is also common to leave the value of a conditional probability undefined, when the probability of the antecedent is zero. Thus if we ally, in some way

Probably if it were that p, it would be that q
Probably if it were that p, it would be that -q

with

$$P(q/p) > 1/2$$
$$P(-q/p) > 1/2$$

then the fact that the two conditional probabilities cannot in general both be greater than 1/2 might incline us to follow Adams and take the result to be available always, and so say that the two probability conditionals cannot be asserted together, and hence cannot be true together. But what happens to the conditional probabilities when $P(p)=0$ is patently crucial to this way of getting the general conclusion, since, even though in all other cases the incompatibility result can be maintained, it is just what happens when there is no probability of the antecedent which is centrally in question. Adams admits this

> Finally, honesty compels us to acknowledge the inconclusiveness of much of what we have said both about inconsistency and denial in application to conditionals, which arises from our neglect of the possibility that the antecedents of the conditionals involved may have zero probability and we have no theory which applies in that case. Are we really entitled to say that 'if A then B' and 'if A then not B' cannot be simultaneously probable if we don't know what probabilities these propositions should have in case p(A) is 0? As a matter of fact, in my earlier articles...I arbitrarily stipulated that if p(A)=0 then both p(A [D] B) and p(A [D] -B) equal 1, from which it would follow that the contrary A [D] -B could not be a 'true' denial of A [D] B since in fact the two would be probabilistically consistent. Lacking a satisfactory theory of the zero antecedent case, all that can be argued is that results which hold true of conditionals when their antecedents don't have probability zero constitute <u>prima facie</u> evidence for their validity in general, although we must always be prepared to find that our supposed generalities admit exceptions in the zero antecedent case.

Now we shall, in a moment, locate a way of determining the conditional probability in this exceptional case, which will show us that indeed there P(B/A)=P(-B/A)=1, but even in the absence of such a decision it is clear that the general incompatibility result fails to follow because the classical definition

P(B/A)=(P(B.A)/P(A))

necessarily leaves the zero antecedent case undecided, and so it is that definition which is causing the trouble.

Now we can, in fact, firm up the above alignment between the probability of a conditional and a conditional probability, if we take for that conditional one of the pronominal form distinguished before, namely

(Ex)Ax D BexAx.

For the probability of this is the probability of

-(Ex)Ax v BexAx,

and, if (Ex)Ax, this is the probability of BexAx, which is the standard P(B/A), since this is defined in this case, but also then AexAx, and so the epsilon term selects at random just from amongst the A's. But if -(Ex)Ax, we can improve upon the classical account of conditional probability, since a probability for the given conditional is now still available, indeed it is, as Adams suspected, 1. This means, for one thing, that in place of the above definition, we should take

P(B/A)=P(if anything is A, it is B),

giving us an unrestricted definition as opposed to one which is not fully applicable, but the zero antecedent case having a probability of 1 also settles in the negative Adams' other conjecture, about the incompatibility of certain probabilistic conditionals, since very much as with non-probabilistic conditionals, we see that the two probabilistic conditionals above are consistent, both being true in the exceptional case.

This point, and those immediately previous, bear on the supposed connectedness of conditionals, since, by definition, p cannot be connected with both q and -q, and so if 'if p, q' and 'if p, -q' can be both true it follows that true conditionals need not be connected. The fact that <u>Reductio</u> presumes that both such conditionals can be true is then a further argument for possible non-connection; it also follows from the above point about the denials of conditionals.

Faris has tried to defend the connectedness even of the truth-functional conditional [9]. Talking about 'Condition E', i.e. 'There is a set S of true propositions such that q is inferrable from p together with S', he argues that this is both a sufficient and a necessary condition of the truth of 'if p, q', going on to show that, since condition E is satisfied when 'S' is 'p D q', if indeed the latter is true, then 'if p, q' is entailed by 'p D q'; and the reverse entailment is commonly undoubted. So, on these grounds, 'if p, q' is equivalent to 'p D q'. This is a very good argument for the interderivability of the natural and symbolic forms, but the 'connection' thereby established to fulfill Condition E, reduces merely to occurring together in a true material conditional, which is not the connection by topic, cause or meaning usually supposed.

Other writers, as we shall see in more detail in the next section, have tried to insist that conditionals do indeed require such 'relevance'. Unfortunately for this point of view there are plenty of conditionals which do not require relevance, including most of those considered above. For there is only an 'intentional' connection between the parts in 'If it rains, the match will be cancelled/the game will be postponed/the exercises will be held indoors': these either record, or express a mere choice. Equally with 'If it rains, I shall eat my hat', there is no causal or meaning relation involved, merely a decision, and neither need that decision be 'rational' by being topic related to the rain, since irrational choices may still be made. Likewise there are even subjunctives which are 'unconnected', viz 'If you were to do that, I would eat my hat'. Irrationality, disconnection, and irrelevance, one must remember, are logically possible. Moreover, they are morally valuable. Stalnaker misses the value of the disconnection in the material conditional in his discussion of Fatalism [10]. For he finds no easy way out of the following argument:

Either I will be killed in this raid, or I will not be killed.
Suppose that I will be killed [K].
Then, even if I take precautions I will be killed [K.(P D K)],
so any precautions I take will be ineffective.
But suppose I am not going to be killed [-K].
Then I won't be killed even if I neglect all precautions [-K.(-P D -K)],
so no precautions are necessary to avoid being killed.
Either way, any precautions I take will be either ineffective or unnecessary, and so pointless.

The mistake in Stalnaker's reasoning in that although '-P D -K' is entailed by '-K' that does not mean that no precautions are necessary to avoid being killed. For if precautions are necessary (-P D K) and one isn't killed (-K), that only means one took the necessary precautions (P), not that there aren't any. Stalnaker has difficulty seeing this since for him the two conditionals '-P > -K' and '-P > K' can only both be true if '-P' is impossible, and, of course, it is contingent whether one takes precautions. But the fact of the matter is that both '-P D -K' and '-P D K' are both true, when those contingent precautions are taken.

ENTAILS

There is a well known argument by C.I.Lewis defending the view that contradictions entail anything. It has been open to much discussion, notably by 'relevance logicians'. They would argue that two senses of 'or' are involved in the puzzle, an 'extensional sense' in which 'p or q' is derivable from 'p' and an 'intensional sense' in which it isn't. In fact the distinction between these two senses also had its origin in C.I.Lewis [11]. One hopes no one is denying that in some contexts a disjunction is derived from one of its disjuncts, and that in other contexts it is not: what is at stake is whether the two context-dependent aspects derive from two context-independent senses. Anderson and Belnap say [12]:

> It will be insisted that...to deny the principle of disjunctive syllogism surely goes too far: 'from -A and A v B to infer B', for example, is surely valid. For one of the premises states that at least one of A and B is true, and since the other premise -A, says that A can't be the true one, the true one must be B...Our reply is to remark again that this argument commits a fallacy of ambiguity. There are indeed important senses of 'or', 'at least one', etc. for which the argument from -A and A-or-B is perfectly valid, namely, senses in which there is a true relevance between A and B, for example, the sense in which 'A-or-B' means precisely that -A entails B. However, in this sense of 'or', the inference from A to A-or-B is fallacious, and therefore this sense of 'or' is not preserved in the truth-functional constant translated by the same word.

The fact of the matter is, however, that there are not two senses of 'or': there is a composite symbol 'Either p or q' which is negated by saying 'Neither p nor q', and in connection with this latter symbol we have the inference

    Neither p nor q
    Therefore, not-p.

So anybody who wishes to show there is a sense of 'Either p or q' which allows the disjunction not to be entailed by its disjuncts must find a sense of 'Neither p nor q' for which the reverse entailment does not hold. Of course, there is no such sense. Immediately before the above quote, Anderson and Belnap had said with regard to their thesis

Such a thesis so strongly stated will seem hopelessly naive to those logicians whose logical intuitions have been numbed through hearing and repeating the logicians' fairy tales of the past half century, and hence stands in need of further support.

Much the same point may be made here, except that the argument from 'Neither p nor q' is final, and stands in need of no further support.

However we can still speculate about the origins of Anderson and Belnap's own fairy tale. Immediately after the above quote Anderson and Belnap had said

As Lewis himself argued in some early articles, there are intensional meanings of 'or', 'not both', 'at least one is true' etc., as well as of 'if...then...' Those who claim that only an intensional sense of these words will support inferences are right - Lewis' only error was in supposing he captured this sense by tacking a modal operator onto a fundamentally truth-functional formula.

Now Lewis' own original disjunctive examples were

Either Caesar died or the moon is made of green cheese,
Either Matilda does not love me or I am beloved,

with regard to which he said that to suppose it false that Caesar died would not force one to suppose the moon was made of green cheese, 'if conditions contrary to fact have any meaning at all', whereas with the second disjunction not only is one of the disjoined propositions true, but one of the disjoined propositions is 'necessarily true', by which, I take it, he meant that it is necessary that one of the disjoined propositions is true. It is clear, therefore, that in the second case he was talking about a necessitated subjunctive of the form

(i)(Wip v Wiq).

But Lewis was not 'in error' in thinking he captured a

sense of 'or' simply by 'tacking a modal operator onto a fundamentally truth-functional formula', for, as before, there is a way of transforming this quantified disjunction into a plain disjunction, so the expression is still a disjunction, merely one with different parts, viz

Wkp v Wkq

where k=ei-(Wip v Wiq). Moreover this disjunction is then still a disjunction implied by its disjuncts, if not by p and q, and so involves not a new, but still the old, extensional sense of 'or'. It is notable, of course, that Lewis himself was not troubled by any ambiguity in this area, as a source of breakdown of his proof that contradictions entail anything: in present terms, the fact that p does not entail the above quantified disjunction is irrelevant to his point, since the whole of Lewis' argument is pursued just in terms of Wap and Waq, i.e. p and q. That argument proceeds

(p.-p) D p,
p D (p v q),
(p.-p) D -p,
(-p.(p v q)) D q,

therefore

(p.-p) D q,

and to fault this it would need to be shown that in the 'extensional' (i.e. one and only) sense of 'or', disjunctive syllogism fails. Now Anderson and Belnap allow that Lewis' proof goes through, if valid inferences merely involve its being necessary that either the premises are false or the conclusion is true, but they demand more than this: they demand 'relevance'. But in the disjunctive syllogism there is relevance. For the two premises '-p' and 'p v q' interact to discharge the conclusion 'q', so there is pairwise sharing of variables. Furthermore, while there is relevance in this place, there is also an irrelevance in 'p v q', when this is deduced from 'p', since there a new, unmotivated variable 'q' is brought in. Hence Anderson and Belnap's demand for relevance is not all embracing, since they allow there is an entailment at this previous point. Moreover, it is that irrelevance which has let in the 'q' which eventually gets derived, in Lewis' proof, from 'p.-p'. So what Anderson and Belnap need to block is 'p's entailing 'p v q' (in its one and only extensional sense), before they can hope to stifle all irrelevance. Of course, they have no hope of doing this.

But the whole issue is irrelevant, in another sense, since 'p.-p' cannot arise, and so what it entails is quite academic. Indeed, in the cases where a disjunction is obtained from a disjunct, the disjunctive syllogism is either not usable, or not useful, since deriving 'p v q' from 'p' means that we cannot also get '-p' to use the result above, while if one also gets '-q' one can then only derive what one originally had, namely 'p' again. So what is true is that only when the disjunction is obtained in some other way than through a disjunct will disjunctive syllogism be <u>useful</u>, i.e. enable one to derive something previously unknown, but usefulness is not validity: covered by the latter are also pointless irrelevances and academicisms.

Certainly we may say that the disjunction gains a different aspect in the two cases, but these two aspects are merely reflections of the differing contexts in which the disjunction arises, and are not to be formulated in different symbols. The situation is somewhat like that of the 'exclusive disjunction': given Sydney is not Canberra then 'She is in Sydney or Canberra' has an exclusive aspect, but since it is an external fact which gives it this aspect, there is no need for, indeed no possibility of, any special symbol - its symbolisation is just 'p v q', and this gains an 'exclusive' aspect when, additionally, '-(p.q)' is known. There is indeed, in this connection, the symbolisation 'p CL -q', sometimes called 'exclusive disjunction', though more properly just a material bi-conditional, but it is expressly the fact that this is non-context-dependent which allows it a formal expression. Jonathan Bennett's example, defending Lewis, shows that the same disjunction may be taken both 'extensionally' and 'intensionally', so there are no grounds for two symbols in this area, since the distinction is, thereby, entirely context dependent [13]. Bennett's example involves Helen, who believed Mary went out with a woman last night, and said

Mary went out with someone (i.e. a man or woman) last night,

also Jane, who believed Mary went out with no one last night, and said

Mary did not go out with a woman last night.

Bennett concludes, from what was said, that Mary went out with a man last night, and the question is whether Helen's disjunction is 'extensional' or 'intensional', Bennett's judgement being that these notions are 'person-relative'. But clearly the disjunction is definitely an 'extensional' one, since it was derived from one of its disjuncts, so any 'intensional' aspect merely arises through ignorance of this source.

Similarly with the parallel case of implication. A long tradition from von Wright has tried to extract those implications which are neither entailed by the denials of their antecedents, nor entailed by their consequents [14]. If an implication is not derived in either of these ways it certainly has a unique aspect, i.e. a unique origin and place in inferences. But it is not a special implication on that account, and does not have its own kind of logic: it is just the everyday material implication in a distinctive context, and that context is not the only one it might arise in. Certainly there are more forms of antecedent and consequent than were dreamt of in some philosophies of logic, but that, as we have seen, is no argument for implications being non-material, even if it shows that it can be immaterial what is in such implications.

So spreading out the natural variety of material conditionals and associated forms helps us to accommodate ourselves to the 'paradoxes', i.e. freedoms of material implication. There is no real trouble with one of these freedoms, namely that involving a true consequent and arbitrary antecedent, for, as we have seen, 'even if' implications clearly involve an antecedent which is detachable without weakening of the truth, and hence an antecedent which is not necessarily a condition on, or relevant to, or connected with that truth, and so the departure from other 'conditionals' in this respect is understandable. But with the other freedom - the one allowing an arbitrary consequent - there is more trouble. In Bennett's case, according to this licence, Helen, who believed Mary went out with a woman last night, might have said that if Mary didn't go out with a woman last night then she went out with a man, and one might be inclined to ask: isn't the introduction of a man illogical? But, of course, it is no more illogical than with the conditional's equivalents, namely the given disjunction 'She went out with someone, i.e. a woman or a man', which draws mention of a man from nowhere, and the other sort of free conditional 'She went out with a woman, if she didn't go out with a man', which again cooks up a supposition from out of the blue. However, these examples are perhaps too comforting, for the topic of a man is not so far off the point, when women are at issue, and so one can settle one's nerves by thinking licence is not so bad, so long as it is perhaps contained, or restrained. But the logic of the matter is the same as with 'If she didn't go out with a woman, I'll eat my hat', which has equivalents 'Either she went out with a woman, or I'll eat my hat' and 'She went out with a woman, if I don't eat my hat', and these clearly involve no topic connection or relevance, and are thus completely mad, which reminds us that the relevance of 'man' to 'woman' is itself context dependent, for in certain circles it may be taken to be terrifying to stray so far off the question of women as even to mention those other earthly creatures.

But now, since we have a false antecedent in 'If she didn't go out with a woman, I'll eat my hat', another red herring may lead us off the track. For the comparison with 'counterfactuals' now becomes appealing, and thinking confusedly these must be subjunctives, we are likely to get cross thoughts from the non-derivability of 'If she hadn't gone out with a woman, I would have eaten my hat' from 'She did go out with a woman'. So we must be careful not to cross over from the indicative counterfactual to the subjunctive one. For while p licenses -p D q, and we also have that Wip licenses Wi-p D Wiq, we do not have, unless i=a, that p licenses Wi-p D Wiq, any more than we have that Wip licenses -p D q, so there is no way that any elementary fact/supposition can interfere with any conditional supposition/fact.

The demand for 'relevance', of course, is indefensible on other grounds. Thus it is integral to tautologies that they be provable given nothing - by means, for example, of Conditional Proof. So they are not dependent on anything (and so need, for instance, no evolutionary support.) Lewis' second proof, deriving a tautology from an arbitrary proposition, merely displays this fact in graphic form, for if such are deducible given nothing, then they are deducible given anything. Of course, in connection with deductions, the freedoms of material implication are, as above with disjunctions, either not usable, or not useful, so the irrelevances in them are quite academic in this central context. Indeed, it may be said, it is just because these arbitrarinesses can do no harm in this crucial place that their grace, charm or ferociousness may be allowed into the pragmatic universe. Contrariwise it is, I suspect, fear of the harm true contradictions might do which exercises many thinkers in this area: remembering all the paradoxes that have been generated this century, perhaps, after all, 'p.-p' can be true, so the hope has to be that such a contradiction can at least be contained, i.e. that one can contrive things so as not to have it that such a form entails anything very much.

Richard Routley [15] is representative of many 'Paraconsistent Logicians' when he argues, for instance, against Disjunctive Syllogism on this basis. He claims that this is not in fact a valid form of inference, since it is falsified by 'inconsistent situations'. In such situations, he believes, both A and -A may hold, though B does not, and hence both A and -A v B may hold although the standard conclusion drawn from them does not, invalidating the logical principle. Routley admits that this is an 'intuitive' argument, but while one might envisage, or describe,

an inconsistent situation, no such situation could be
realised, so Routley's argument is no more than
'intuitive', as his later attempts to substantiate it
show. Thus he argues later that important
mathematical theories are simply inconsistent, though
non-trivial, and hence that the need for a
paraconsistent 'logic' cannot be dismissed. In
particular he instances naive set theory as such a
mathematical theory, and argues that only given an
appropriate non-classical logic can paradoxes like
Russell's be properly accommodated within a non-
trivial set theory. But, as we saw in chapter one, a
non-classical, 'naive' set theory can be given in
terms of second order logic which is even more
appropriate, since not only is it non-trivial, it is
also consistent. Certainly fear of Frege's fate has
been a great motivating factor in recent logical
research, but the correct approach to a paradox such
as Russell's is to solve it, not stick, negatively,
with being nonplussed. Later again Routley argues
that other historical mathematical theories, notably
the theory of infinitessimals and early theories of
the calculus, and analysis, were inconsistent, but
that they were still thought, historically, to be
viable. And indeed, inconsistent thoughts may have
had a central and crucial role in portions of history,
but the fact that it is possible for thoughts to be
inconsistent does not show that things are
inconsistent, any more than the possibility of
attempting to square the circle shows the possibility
of squaring the circle. If we were to follow how
people's minds often do work, we should need a 'logic
of fallacious reasoning', which is a contradiction in
terms. Routley even itemises the policeman-prisoner
situation, as a readily arranged, real-life,
inconsistent situation, where no catastrophic
breakdown would occur. In that situation the prisoner
states only that everything the policeman says is
true, while the policeman, whose statements are
otherwise true, asserts that whatever the prisoner
asserts is false; and the fact that a 'paradoxical'
situation could thus arise, and yet not 'spread and
effect' everything else, Routley takes to show that
such situations do not have the properties which
classical logic attributes to them. But that is
because there are no true contradictions, when the

situations are properly analysed: here

$$Sr(p)(Snp \ D \ p).(q)(Srq \ D \ q=(p)(Snp \ D \ p))$$

and

$$Sn(p)(Srp \ D \ -p).(q)((Snq.-(q=(p)(Srp \ D \ -p))) \ D \ q)$$

are inconsistent, so logic stops such a situation occurring, although such a propositional fact does not stop the prisoner and the policeman asserting whatever sentences they like (c.f. the discussion of the paradox of The Preface, before.)

Accommodating logic to the many arguments which have led in recent years to contradictory conclusions is, as a result, an imaginative exercise without a rational justification. Certainly if contradictions were true then a new logic would be necessary, but it would also not be necessary, since, by definition, contradictions cannot be true, and so the rational effort must be directed instead to seeing how it can seem otherwise, in all those many cases - 'many' because there is no form of the bad. Centrally, the impossibility of true contradictions does not mean that it is not possible to believe a contradiction is true, which matter will exercise us considerably in chapters five and six. We will there be concerned with what might be called the 'Logicising of Psychology', i.e. the attempt there has been to see human minds as being represented in terms of possible worlds, and being, therefore, 'deductively omniscient'. The reverse aspect of this is the Psychologising of Logic, which Frege notably argued against: we should not conceive of Logic as the Laws of Thought in the sense of the actual way in which minds or brains function, and in particular, therefore, we cannot define impossibility in terms of what is or isn't mentally conceivable. Someone might conceive some contradictions are true, indeed we have just seen there is a considerable stream of research, into 'Paraconsistent Logic', which is very much occupied with this idea. But that does not mean that some contradictions are true: it is quite possible that $Bx(p.-p)$, but that doesn't make it at all possible that $p.-p$. Certainly some people slackly say

'Well, it is and it isn't', but what they should say
is 'Well, in one sense it is, in another sense it
isn't', for while it is quite possible that
$(Ex)(Mxp.Mxq.p.-q)$, that again does not make it
possible that $p.-p$.

SUBJUNCTIVES

The logic of subjunctives is often said to differ from
the logic of indicatives. This difference is also
often taken to extend to the area of counterfactuals,
and to 'conditionals' as opposed to material
conditionals generally [16]. We have seen in previous
sections that counterfactuals can arise in both
indicative and subjunctive forms, and that all
conditionals are material conditionals, but what is
the basis for the idea that some compounds in this
area have a different logic?

Adams says, with respect to the following example of
Contraposition

> If it rains tomorrow there will not be a terrific
> cloudburst, so
> If there is a terrific cloudburst tomorrow, it
> will not rain,

that it does not hold, taking the assertion of these
conditionals to go with the related conditional
probability, and noting that $P(-q/p)>1/2$ does not
necessarily mean $P(-p/q)>1/2$. Now it certainly is not
the case that

> Probably if it were to rain tomorrow, there would
> not be a terrific cloudburst,

entails

> Probably if there were a terrific cloudburst
> tomorrow, it would not rain,

but that does not cast doubt upon whether the above
contraposition holds, any more than it casts doubt
about whether

133

Necessarily, if it were to rain tomorrow, there would not be a terrific cloudburst

entails

Necessarily, if there were a terrific cloudburst tomorrow, it would not rain.

Moreover, since $P(-q/p)=1$ does necessarily mean $P(-p/q)=1$ (supposing $P(-p/q)=1$, if $P(q)=0$), whatever goes in the inductive case, in both of the non-inductive cases there would seem to be every reason, on Adams' own grounds, for accepting Contraposition. The truth of matter, however, is more complex than that three different forms of expression may be involved. For while the plain expression

If it rains tomorrow, there will not be a terrific cloudburst,

is a conditional of the form 'p D -q', and the necessitated expression

Necessarily, if it were to rain tomorrow there would not be a terrific cloudburst,

is a quasi-conditional of the form '(i)(Wip D Wi-q)', which may be readily transformed into a conditional proper, with the probability expression

Probably if it were to rain tomorrow, there would not be a terrific cloudburst,

we have a non-conditional of the form 'P((Ei)Wip D W(eiWip)-q)>1/2', and this may not be transformed into a conditional, being otherwise expressed

$P(-q/p)>1/2$.

Hence while the inductive case does not obey Contraposition, there are no grounds for denying that this law holds universally for conditionals: it is with a different form of speech that the law fails to apply. Adams takes the assertion of the indicative conditional to 'go by' the conditional probability,

134

and indeed, for instance

$$P(-q/p)=1 \text{ entails } P(p \ D \ -q)=1,$$

but there is not an entailment in the reverse direction, and, in any case, the relationship does not interfere with the validity of indicative contraposition. A peculiar feature of the actual given case, however, might interfere with the full apprehension of this, for commonly if there are cloudbursts it rains, and so the conclusion of the contraposition, if one keeps this fact in mind, might gain a strange aspect. But even if q D p, still p D - q entails q D -p, and the strange aspect of the two latter forms is then merely that they are each materially equivalent to -q. Hence classical propositional logic is saved in all cases, for it applies to the indicative conditional, and to the necessitated subjunctive, even if not to the probability of another sort of conditional in the area.

Stalnaker says with respect to the following example of Syllogism

> If J.Edgar Hoover were today a Communist, then he would be a traitor,
> If J.Edgar Hoover had been born a Russian, then he would today be a Communist, so
> If J.Edgar Hoover had been born a Russian, then he would be a traitor,

that it does not hold, since on his account the conditional 'if A then B' would be true in w iff B was true in f(A,w), where f(A,w) is a selected, 'minimally different' world in which A is true, and the selected world in which J.Edgar Hoover would be a Communist is not necessarily the selected world in which J.Edgar Hoover would be born a Russian, preventing a syllogistic inference in the case. Certainly

$$(Ei)WiC \ D \ W(eiWiC)T$$

with

$$(Ei)WiR \ D \ W(eiWiR)C$$

does not entail

(Ei)WiR D W(eiWiR)T

since eiWiC is not necessarily eiWiR. But the formal subjunctives then have a suppressed credit which is not the same each time, being 'In story eiWiC' one time, and 'In story eiWiR' the rest, and so they do not have the syllogistic form of the natural subjunctives before. Only if we take the shift from indicative to subjunctive to involve implicit reference to the same story do we get the syllogistic form, and then, clearly, Syllogism is not threatened, since we have an argument of the kind

WiC D WiT
WiR D WiC, so
WiR D WiT,

which is exactly parallel to the indicative case where i=a. So the only relevant symbolisation of Stalnaker's argument is not fallacious; moreover, making the suppressed credits explicit shows why it is not fallacious: it is straightforwardly of the form to which the rule of Syllogism applies.

David Lewis says with respect to the following example of Strengthening the Antecedent

If Otto had come, it would have been a lively party, so
If Otto and Anna had come it would have been a lively party,

that it does not hold, since, on his account, the counterfactual 'If it were that A, it would be that B' would be true in w iff if there were worlds in which A was true, B would be true in those which are closest to w, and in a similar way to Stalnaker, though quite different in detail, the closest worlds in which Otto would come are not necessarily the closest worlds in which Otto and Anna would come, invalidating the inference. So the same points about the need to supply missing credits with subjunctives, about the then available possibility of a non-changing antecedent world, and the resulting validation of the inference in its proper form, which applied to Stalnaker, also apply here. But Lewis has also shown that there cannot be conditionals whose probability is a conditional probability, if that probability can also be conditionalised, and so he seemingly has distanced himself from Adams' approach [17]. Certainly conditionals whose probability is a conditional probability are a rare breed, but the fact, for instance, that one precisification of Lewis' argument is:

(Ei)WiO D W(eiWiO)L, so
(Ei)Wi(O.A) D W(eiWi(O.A))L,

and this inference is invalid for reasons very much like those Lewis gives, shows his approach is only different in detail from Adams'. For these conditionals are of the very type whose probability is a conditional probability.

It is clear from these points and objections that the current state of speculation about the logic of subjunctives/counterfactuals/conditionals is in some confusion. The account I have developed from Hilbert's enriched predicate calculus and the ordinary modal notion 'V(p,w$_i$)=1' is closest to Stalnaker's, although, following from the points made against Adams and Stalnaker and Lewis, it allows there are three types of subjunctive conditional: for, in addition to the necessitated one, there are two contingent conditionals, one in which there is an external reference to a story which is being continued, i.e. a conditional of the form 'Had it then been that p, it would then have been that q', and one in which there is no external reference, but an internal one to a story started in the antecedent, i.e. a conditional of the form 'If it ever were that p, then it would be that q'. The former has a logic which parallels exactly the logic of indicatives, the latter has a probability which is a conditional probability. The latter has the same overall form as the former, namely

Wip D Wiq

but depends upon a formulation of the 'then' in the

consequent as a pronoun for the world brought up in the antecedent: the conditional

$$(Ei)Wip \quad D \quad W(eiWip)q$$

being

$$W(eiWip)p \quad D \quad W(eiWip)q,$$

as before.

The important thing about this conditional with no external reference is how it obeys Adams' requirement about its probability being a conditional probability without infringing Lewis' triviality results about these things. It does so by being an _a priori_ or absolute conditional, so that the associated conditional probability cannot be further conditionalised; by contrast, the conditional with the external reference is a temporal or relative conditional, which can thus be conditionalised but whose probability is, as a result, not a conditional probability. The possibility of this conditionalisation means that what its truth value and probability is is dependent upon which external story is told, for what the assessment of

$$Wip \quad D \quad Wiq$$

is depends upon i. But while

$$(Ei)Wip \quad D \quad W(eiWip)q$$

is likewise dependent upon eiWip for its truth, and so this cannot, in general, be determinate - it has an objectively determinate truth value only if Lp.L-q, or L(p D q) - that does not mean that its probability is equally indeterminate, and indeed, if its probability is large we have a good representation of a causal law. If we write 'Most probably, if it ever were that p then it would be that q' as 'p causes q', then causation is, for instance, defeasible (since Strengthening the Antecedent fails), non-transitive (since Syllogism fails) and directional (since Contraposition fails). The contingency of causal laws is then not a non-a-prioricity, but just their probabilistic, non-universal, form [18].

This account thus allows Adams' programme to survive Lewis' criticisms, supposing that programme is just pursued with the inductive case, i.e. restricted to where the probabilities involved cannot be further conditionalised. But the account also details how the selected world comes to be defined in terms of the antecedent and so links Adams' theory in detail with Stalnaker's and Lewis' theories, while avoiding the 'closeness' conditions in the latter two, which have given so much trouble: 'eiWip' may be taken to be a typical p-world rather than the closest of them (whatever that would mean).

The account was actually derived from Loux [19]. Loux' sketch of an account was that 'If it were that p it would be that q' is, in the present terminology, 'Wi(p.q)', where 'i' is defined simply in terms of 'closeness to the actual world'. This, for one thing, does not allow for subjunctives with impossible antecedents - hence the formulation, instead, 'Wi(p D q)'. But in place of the 'closeness' condition, there is now either no condition or simply i=ejWjp, i.e. i is a chosen world in which (if possible) p is true. Stalnaker [20] defines 'A > B' to be true in world w if B is true in world f(A,w), where the selected world f(A,w) obeys

> (1) For all antecedents A and base worlds w, A must be true in f(A,w),
> (2) For all antecedents A and base worlds w, f(A,w) is the absurd world (i.e. the world in which 'everything is true') only of there is no world possible with respect to w in which A is true.

The former condition ensures that all statements like 'If A then A' are true; the second condition ensures that 'If A then B and not B' is only true when A is inconsistent. But the world selected for the a priori conditional can be just any world in the case where A is impossible. For, concerning ourselves with our one base world a, and so writing 'f(A,a)' as 'eiWiA', then, against (1), A need not be true in eiWiA, since W(eiWiA)-A is just -(Ei)WiA, and so, against (2), eiWiA is never a world in which everything is true, for if -(Ei)WiA that merely makes eiWiA any world we choose. And the former fact does not invalidate 'If A were true, then A would be true', i.e. 'If (Ei)WiA then W(eiWiA)A'; nor does the latter fact allow 'If A were true then B would be true and false', i.e. 'If (Ei)WiA then W(eiWiA)B.W(eiWiA)-B', not to entail '-(Ei)WiA'. Stalnaker has to suppose there is a world in which everything is true to try to maintain his condition (1), but such a world is impossible, as we saw in the last section, so what happens when A is impossible as well is only that it becomes immaterial which world we choose, no one being any better than the rest.

Stalnaker goes on to try to ensure that f(A,w) differs minimally from w, by adding two further conditions:

(3) For all base worlds w and all antecedents A, if A is true in w then f(A,w)=w.
(4) For all base worlds w and all antecedents B and B', if B is true in f(B',w) and B' is true in f(B,w), then f(B,w)=f(B',w).

The third criterion Stalnaker justifies by asserting that no other possible world is as much like the base world as the base world itself. The fourth criterion establishes a total ordering of selected worlds for each base world w. But, against (3), only if A is only true in a will it definitely be the case that eiWiA=a, for even if A is true, if it is otherwise possible then eiWiA has an option. Clearly the point to remember here, in defense of the present selection function, is that what the likelihood is, say of a spade being drawn from a pack when a card is drawn from a pack, is not determined by just seeing what happens when an actual card is drawn from the pack. Other possibilities must be considered to assess the likelihood of this consequence. The same model falsifies (4), for if B is 'a spade is drawn' and B' is 'an honour is drawn', say, then one might well have W(eiWiB')B and W(eiWiB)B' without eiWiB=eiWiB', though, again, the result would be different if there was, say, only one B-world, for W(eiWiB')B alone, with (Ej)(i)(WiB D i=j) would entail eiWiB=eiWiB'. No total ordering of worlds is available in classical probability theory, and the epsilon term analysis respects this: likewise the notions of closeness and minimal difference are now out of place - unless 'closest' means 'most probable', but then, another point (3) forgets is that what is most probable may turn out to be quite unlike the actual case.

But the present definition not only links certain conditionals straightforwardly with classical probability theory, it also shows how those conditionals are distinct from probability judgements. It is only because of this we can give a general probabilistic account of the so-called 'fallacies of conditional logic' at the same time as leaving classical logic intact. For while the general logic of 'Wi(p D q)' is just the same as the logic of 'p D q', the logic of the former, when 'i' is restricted to chosen p-worlds, is not the same as, even though it is directly related to the logic of, judgements like 'given p, probably q' (with this probability being 1, if p has probability 0.) Thus, for instance, with Strengthening the Antecedent: it is because Wg(p D q) does not entail Wh((p.r) D q), if g=eiWip and h=eiWi(p.r) that P(q/p)>1/2 does not entail P(q/(p.r))>1/2, for if there was an entailment the probability of the second would be greater than or equal to that of the first. Likewise with Syllogism and Contraposition. Note in a similar way that the fact that one needn't have P(q/p)=1 or P(-q/p)=1 does not mean Stalnaker's principle, Conditional Excluded Middle, does not hold, for, as before, 'Wi(p D q) v Wi(p D -q)' is true, no matter what i. Also we have another feature of Stalnaker's account, namely that with the same contingent antecedent, but contradictory consequents, two of these conditionals are material contradictories, for

Mp D ((Wjp D Wjq) D -(Wjp D Wj-q))

where j=eiWip, since Mp just is Wjp in that case.

However we can now improve Stalnaker"s account of 'might', since he could do little better than formalise 'q might be true, with p' as 'M(p.q)'. It is one of the virtues of Lewis' account, in contrast to Stalnaker's, that Lewis can find a distinct place for the 'might' form, and indeed we may contradict

$$Wjp \ D \ Wjq$$

by saying

$$Wjp.Wj-q,$$

which is distinct from M(p.-q) i.e. (Ei)(Wip.Wi-q), i.e. Wkp.Wk-q where k=ei(Wip.Wi-q). The latter, i.e. 'M(p.-q)', must be read 'In some circumstances it would be true that p and that -q', while the former, i.e. 'Wjp.Wj-q', must be read 'In some circumstances it would be true that p, and there that -q'. This means that unlike M(p.q) and M(p.-q), which may be true together, since M(p.q) is (Ei)(Wip.Wiq), i.e. Whp.Whq where h=ei(Wip.Wiq), which may be distinct from k, it is not the case that we may have 'Wjp.Wjq' and 'Wjp.Wj-q' true together. Hence the present account of 'might' is no threat to Conditional Excluded Middle, as is Lewis' account. There the two 'might' forms may be true together, making it possible that their contradictories, the two 'would' forms, may be false together, invalidating the principle. Certainly, in connection with that principle, only inside a story is either conditional settlable as true, but the fact that there is no way outside a story of deciding, say, what nationality Bizet and Verdi would have been, if they had been compatriots, does not prevent some judgement being made, i.e. a story being written, as we saw before. There is a truth to the matter, even if it is a truth about what would have been, indeed if there were no truth to the matter there could be no estimate of the probability - based perhaps on these musicians' patriotic allegiances, and how cosmopolitan they were - for estimates of the probability are estimates of what it is likely would have been true, even though what would have been true might have been quite unlikely.

It is the desire to settle the truth of such conditionals outside of stories which has led to the formulation of the various closeness conditions, but once it is realised that the non-necessitated a priori ones are not themselves probability judgements but the

142

'indefinite propositions' which figure within them, the call for such closeness conditions vanishes. Equally, the other contingent subjunctive conditional is not a probability judgement and figures only in connection with stories, but, clearly, again, if a story contains 'if p, q' then, no matter how close or remote this story is to the actual truth, there is no doubt that, in that story it would be that if p, q.

This 'choice' account of subjunctives is the most novel contribution to logical theory in this book. That is not because these conditionals are thereby taken to have no objective truth value - for Quine also held that. But by formulating the classical semantic expression 'V(p,wi)=1' as a Priorian indirect speech form, and taking it out of the 'meta-language', we make a considerable movement in thought, since it involves a radical consequence of the semantic closure of natural language established in the last chapter. Without that preparation the expression 'Wip' could not have been extracted from semantical theory and placed in the 'object language' as an entity in proof theory, since these two realms were once thought to be quite distinct. Note that, as a result, another myth about meta-languages is exploded: there are no distinct 'meta-connectives', so our account of conditionals is complete.

NOTES

[1]   For Strawson's views see <u>Introduction to Logical Theory</u>, Methuen, London, 1952, Ch.3.
[2]   For the basics of Modal Logic, see G.E.Hughes and M.J.Cresswell's <u>An Introduction to Modal Logic</u> Methuen, London, 1968, Ch.4, and see, for instance, J.van Benthem's <u>Modal Logic and Classical Logic</u> Bibliopolis, Napoli, 1983, for a general account of classical modal logic in quantificational terms.
[3]   R.Stalnaker's views on conditionals are in 'A Theory of Conditionals', in N.Rescher ed. <u>Studies in Logical Theory</u> Blackwell, Oxford, 1969, for his discussion of the epistemology of subjunctives see p99. D.K.Lewis' views are in

Counterfactuals Harvard U.P. Cambridge Mass.,
1973.

[4] W.Hodges Logic, Penguin, Harmondsworth, 1977,
sec.18.

[5] Strawson, op. cit. note 1, Ch.3, see pp88-9,83-4
for the present and following quotes.

[6] For Lewis Carroll's story about the barbers see
Mind, III, 1894, p436.

[7] D.Mitchell's Introduction to Logic, Hutchinson,
London, 1962, Ch.3, p64.

[8] For his attempt at a probabilistic analysis of
conditionals see E.Adams' The Logic of
Conditionals, Reidel, Dordrecht, 1975; the two
quotations given being from p38, and pp40-41,
Copyright © by D.Reidel Publishing Company,
Dordrecht, Holland, 1975;

[9] For J.A.Faris' attempt at a connection analysis
of hook, see his Truth-Functional Logic,
Routledge and Kegan Paul, London, 1968, p118.

[10] Stalnaker's fatalistic argument is in 'Indicative
Conditionals' Philosophia 1975, see also Ifs eds
W.L.Harper, R.Stalnaker, G.Pearse, Reidel,
Dordrecht, 1981, p204.

[11] C.I.Lewis' original article was 'Implication and
the Algebra of Logic' in Mind, XXI, 1912, see
p523 for the subsequent discussion here of
different disjunctions; see also Lewis and
C.H.Langford's Symbolic Logic, Century, New York,
1932, p250, for the argument showing
contradictions entail anything.

[12] A.R.Anderson and N.D.Belnap's work is in 'The
Pure Calculus of Entailment' Journal of Symbolic
Logic, 21.1, 1962, and 'Tautological Entailments'
Philosophical Studies, XIII, 1962; see p20 of the
latter for the quote, copyright © (1962) by
D.Reidel Publishing Company, reprinted by
permission.

[13] J.F.Bennett's defense of C.I.Lewis is in
'Entailment' Philosophical Review, LXXVIII, 1969,
see p219 for the given example.

[14] G.H.von Wright's account of implication is in
'The Concept of Entailment', see his Logical
Studies, Routledge and Kegan Paul, London, 1957,
see in particular the views of the classical
apologists Johnson and Pap, pp171,173.

[15] R.Routley's discussion is in Relevance Logics and

their Rivals, Ridgeview, Atascadero, 1982, see especially pp25,54,55, and 63 respectively.

[16] For Adams', Stalnaker's, and D.K.Lewis' views on Conditional Logic see their works cited in notes 8 and 3, the illustrative examples used here being drawn from pp14,104-6,and 10, of those works, respectively.

[17] For D.K.Lewis' triviality results see 'Probabilities of Conditionals and Conditional Probabilities' in Philosophical Review, LXXXV, 1976,and XCV, 1986.

[18] For a probabilistic account of causation see, for instance, P.Suppes' A Probabilistic Theory of Causality, North Holland, Amsterdam, 1970.

[19] See M.J.Loux' editorial introduction to The Possible and the Actual, Cornell U.P., Ithaca, 1979, p34.

[20] Stalnaker, op. cit. note 3, p104.

4 Reference

EXISTENCE

One of the seeming problems with classical predicate logic is that using it means that the existence of the world is provable. Given 'Fa' entails '(Ex)Fx', and '-Fa' entails '(Ex)-Fx', the fact that we must have one or other of 'Fa' and '-Fa' means we must have '(Ex)Fx v (Ex)-Fx', i.e. '(Ex)(Fx v -Fx)'. To avoid this conclusion it is possible to deny that we must have one of 'Fa' and '-Fa' - Aristotelians and Presuppositionists, in different ways, do this - and it is possible to deny Existential Generalisation - Aristotelians and Free Logicians, again in different ways, do this. I shall talk about the Presuppositionists' position more at the end of this chapter, and that of Free Logicians in a moment, but it is important not to ignore the Aristotelian position, for not only Sommers, say, is still an Aristotelian in the appropriate sense, but Russell and Quine also were.

This comes about because of their analyses of sentences involving names and descriptions for their subjects, i.e. most singular predicative expressions like 'Socrates is wise' and 'The king of France is bald'. According to these theorists, such expressions have two different negatives, an internal negative, perhaps 'Socrates is foolish', 'The king of France is hirsute', and an external negative 'Socrates is not wise', 'The king of France is not bald'. The distinction between the two negatives is in fact mirrored with the positives as well, for 'Socrates is not foolish' is to be now distinguished from 'Socrates is wise' while 'The king of France is not hirsute' is to be distinguished from 'The king of France is bald'. The way to distinguish them is to take the external negation forms not to entail the existence of their subject, and the internal negation forms to entail this. Hence we get a fourfold pattern, for singular predicative expressions involving proper names, or identifying descriptions, viz:

(A) Socrates is wise (Ws)
(E) Socrates is foolish (W"s)
(I) Socrates is not foolish (-W"s)
(O) Socrates is not wise (-Ws)

the 'A','E','I' and 'O' designations arising through the similarities to the classic quantified forms in Aristotelian logic.

Now this account seems to relieve us of the burden of acknowledging the world in the following way. We can still say 'Fa' entails '(Ex)Fx', and also that 'F"a' entails '(Ex)F"x', but since we cannot now say '-Fa' entails '(Ex)-Fx', the necessary 'Fa v -Fa' does not entail '(Ex)Fx v (Ex)-Fx', even if the contingent 'Fa v F"a' does entail '(Ex)Fx v (Ex)F"x'. Either way the existence of the world becomes a contingent matter, and so something we can apparently ignore when doing logic. But the trouble with this account is that, while it seems to relieve us of attending to the world, it in fact only postpones it, since it tries to treat all singular referring phrases as individuating predicates, and certainly some are not. Thus if 'Sx' is 'x socratises' we can equally represent the four forms

(A) (Ex)(Sx.Wx)
(E) (Ex)(Sx.-Wx)
(I) (x)(Sx D Wx)

(0) (x)(Sx ⊃ -Wx)

and the previous relationships still hold. But singular referring phrases would not be done away with on this account, for some would remain. Indeed on this formulation it is evident that a further form of expression is presumed, namely something of the form 'Sx', where '-Sx' cannot be distinguished from 'S"x', since, now, irrespective of whether or how there is a negative in 'Fx', this entails '(Ey)Fy', hence here 'x' must be replaced not by a predicate, but by a referring phrase. This was Russell's position, explicitly, and his preferred substituends for 'x' were (eventually) demonstratives. Quine had a rather different account, holding that only the above quantified forms are required by logic, so we are relieved of the necessity of providing any constants for our variables to range over [1]. But this doctrine sits unhappily with Quine's other tenet that 'to be is to be the value of a variable', for if there cannot be values of variables that means we can show, by logic, nothing can be, i.e. the world cannot exist. But if there can be values of variables it must be required of logic that it give an account of them, and, moreover, a non-predicative account of them. For Russell, therefore, the above proof of the existence of the world resurfaces, supposing we restrict 'a' appropriately. Quine is more prepared to believe that 'Fa' (for constant 'a') never on its own entails '(Ex)Fx', since such an entailment would presume a was a real existent.

Lejewski has taken Quine to task about this [2]. He points out that, on such an understanding, before we could use the classical law of Existential Generalisation, we would have to find out whether the noun-expression employed was empty or not - which would seem an empirical question. But the thought that some rules of inference should depend on contingent data, which even may not be available, Lejewski takes to be so alien to the tradition of logic that a thorough overhaul of the classical interpretation of the quantifiers is called for. According to Quine the strange theorem we started with means that standard logic only applies to universes which are non-empty, granting thereby that a stricter logic should not assume this, but allow for empty universes, as well. Lejewski's free-logic way out, following Lesniewski, is to distinguish between two senses of the quantifier: a Quinean objectual, 'restricted' sense in which it ranges only over extensional individuals, i.e. real existents, and a substitutional, 'unrestricted' sense in which it ranges over noun expressions, which may relate to fictions, as well. In the former Realist sense we need to know that a exists before we can step to the existential conclusions in our theorem; in the latter quasi-Idealist sense the steps are immediate, but the conclusion weaker, as a result.

Lejewski's own position has been questioned, for instance by Cohen [3]. Cohen complains that Lejewski has defended classical logic at the expense of leaving some statements in it quite without truth-grounds. He argues that, since, in 'the empty universe',

    Fa v -Fa

and

    -(Fa.-Fa)

are still logical truths, for any 'a' and 'F', it follows that still one and just one of 'Fa' and '-Fa' is true. But there can be no way of telling which is true, in general: there are no grounds for assigning one truth value to 'Fa' and the other to '-Fa', for while there can be no evidence against any assignment there can be no evidence in favour of any assignment, either. Cohen, as a result, believes the classical theorems can be given an unrestricted interpretation, in which a may be a fiction, only so long as 'F' is a predicate like 'exists', and not if 'F' is one like 'is winged'. And one might well want to say it was definitely true that nothing pegasises, but not be able to make up one's mind whether Pegasus was winged. Certainly Lejewski provides no decision procedure. But it is clear that Lejewski does not need to be defeated by this criticism, for it is open to him to say that there are indeed no truth grounds, evidence, or decision procedure for fictional statements, so that they are given truth values merely through choice

149

and stipulation (except with regard to the non-existence statements which define them). What is more of a proper objection to Lejewski's position, therefore, is its position on Ontology. If the unrestricted interpretation of the quantifiers is taken to be <u>linguistic</u> i.e. non-referential then we shall have lost any connection to the Realist universe, and the Russellian 'robustness' it engenders. On the other hand, of course, if the unrestricted interpretation is taken to be referential in the classic sense then it seems inevitable we shall have to subscribe to some Idealist expanded universe including not just extensional, but also intensional objects, as well. It is therefore best not only to choose the truth value of fictional statements, but also to do so by choosing the referents of their subject terms: fictions are then not creatures in some other world, but still creatures in this world, and we can have the Realist benefits of reference along with the Idealist benefits of a non-empirical logic. Plantinga noted this option some years ago [4]:

> For if descriptivist intuitions are satisfied by the suggestion that a story describes its characters as they are <u>in other possible worlds</u>, why not hold instead that a piece of fiction is about n-tuples of <u>actual</u> objects, ascribing to them properties <u>they</u> have in other worlds? If we think stories must be <u>about</u> something, why not think of them as about existent objects? No doubt there are possible worlds in which Ronald Reagan, for example, is named 'Rip van Winkle' and has the properties depicted in Irving's story. If we are bent upon a descriptivist account we may suppose that Irving is describing Reagan as he is in these worlds (and the rest of us as we are in our Rip van Winkle worlds). For any fictional character there will be real objects and worlds such that the former have in the latter the properties credited to the fictional character. And hence we have no reason for supposing that stories about Pegasus, Lear and the rest are about possible but unactualised objects.

There is thus a third option in this area, besides

the classic Realist and Idealist ones, which is not
commonly considered. Formally it derives from using
the enriched predicate logic called Hilbert's epsilon
calculus which has already figured extensively in this
book, the characteristic axiom of the system being

Fa D FexFx,

where 'exFx' is a term defined for all predicates in
the language. Indeed this axiom is all that is needed
(although sometimes a second one is also added) to
form a Hilbertian predicate logic from standard
propositional logic. For we can then define the
quantifiers by means of

(Ex)Fx = FexFx,

and

(x)Fx = Fex-Fx,

showing that exFx is an F just so long as there are
F's, and conversely that ex-Fx, despite its name, may
be F. It is this feature which gives us the novel
account of fictions above, for if Pegasus=ex(x
pegasises), i.e. p=exPx, then if nothing pegasises,
Pegasus is a fiction, but exPx is still a referring
term, and we have, since -(Ex)Px = -PexPx, merely that
Pegasus does not pegasise, not that Pegasus does not
exist, i.e. -(Ex)(x=p). Hilbert called 'exFx' 'the
first F', in which case 'ex(Fx,-(x=eyFy))' would be
'the second F', giving a representation of the
ordinals. But, as we saw in chapter one, 'exFx' can
also be thought of as 'what would be F if anything
was', i.e. 'the paradigm F', although its referent is
invariably to some degree arbitrary except in the case
where there is just one F. In all, if there is just
one F its referent is that F, if there are no F's its
'non-existent' referent is anything, while if there
are many F's its 'generic' referent is any one of the
F's, although still a certain one of them.

Hilbert's epsilon calculus is sometimes thought to
formalise indefinite descriptions, like 'an F',
'some F', on account of the choice thus often
available for the referent of 'exFx'; but this is a

misapprehension. 'Some F is G' with 'Some F is H' does not entail 'Some G is H', yet 'GexFx' with 'HexFx' does entail '(Ex)(Gx.Hx)'; moreover 'Some F is G' does not contradict 'some F is not G', but 'GexFx' does contradict '-GexFx'. Certainly epsilon terms may be used in the symbolisation of indefinite descriptions, for '(Ex)(Gx.Hx)' is

Gex(Gx.Hx).Hex(Gx.Hx),

but that is not 'HexGx', so 'exGx' does not symbolise 'some G'. The indefinition in the epsilon term therefore arises in some other way than through representing an indefinite description. Demonstratives are in the right class to be symbolised by epsilon terms, since they may have a variety of referents, on different occasions of use, yet each time they have a single, unique, and definite referent. But the interpretation of epsilon terms is not limited to demonstratives, for, as we shall see in more detail in the next section, they are also usable to formalise definite descriptions, i.e. expressions like 'The king of France', when used as subject terms. The classic theory of descriptions concentrates on the case where there is just one king of France, with the expression then denoting that thing, but when there are, or have been several such kings this phrase can be used in connection with any one, and when there are or have been no such kings the phrases can still be used, though now used quite arbitrarily - say for one's grandiose next-door neighbor.

On this account, therefore, 'fictions' become selected real objects, whether the fiction is of a 'generic' or a 'non-existent' variety, and so, with respect to quantification, the two forms Lejewski isolated fuse into one. But that means that the certainty of the conclusion, (Ex)(Fx v -Fx), in the unrestricted case, flows through into the other case, as well. Hence we have indeed proved there is something, (Ex)(x=x), and so the world exists, (Ey)(y=ex(x=x)).

Use of 'the world', 'ex(x=x)', here, however, shows how crucial it is to the proof that referring terms, paradigmatically demonstratives, are not just inescapably present in language, but also available, as a result, for demonstration purposes. For no substantive conclusion, about the necessity of the world, would follow on Lejewski's own, linguistic understanding of his unrestricted quantification. One cannot learn that the world necessarily exists from the fact that a sentence is true, even the sentence 'the world exists'; for the sentence needn't have been true, since it is contingent that it means what it does. But one can learn that the world necessarily exists from the fact that the world exists, since it is necessary that $(Ey)(y=ex(x=x))$. So the proof of the existence of the world consists essentially in just pointing to it, i.e. acting in a certain way.

Now the necessary existence of the world shows that existence is not a (first order) predicate, for that there is nothing of a certain kind, i.e. nothing falling under a certain first-order predicate, is conceivable, even while that there is nothing is not. Existence is thus essentially formulated by means of quantification, 'Pegasus exists', as before, being '$(Ex)(x=p)$', and 'Something pegasises' being '$(Ex)Px$'. Moreover the latter is contingent, expressly because it says there is something of a certain kind, unlike '$(Ex)(x=p)$', which is necessary, and merely says there is something with a certain name. It is presumably a confusion between these two forms which has been the basis of the Quinean and Lejewskian arguments about the legitimacy of Existential Generalisation, i.e. the move from 'Fa' to '$(Ex)Fx$'. For if the term 'a' here is indeed a referring phrase then '$(Ex)(x=a)$' is guaranteed, and so there is clearly no need for a further premise, whereas if 'a' is an attributive phrase, so that 'Fa' is to be interpreted as '$(x)(Ax \supset Fx)$', then equally clearly one does need the extra assumption, '$(Ex)Ax$' before 'generalisation' to '$(Ex)Fx$' can take place. This distinction, that it is possible that nothing pegasise, but not possible that nothing is Pegasus, also means that stories about Pegasus were certainly stories about a real creature, but it is quite possible, for instance, that it did not have wings, indeed that the stories were all falsehoods, and the storytellers all liars [5].

Note that, while it is possible to prove the

existence of the world, it is not possible to go
further than that and say there is more than one
entity in it. The point is important in a number of
connections, for instance in connection with the
supposition that propositional logic requires there to
be two objects of reference, say the True and the
False, which are distinct. Now it is certainly
possible to prove

$$(En)(((n=T).p) \lor ((n=F).-p)),$$

for, using Reductio, if

$$-(En)(((n=T).p) \lor ((n=F).-p))$$

then

$$(n)((n=T \ D \ -p).(n=F \ D \ p))$$

and so, instantiating to T and F, we get that -p.p,
which is impossible. Hence it might seem that, since
we can go on to write

$$((V=T).p) \lor ((V=F).-p)$$

where $V=en(((n=T).p) \lor ((n=F).-p))$, i.e. 'the truth
value of p', we cannot have T=F, since we cannot have
p.-p. But from this disjunction there is no way to
show -(T=F), indeed in contrast to the above theorem,
nothing like

$$(En)(n=T \ CD \ p)$$

is provable, since, attempting Reductio on this, we
find

$$-(En)(n=T \ CD \ p)$$

entails

$$(n)(n=T \ CD \ -p)$$

and while this entails -p, we would need the express
thing we cannot get, namely

$$(En)-(n=T)$$

in order to derive, as well, p. Karel Lambert says [6]:

> The matter can be summed up this way. If the world were empty then, of course, all singular terms would fail to refer; but if the world had things in it, it might still be the case that not any of them would be specified by a singular term such as 'Pegasus'. A free logic recognising the empty world is, to be sure, easy to develop. A free logic making room for the empty world is conventionally called a universally free logic.

But there is no way to develop a totally free logic. For if the world were empty, or even just recognised or made room for, then still (Ex)(x=the world). Certainly if the world had things in it, and was not just an undifferentiable 'soft shapeless dough', it might have been the case that not any one of the things in the world was called 'Pegasus', but that does not prevent what we do call 'Pegasus' from existing, and indeed its being necessary that (Ex)(x=that thing) i.e. (Ex)(x=Pegasus). If the world were empty, i.e. absurd, what would then also be the case would be that Pegasus=the world, and indeed (x)(x=the world), so what Lambert is merely saying is that the reverse of this latter, i.e. that there is more than one thing, is not provable.

RUSSELL

One traditional philosopher who held the unrestricted (Idealist) point of view on Reference was Meinong [7]. Meinong attacked what he called the 'prejudice in favour of existence', which made realists speak of the properties of things (their Sosein) only when their existence (their Sein) was given. Mathematics pre-eminently showed that this prejudice was untenable, Meinong said, for the figures in Geometry, he thought, did not exist, although their properties could still be established. In the area of the a posteriori, he admitted, there might be reasons for disinterest in such facts, but that did not alter the Sosein of an object being unaffected by the object's non-existence (<u>Nichtsein</u>). As a result of this reasoning, Meinong formulated his famous 'Principle of Independence' - of <u>Sosein</u> from <u>Sein</u> - and uttered his no less famous opinions that not only was the gold mountain made of gold, but also the round square was as round as it was square. But since nothing is round and square, i.e.

$$-(Ex)(Rx.Sx),$$

then the round square, i.e. ex(Rx.Sx), cannot be both round and square, since expressly the non-existence statement is equivalent to

$$-(Rex(Rx.Sx).Sex(Rx.Sx)).$$

Only, indeed, in this way can the round square's necessary <u>Sosein</u> be quite independent of its contingent <u>Sein</u>, since its <u>Sosein</u> is asserted in

$$(Ey)(y=ex(Rx.Sx)),$$

whereas its <u>Sein</u> is asserted in the existence statement previously denied. The defining properties of an Object are thus merely inscribed in the term, and are not necessarily predicable of it, i.e. it is the <u>Sein</u> and not the <u>Sosein</u> which properly relates to the possession of the properties. The figures with which geometry is concerned may indeed lack <u>Sein</u>, but also, in this sense, may possess <u>Sein</u>, given, for example, SexSx, i.e. (Ex)Sx; while exSx, i.e. the Object the square, is never in some other world. As a result there is no prejudice in favour of existence, for although calling a house large ((Ex)(Hx.Lx)) does entail there is a house ((Ex)Hx), calling <u>the</u> house large (LexHx) does not.

Russell held Meinong's Idealist view at one time, but later became a Realist; he did so as a result of formulating his classic 'Theory of Descriptions' [8]. The theory Russell formulated was that 'The king of France is bald' had three constituents:

There is a king of France   - (Ex)(Kx
and only one king of France - .(y)(Ky D y=x)
and he is bald   - .Bx),

and so he could not make the distinction Meinong made between _Sosein_ and _Sein_, since, given his analysis, 'The king of France is bald' entailed 'There is a king of France', and likewise 'The house is large' would have to entail 'There is a house'. Moreover it is a straightforward theorem of Hilbert's epsilon calculus that

$$(1):(Ex)(Kx.(y)(Ky \supset y=x).Bx),$$

is equivalent to

$$(2):(Ex)(Kx.(y)(Ky \supset y=x)).Bk,$$

where $k=ex(Kx.(y)(Ky \supset y=x))$, for (2) entails

$$Kk.(y)(Ky \supset y=k).Bk,$$

and hence entails (1), while (1) entails

$$Kh.(y)(Ky \supset y=h).Bh$$

where $h=ex(Kx.(y)(Ky \supset y=x).Bx)$, and hence entails

$$(Ex)(Kx.(y)(Ky \supset y=x))$$

and so

$$Kk.(y)(Ky \supset y=k),$$

making $h=k$, and Bk, and giving (2). Hence, if we take k as the symbolisation of the description 'The (one and only) king of France', we see, directly from his later view, that Russell's former view was nearer the truth, for it is the third element in the above definition which alone formalises 'The king of France is bald', and thus the Principle of Independence is saved.

The point may be put grammatically in terms of the difference between relative and personal pronouns. For while there is a substantial difference between the non-unique

There is a king who is bald

i.e.

(Ex)(Kx.Bx)

and

There is a king. He is bald

i.e.

KexKx.BexKx,

so that the latter entails the former, but not vice versa, there is, as we have just seen, no substantial difference between the pair above, and so not between the same pair transcribed into full English, namely

(1'):There is a king of France, who alone is king of France, and who is bald

and

(2'):There is a king of France, who alone is king of France. He is bald.

Now the 'he' in the second part of (2') is replaceable by 'The one and only king of France', but there is no formulation for this as a term in a separate proposition, in Russell's non-Meinongian logic - only (1') is formulable in that logic, and this cannot be split up into a conjunction there. Hence the whole of (1') comes to seem as though it formalised 'The king of France is bald', since the part of (2') (=(1')) which does formalise this referential sentence cannot be extracted in that logic. It is only once one realises the difference between relative and personal pronouns is important that one comes to appreciate this fact: for unlike 'who', in (1'), 'he', in (2'), can stand alone in a distinct, separate sentence, hence the former kind of pronoun does not allow the articulation which the latter kind permits.

Clearly, however, in the epsilon formalisation, the proper analysis of 'The king of France is bald' does far more than illuminate the difference between these

two types of pronoun. It also locates what Russell
would have to call 'logically proper names', for we
now have something to substitute for 'x' which makes
'Bx' the unambiguous contradictory of '-Bx'.
Demonstratives may be the paradigms of 'logically
proper names' in that their gestural use displays
graphically the referential aspect of singular terms,
but the present 'logically proper names' are now no
more than ordinary names and definite descriptions in
their proper guise - it was Russell's getting the
wrong analysis of these that made him think there was
another category of individual term. Also we have an
improved Idealist cum Realist theory about the
relationship between

There is one and only one king of France

and

The king of France is bald,

to set beside Russell's later one and that of the
presuppositionists. The predicative statement would
entail the existence and uniqueness clauses on
Russell's account, while the predicative statement
would presuppose these clauses on the
presuppositionists' view. But there is in fact no
logical relationship between these two expressions,
for if the former is false that merely gives 'The king
of France' an arbitrary referent, and 'The king of
France is bald' an arbitrary truth value (supposing
baldness is not universal), while if the former is
true the term has a determinate referent and the
proposition a determinate truth value (supposing
baldness is not vague). But in no way is there an
entailment, or even weaker relation, linking the truth
or falsity of the two expressions.

This means the epsilon account formalises not a
Realist or an Idealist, but strictly an Activist, i.e.
choice account of reference. But we also get a
related account of 'possible worlds', as Plantinga
illustrated, the point being that we do not have
different 'possible worlds' in the sense of different
sets of individuals, we merely have the same
individuals with different properties (though, as we

shall see at the end of this section, individuals
might fuse). For it is now a contingent matter
whether

$$Kk.(y)(Ky \supset y=k),$$

i.e. whether the king of France is king of France, so
what could be different in another possible world
would not be that k was not there (for as before
$(Ex)(x=k)$ is necessarily true), but simply that k, who
would still be there, would no longer be king of
France, and could have any existent character, chosen
at will. This makes the epsilon term account
categorically different from Russell's iota term one.
For according to Russell's theory of descriptions
(naturalised)

$$F(ixKx) \ CD \ (Ex)(Kx.(y)(Ky \supset y=x).Fx)$$

and hence

$$(Ez)(z=ixKx) \ CD \ (Ex)(Kx.(y)((Ky \supset y=x).(Ez)(z=x))$$

i.e.

$$(Ez)(z=ixKx) \ CD \ (Ex)(Kx.(y)(Ky \supset y=x)).$$

Hence both remarks are contingent and so what might
happen, in another possible world, on Russell's
account, would be not just that there was nothing with
the character of being a sole king of France, but also
nothing identical with the king of France. Lack of
the defining property would then reduce the identities
in the world, instead of merely making a certain name
a misnomer. This is another way of exposing Russell's
later inability to distinguish <u>Sosein</u> from <u>Sein</u>: he
lost the ability to distinguish 'The round square
exists' from 'A sole round square exists'.

But Russell's later way of formulating the existence
of individuals, making it equivalent to the possession
of properties, is not just of academic interest to
Russellian biographers, for it has had an extensive
influence on subsequent generations of philosophers,
with later logicians, for instance, commonly using
expressions of the form '$(Ex)(x=b)$' to try to do the

job of expressing contingent existence, so making the term 'b' and its associated individuating predicate hard, if not impossible, to distinguish, but also making identity statements seem to be not necessary. Thus Hintikka tries to hold on to the necessity of 'b=b' while taking '(Ex)(x=b)' to be a predicate of contingent existence. He says [9]:

The popularity of (b=b) as a candidate for the role of our 'predicate of existence' Q(b) probably derives from a misguided application of Russell's theory of definite descriptions. It is thought that a proper name or other free singular term behaves, at least in the contexts where it cannot be assumed to have a reference, like a definite description (ix)B(x) derived from some predicate expression B(x). Indeed, if this definite description is allowed to replace b, the identity (b=b) becomes (on Russell's theory) equivalent to
    (31) (Ex)(B(x)&(Uy)(B(y) D x=y))
which is also equivalent (on the same theory) to what becomes of
    (32) (Ex)(x=b)
when the same replacement is made. Hence (b=b) seems to play the role of a predicate of existence quite as well as (32)...
These reasons in favour of (b=b) as a predicate of existence are completely illusory, however. They are due to the fact that certain existential presuppositions have already been built into Russell's theory of definite descriptions...
As I have pointed out elsewhere, we can get rid of these presuppositions by using instead of Russell's contextual definitions such contextual definitions which are illustrated by the following equivalence:
    (34) (a=(ix)B(x)) CD (B(a)&(Ux)(B(x) D x=a)).
If (34) instead of [Russell's definition] is the basis of our theory of definite descriptions, a substitution of (ix)B(x) for b in (32) gives rise to a formula which is still equivalent to (31) and which implies (Ex)B(x). Nevertheless the same substitution in (b=b) gives rise to a formula which is not any more equivalent to (31) and which does not any more imply (Ex)B(x). In general (b=b) does not imply any existential statements

any more even if b is replaced by a definite description.

But that is only because Hintikka, for no other reason, identifies '(ix)A(x) = (ix)B(x)' with '(Ux)(A(x) CD B(x))' (and see the discussion of a second epsilon axiom below.)

That is not to say that the alternative Hilbertian account, which uses names for necessary existence and predicates for contingent existence, might not seem unreasoned also. For one of the peculiarities of the Hilbertian account is that it seems to conflict with 'Buridan's Law', which states that terms in propositions must have the same referent independently of whether those propositions are true or false [10]. With

Kk.(y)(Ky D y=k),

for instance, it might well seem that, depending upon the truth and falsity of this, the term 'k' must vary its referent, for if this proposition is true then k is the one and only king of France, while if the proposition is false, k is not the one and only king of France, and indeed can have a quite arbitrary, chosen character. But if it seems there is a conflict with Buridan's Law here then identity is being thought to be a matter of properties, making it seem necessary that the object possesses them. But it is the same object, with the same identity, which is involved, whether or not the properties are possessed, for it is quite certain that

the king of France is identical with the king of France,

i.e.

ex(Kx.(y)(Ky D y=x))=ex(Kx.(y)(Ky D y=x)).

although it might not be that

The king of France is (predicatively) the king of France

162

i.e.

Kk.(y)(Ky D y=k).

Hence the identity of the object does remain constant, even though it might so radically change its properties.

This important fact we are underlining against Russell is really a re-working, in formal terms, of Donnellan's distinction between referential and attributive uses of definite descriptions, as we shall see in more detail in chapter five. It also shows there is an ambiguity in the area which will eventually give us a way out of Quine's famous problem with necessity [11]. For it can be that LF9 but - LF(the number of the planets), even though 9 is the number of the planets. But that means reading 'the number of the planets' Russell's way, i.e. attributively: it is not necessary that the number of the planets is the number of the planets, i.e. ([en(nx)Px]y)Py, since neither is it necessary that there are just 9 planets, i.e. (9y)Py; but it is necessary that 9=en(nx)Px, i.e. that 9 is identical with the number of the planets - 'the number of the planets' being there used referentially.

The relation between a contingent individuating expression and the associated necessary identity expression is not equivalence, as the Russellian tradition confusedly believes, it is merely entailment, indeed the equivalence in the area is

A'b CD (exA'x=b.(Ex)A'x),

supposing 'A'' includes some kind of uniqueness feature ('one and only', 'smallest', 'nearest' etc.), so the predicative expression 'A'b' adds, but merely adds _Sein_ to the identity expression 'exA'x=b'. Moreover, it only adds _Sein_ to one of the terms in this expression, and not both, and indeed we must be careful not to adopt as a second epsilon axiom [12]

(x)(Ax CD Bx) CD exAx=exBx.

for that would mean that _Sein_ was transmissible across

163

identities, since (Ex)Ax, with exAx=exBx would then entail (Ex)Bx. Hintikka says [13] with respect to a principle he formulates, namely that whenever a and b are identical, and a exists, then b exists, that there do not seem to be any plausible objections to it, but that principle, and the associated epsilon axiom can have no application in a temporal context, since they prevent identifications with what no longer is, and what is yet to be, and hence prevent the proper representation of continuity in time. Thus it is a feature, say of the boy Moore i.e.

ex(Bx.x=m)

that he grew up and became the man Moore, i.e.

ex(Mx.x=m).

But while we can atemporally identify these two term expressions, it does not follow that there ever was a boy and also at that time a man, for

(Ex)Bx.(Ex)Mx

could be at all times false. However, (Ex)(Bx.x=m) would entail (Ex)Mx, given the atemporal identity, and the Hintikkan epsilon axiom, because of the transmission of Sein. Moreover, if that second epsilon axiom were the case then from

A'exB'x

not only could we get 'exA'x=exB'x' and hence '(x)(A'x CD B'x)', we could also get 'A'exB'x CD B'exB'x' and hence 'B'exB'x'. So that would mean exB'x could not have individuating properties without having its own inscribed individuating property, and so long as it was distinguishable it would have to be distinguishable always in the same way. Thus, since, when Moore was grown up, he was (predicatively) the man Moore, i.e.

Mex(Mx.x=m).ex(Mx.x=m)=m,

the atemporal identity gives us

164

Mex(Bx.x=m).ex(Bx.x=m)=m,

and so from Hintikka's epsilon axiom, we would have to have

Bex(Bx.x=m).ex(Bx.x=m)=m

for ex(Bx.x=m) would have an individuating property, and the inscribed property in the name 'ex(Bx.x=m)' would also have to apply to the individual then. Hence

(Ex)(Bx.Mx),

and not only would a boy exist at the same time as a man, a boy would exist at the same time and in the same person as a man, which is impossible.

Note that, although such identities as those above are necessary truths, and hence hold at all times and in all possible worlds, that does not make non-identities necessary; indeed if it was possible, by logic, to prove that two individuals were distinct, then we should know for sure that more than one individual term was needed to make reference to the universe, against the considerations in the last section. But the resulting possibility of fusion between individuals is in line with our account of necessity being basically that given by the system T. It is easy to prove that any identity must be a necessary identity, for if x=y then (F)(Fx CD Fy), and so we can substitute for x in the undoubted truth L(x=x) and get that L(x=y). But for it to be the case that non-identities were necessary we would need to show that actually separate individuals could not marry, and for that it is known we would need, for example, the characteristic axiom of modal system B, i.e. 'p D LMp' [14]. For then

-(x=y) D LM(-(x=y)),

but already

M(-(x=y)) D -(x=y),

since

        x=y D L(x=y),

and so

        LM(-(x=y)) D L(-(x=y)),

giving

        -(x=y) D L(-(x=y)).

But there is no reason why individuals cannot marry, since, as we saw before, there is no reason why 'p D LMp', or any other comparable condition, should necessarily hold.

FREGE

Frege's formal view of reference was Hilbertian: descriptive names in his system had an arbitrary reference if the description did not apply. In his more philosophical works, however, Frege (like Hilbert) was a presuppositionist [15], that is to say he held that one cannot make true, or false, remarks about creatures in fiction. In 'The Thought' he says 'that lime tree is my idea' could be false, but could not be true: in what one might regard as the latter case, where the lime tree was just a figment of his imagination, Frege was unable to give the statement a truth value, since one element in it, he believed, lacked a referent.

   In 'On Sense and Reference' he gives an argument for this claim, for, he says, if the sense of 'Kepler died in misery' contained the thought that 'Kepler' has a referent then its negation would have to be

        Kepler did not die in misery, or 'Kepler' has no referent

and not simply

        Kepler did not die in misery.

166

Now while it is necessary that (Ex)(x=Kepler) it
certainly is a contingent matter whether the word
'Kepler' has or has not a referent, and so if indeed
'Kepler died in misery' entailed not just
'(Ex)(x=Kepler)', but also ''Kepler' has a referent'
its negation would have to be what Frege makes it out
to be. But the fact that that is not its negation
does not show, following Frege, that its relation to
''Kepler' has a referent' is the presupposition
relation, making the truth of ''Kepler' has a
referent' a precondition of the truth or falsity of
'Kepler died in misery', instead of, say, just the
truth of it. For whether 'Kepler' has a referent is
not a given fact but a matter of choice, and so the
use of 'Kepler' in the assertion of 'Kepler died in
misery' or 'Kepler did not die in misery' does not
need to wait upon some precondition in the world to be
legitimate. Asserting or denying 'Kepler died in
misery' makes it the case that 'Kepler' has a
referent, indeed any use of 'Kepler' as opposed to
mention of it does that. Frege says that it is a
'fault' in some languages that they contain terms
which fail to refer, and that a <u>Begriffsschrift</u> should
avoid that incompleteness, but he does not see that
the process he recommends, to correct this 'fault',
where, by a 'special stipulation', all such terms
refer to the number 0, is not a special process. It
is just the Hilbertian process (following,
unnecessarily, Hintikka's second axiom). In fact all
proper names must gain their referent in this
stipulative kind of way, and the application of
individuating descriptions can be equally
conventional. If certain terms in Frege's scheme of
things do lack a referent, therefore, this can only be
because he chooses not to give them one, i.e. chooses
not to use them: so it is Frege's attitude to certain
words which is exposed by his philosophy, not some
natural fact about them.

In 'On Sense and Reference', just which words Frege
was reluctant to use start to appear: such a statement
as 'Odysseus was set ashore at Ithaca while sound
asleep' is there doubted to be a source of truth,
since it is taken to be doubtful whether it is subject
to scientific investigation, and is not rather just an
object of aesthetic delight. But which statements and

words are in this latter class cannot be decided <u>a priori</u>, as we saw before, with Lejewski, and as Frege, finding the matter merely doubtful, clearly realises. It might be that both the truth value of the statement 'Odysseus was set ashore at Ithaca while sound asleep', and the referent of 'Odysseus' would have to be chosen, but only after we have found that the storytellers are liars, for tracing the myth to its origins and finding who was set ashore at Ithaca would be one scientific investigation we could certainly start on, possibly locating a referent for 'Odysseus', and then there would be no opening for aesthetic favour. So there is no way that Frege can eliminate fictions from his logic, since it is not logic which delimits them. And if logic cannot exclude them, it must be prepared, however reluctantly, to deal with them. The described object clearly needn't be properly described as having been set ashore at Ithaca, since it may be misremembered, or simply misdescribed, indeed in the truly delightful case it must be misdescribed, otherwise there would be no choice about locating it. But while what can be definitely located is, by contrast, a non-fiction, it is only as a matter of fact not misdescribed, or misremembered in this pleasurable way.

Now it is not just a better attitude to pleasure which emerges as a result of seeing that the referents of all names are physical objects: we get a better view of a number of other central matters in Psychology and Aesthetics, as a result. Thus, for a start, there is now no difficulty with the psychological correlate of non-fictional names in indirect speech, i.e. with images where no choice or misdescription is involved, 'memory images'. Sartre says generally about images [16]

> The consequences for images are immediately apparent. An image, too, is an image <u>of</u> something. We are dealing, therefore, with a certain consciousness of a certain object. In a word, the image ceases to be a psychic <u>content</u>. It is not <u>in</u> consciousness in the guise of a constitutive element.

He goes on, in particular, about memory images,

The image of my friend Peter is not a dim
phosphorescence, a furrow left in consciousness by
a perception of Peter. It is an organised form of
consciousness which refers in its own way to my
friend Peter; it is one of the possible ways of
aiming at Peter. Thus, in the act of imagination
consciousness refers to Peter directly, not by
means of a simulacrum _in_ consciousness. At one
stroke vanish, along with the immanentist
metaphysics of images, all the difficulties
adduced in the preceding chapter concerning the
relationship of the simulacrum to its real object,
and of pure thought to the simulacrum. The 'Peter
in reduced format', that homunculus carted about
by consciousness, was never _of_ consciousness. It
was an object in the physical world that had
strayed among psychic realities. By expelling it
from consciousness and asserting that there is but
one Peter, the object of perceptions and images,
Husserl freed the psychic world of a weighty
burden and eliminated almost all the difficulties
that clouded the classical problem of the
relations of images to thoughts.

The point explains the fullness of our emotional
response to memory images, and thereby to photographs
and portraits, but there is no difficulty now, either,
about the fullness of our emotional response to non-
memory images, and thereby to pictures, films, and
stories where a fiction, and so a choice of referent
is involved, as well.

On other accounts there is considerable difficulty
with this. For, supposing it is not a photograph or
portrait, on the Realist view all there is with a
picture is the picture, and so there is clearly no
defense of any human response, merely a pure aesthetic
response to the technique and structure of the
artwork. But on the Idealist view the picture
transports us to another world, where ghostly,
insubstantial unearthly creatures exist, and so that
account clearly fares no better at explaining the
fullness of our emotional response, for where we are
'transported' to is supposedly a world sealed off from
the real one, and hence terrors and idylls which lie

there cannot affect us, because they cannot get to us, and we cannot get to them. Their 'otherness' is then not just a matter of their remoteness, as if they were on some other planet, or island in the south seas, for on the Idealist view it is crucial that the creatures in fiction do not exist at all in the actual universe, making the lack of engagement complete. But on the present, Activist, view we combine the Realist virtue of real reference with the Idealist virtue of reference to something other than the artwork: there is a set of second objects involved, so there is objective reference just as in photography and biography, but which second objects are involved is not determined entirely by features of the artwork, but either partly or wholly by the reader's/viewer's choice. No identity of the form 'x is Cinderella', where 'x' is not 'Cinderella', is knowable, but still identities of this form may be believed, or thought. We thus escape the danger of 'overdistancing', i.e. weakness of emotional response, because we see something in the artwork, but we are not so 'underdistanced' as to be like the proverbial yokel who jumps onto the stage to save the heroine in the melodrama: it is to the chosen second object that we respond and any action is taken off the stage, to save 'heroines' in misery elsewhere.

Of course there might be two objects involved in another sense: not the representation and the represented, but two things represented, as with the duck-rabbit and similar pictures. The duck-rabbit case, indeed, quite defeats any Realist or Idealist analysis, and so is a paradigm on which to build the Activist one. For how can an Idealist conceptualise, say a satire in which politicians are portrayed as animals, and vice versa? Such a fiction has a double reading in order to convey and yet mask the satirical reference. But what could be the ideal object portrayed in that case: a curiously disjunctive intension, a politician-or-animal? No: for no one object is portrayed, so while we can formalise the topic of the satire by means of a disjunctive epsilon term 'ex(Px v Ax)', it is crucial that this can have a choice of real referents rather than a single, unreal, Idealist one. The fact that real referents are involved might suggest, by contrast, that some Realist analysis was possible, but the further fact that imagination must be used to make the choice between the two referents means that neither is 'really' there: the only thing really there being again the artwork, i.e. the satire. If it was not an artwork but a piece of technology, like a photograph or aeolian harp, the Realist would have no trouble, even though a second object was involved which he might not like to follow Sartre and say was seen or heard. But it is the fact that, in general, there is a choice of second objects with artworks which quite defeats the Realist's thesis. Frege took fictional names to have merely a sense but no reference, in an attempt to escape the Realist's dilemma at such a point, but the Idealism of his senses tried to reify as an extraordinary entity what is merely a choice between ordinary ones [17].

But Frege's distinction between sense and reference had another source than this about the contrast between what has a definite referent and what can only have an imagined one. He was also concerned with a puzzle about identity: the medians of a triangle, a, b, c all meet at one point, so the point of intersection of a and b is the point of intersection of b and c. But this identity, it seems, can hardly be the same as the identity between the point of intersection of a and b and the point of intersection of a and b, as substitution of identicals would require, hence Frege conceived of all referring terms having a sense, whether or not they had a referent. Although they have the same referent the two ways of pointing to the intersection have different senses, according to Frege, and that is what gives the identity statement its content over and above the tautology.

We can now see what this aspect of the distinction between reference (denotation) and sense (connotation) amounts to. For to say $x=ey(Ky.(z)(Kz D y=z))$ is not to say $Kx.(y)(Ky D y=x)$, as we realised in the last section. Hence there are two statements here which might loosely be transcribed 'x is the king of France' - one in which there is a term (with a referent, i.e. an object), in the other of which there is a predicate (with a sense, i.e. entailments). To make the

171

separation in speech we must clearly be careful to distinguish 'is identical with' from 'is', and subject from predicate: a subject is 'the king of France', but a predicate is 'is the king of France', or 'is identical with the king of France', and, as we have seen, 'the king of France is king of France' is contingent (though not a 'contingent identity'), while 'the king of France is identical with the king of France' is necessary, being the only proper identity.

Kripke says on this point [18] that if 'Aristotle' meant 'the man who taught Alexander the Great' then 'Aristotle was a teacher of Alexander the Great' would be a tautology, which clearly it isn't. He deduces that the predicate can be no part of the sense of the name. But it is 'Aristotle is identical with the man who taught Alexander the Great' (a=eyT'y) which would be a referential tautology, allowing that 'being the teacher of Alexander the Great' (T'x) might be false of the name, while still requiring 'Aristotle' meant as supposed. And then the predicate could be no part of the sense of the name only because

    x is Aristotle (x=a),

which would entail

    x is identical with the teacher of Alexander the Great (x=eyT'y),

would not thereby entail

    x is the teacher of Alexander the Great (T'x),

even though the reverse entailments would hold.

Kripke says later that if 'Moses' means 'the man who did such and such', e.g. 'the man who led the Israelites out of Egypt', then if no-one did such and such, Moses didn't exist, complaining against this that if Moses had just decided to spend his days in Egypt that would not mean Moses wouldn't have existed. Kripke concludes that 'Moses exists' must mean something different from 'the existence and uniqueness conditions for a certain description are fulfilled'. Now, indeed, 'Moses exists' is '(Ex)(x=m)', and even if necessarily m=exM'x that does not mean necessarily M'm, i.e. that the existence and uniqueness conditions for a certain description are fulfilled. Certainly in this world, i.e. in actual fact, Moses led the Israelites out of Egypt, i.e. L'm, and hence, since it follows that (Ex)L'x, and so L'exL'x, we get m=exL'x, but it is as a result quite possible not only that Moses had not led the Israelites out of Egypt (-L'm), but, what Kripke could not even consider, that the man who led the Israelites out of Egypt had not led the Israelites out of Egypt (-L'exL'x), so the definite description is a 'rigid designator' along with the name - when used in subject position. Kripke realises there is an alternative view of subjects, due to Donnellan, according to which referential descriptions need not describe, but follows instead Russell's view, which leads him to take names alone to be such that in any possible world they designate the same object. Or, at least, he does this in theory, for in practice he talks often enough about such things as 'this table', meaning thereby to identify the table in another world irrespective of its properties, and hence even of the central property it might lose, namely that of being a table. Likewise, in places, he stipulates he is talking about our hands, although 'our hands' is not a Kripkean rigid designator, any more than 'this table'. The only difference between such referring phrases and Kripkean rigid designators, i.e. names, is that names may not occur in predicate position, i.e. 'is Hesperus' means 'is identical with Hesperus', while 'is the Evening Star' is distinct from 'is identical with the Evening Star'.

This last point helps to explain how it might seem (to people like Kripke) that certain necessary truths are to be known a posteriori. For it might well seem that, in opposition to the clearly conventional 'Phosphorus is Hesperus', the truth of 'The Morning Star is the same as the Evening Star' was merely an astronomical discovery. But what was discovered here was rather complex, since 'The Morning Star' and 'The Evening Star' are very good examples of Hilbertian referring phrases, neither, of course, referring to a star. If they had referred to one and the same star then what might have been discovered was, say, that

173

The Evening Star is the one and only star which rises in the morning,

which has the form

O'exV'x,

and this is indeed contingent, but from it there follows (Ex)O'x and hence O'exO'x and

exV'x=exO'x,

because of the uniqueness. The latter is ‹ the necessary truth, but that doesn't stop it being entailed by the original contingent truth, and hence it does not stop one route to its realisation being _a posteriori_. In the actual case, of course, the Evening Star is not a star but a planet, and the _a posteriori_ truth which was discovered was that the Evening Star is the same planet as the Morning Star, i.e. some truth of the form

(Ex)(Px.x=exV'x.x=exO'x).

From this it follows that exV'x=exO'x, making the route to the _a priori_ truth again experiential, but the truth is still independent of experience, as is shown by the alternative derivation available from the conventional 'v=exV'x' and 'v=exO'x', where v=Venus.

Note that a similar point is involved when only indefinite descriptions are in question, i.e. when the relationships are purely a matter of 'sense'. There is a considerable similarity between Frege's puzzle about identity and the Paradox of Analysis, for in the one case the question is 'How can 'a=b' have a meaning different from 'a=a', if it is true?', while in the other case the question is 'How can '(x)(Bx CD Ux)' have a meaning different from '(x)(Bx CD Bx)' if it is logically true?' In the former case the answer is that the referential terms 'a' and 'b' do not have different referents in the given circumstances, though that does not prevent any descriptions in them having different senses - for it is not necessary that a planet which rises in the morning sets in the evening. In the latter case the given necessity of the descriptive entailment prevents any precisely similar discrimination: just what is necessary is that bachelors are unmarried men, hence, the two forms '(x)(Bx CD Ux)' and '(x)(Bx CD Bx)', with this substitution, mean exactly the same. But in this case, as we saw with Prior and Stalnaker before, the content of the necessary truth is related to the contingency of the fact that 'bachelor' and 'unmarried man' describe the same things: someone might be ignorant of the contingent convention that we choose to so use these words that they are synonymous. But by learning the contingent convention he can come to learn the necessary truth. A similar story will give us the content of 'Phosphorus is Hesperus' where referential terms with no sense are involved. However, that does not make the content of all necessary truths a matter of convention, as we shall see at the end of chapter six.

PRESUPPOSITION

There have been other presuppositionists than Frege and Hilbert within the logical tradition, notably van Fraassen, who gave the idea a formal definition in his account of 'super-valuations'. This standardly involves a third truth value, but it is recognised in certain cases that, instead, one could assign one or other of the standard truth values - though it doesn't matter which. Thus J.D.McCawley [19] describes a supervaluation as an assignment of T,F and U such that T or F is assigned to a complex proposition so long as those constituents of the proposition which are U 'don't matter', in the sense that whatever their truth value it would not affect the truth value of the whole. Clearly this immateriality parallels the 'choice' element in our Hilbertian account.

Of all the extant accounts of these and related matters the super-valuation account is thus nearest to the present account, and not just here but with other applications as well. For it has been applied to give an account of vagueness, and the Liar Paradox, as well as a semantics for fictions and free logic, and so it opens up a whole non-classical approach to things, and is not just an ad hoc stratagem to deal with one area [20]. Unfortunately, van Fraassen's extant account of the Liar requires that the T-scheme be reduced to an interderivability result, moreover, a weakening of the traditional bi-conditional to a conditional is introduced to allow for non-truth-or-falsity, and, as a result, to avoid the Strengthened Liar, iterations of the truth predicate must be completed at least up to the ordinal omega, since the Liar sentence then turns out to be neither true nor false for each integral iteration of the truth predicate. Hence the possibility is overlooked, which is clearly available in the fiction case, of simply choosing an operational truth value for the sentence: one thing the Liar sentence means is true, another thing it means is false. This possibility is also overlooked in Kit Fine's supervaluational treatment of Vagueness, for to allow the distinction between truth and neither-true-nor-falseness to itself be vague, and so on for even higher order vaguenesses, again an integral hierarchy of iterated truth predicates is used to make discriminations, and the fact that the steps in that hierarchy are, in general, distinct means a simple chosen judgement of first-order operational truth or falsity is ruled out, in most cases. It is the possible arbitrariness of the truth value which is thus what is primarily not respected in the super-valuation account, even though this is a known re-interpretation, in the case of presuppositions with fictions.

It is not too difficult, however, to modify the standard supervaluational accounts of the Liar and Vagueness to put them into something more like present terms. Thus if we read 'T' and 'F' as operators, as before, then 'U' becomes not a third operator, but an arbitrary one of the two, i.e. simply an operational truth value which is unspecified. This makes its negative not 'U' again but '-U', where specifications, i.e. 'precisifications', are governed by the standard truth table for negation

U	-U
T	F
F	T.

We can then also say (T.U)=U and (F.U)=F and construct truth tables accordingly. So with the Liar in the form

Ms-epMsp,

since this entails, as before

MsepMsp,

when the question arises whether we are to assert what s expresses or its negation, i.e. assert epMsp or - epMsp, we can say

UepMsp

since there is no one definite sense for 'epMsp', and saying 'UepMsp' is then one way of sitting on the fence and not saying anything. A similar device will enable one to be non-committal with respect to some vague expression like 'He is bald'. Moreover it helps us to resolve the Sorites Paradox more clearly. On this Fine says:

> Consider the following instance, which is said to go back to Eubulides:
> A man with no hairs on his head is bald
> If a man with n hairs on his head is bald then a man with (n+1) hairs on his head is bald
> So, a man with a million hairs on his head is bald.
> The conclusion follows from the premises with the help of a million applications of modus ponens and universal instantiation...
> In fact, on the super-truth view, the second premise is false. This is because a hair splitting n exists for any complete and admissible specification of 'is bald'. I suspect that the temptation to say that the second premiss is true may have two causes. The first is that the value of a falsifying n appears to be arbitrary. This arbitrariness has nothing to do with vagueness as such. A similar case, but not involving vagueness, is: if n straws do not break a camel's back, then nor do (n+1) straws. The second cause is what one might call truth-value shift. This

also lies behind LEM. Thus A v -A holds in virtue
of a truth that shifts from disjunct to disjunct
for different complete specifications, just as the
sentence 'for some n, a man with n hairs is bald
but a man with (n+1) hairs is not' is true for an
n that shifts for different complete
specifications.

Indeed the second premise in the Sorites inference is
false, but different complete specifications of the
concept of baldness are produced by arbitrarily
asserting or denying certain instances of the
conditional quantified there, so vagueness is just a
kind of arbitrariness, The camel case in fact no more
illustrates arbitrariness than it exhibits vagueness,
for it merely illustrates possible ignorance. There
are observable facts about the breaking points of
different camels which we might be ignorant of, but
there are no comparable facts about complete
specifications of baldness, and any lack of knowledge
there just shows indecision. It is not clear
therefore that Fine distinguishes indecision from
ignorance: for he isolates several fallacies in this
area, but while we can be academic and merely say, for
most n

U(If a man with n hairs on his head is bald then a
man with (n+1) hairs on his head is bald),

it is clear we must also beware of a fallacy Fine does
not mention: that of thinking that we must be hesitant
for middling n. For the U operator expressly allows
us not to be hesitant, but to affirm or deny the
remark as we wish, thereby fixing, or helping to fix
our concept of baldness. Failure to allow for this,
indeed, would make

p, but not definitely p

not a possibility in the modal system, isomorphic to
T, which Fine constructs for the 'Definitely'
operator, and indeed he does seem often to want to say

A is true CD It is definitely the case that A,

which would rule the indefinite truth option out. But

178

it is crucial that we not be restricted, as with a traditional supervaluational 'U', to just commenting on the indefiniteness of vague expressions, otherwise they would hardly be part of our language. The reluctance to use fictional sentences we noted with Frege in the last section, and this same reluctance is thus present in other presuppositional areas, as well. It is no dry academicism, however, that, as a result, 'truth-<u>value</u>-less-ness' comes to be attributed to vague and fictional statements: these would indeed hardly have any value if they were not used.

Now it is Strawson who, in recent times, was first identified with presupposition, and that in its fullest sense, where a truth-value is denied to fictional statements, not just allowed to be what one wills. It was partly on this basis that Strawson argued against the Russellian account of descriptions: Russell would make all fictional statements not truth-value-less, but simply false. So, according to Strawson, Russell mistook the place of the existential and uniqueness clauses in the functioning of descriptive phrases, indeed Strawson places '(Ex)(Kx.(y)(Ky D y=x))' in something like the position we have placed it - as not part of the statement 'Bex(Kx.(y)(Ky D y=x))'. But presuppositionists take the truth of the former to be necessary before the latter can have a value, whereas, of course, we now see, it is only necessary before the latter can have a definite value. The same point would seem to arise in other cases where presupposition is said to occur than the standard cases of fictions, the Liar, and vagueness. Thus, as McCawley points out, it is sometimes thought that with such pairs as the following, for the first sentence to have a value the second sentence must be true

(A) The Senator didn't reveal that he had spent the winter in Monaco
(A') The Senator spent the winter in Monaco,

(B) The public doesn't realise that Nauru threatens security
(B') Nauru threatens security.

By contrast, it is sometimes said that this phenomenon

does not arise with 'The Senator didn't state that he spent the winter in Monaco', or 'The public doesn't believe that Nauru threatens security'.

But it would seem to be all a matter of seeing the use, and the correct use at that, of these and related expressions, for 'presuppositional' and 'non-presuppositional' cases arise with both 'factive' and 'non-factive' predicates. Thus a significant grammatical difference between the two sets is that, when they seem 'non-presuppositional', the latter do not involve 'the fact that', while, when they seem 'presuppositional', the former, implicitly, do. But both types may have or lack this feature, and making 'the fact that' explicit would give us four types in all. Thus, in addition to the above, the Senator might not have revealed the fact that he had spent winter in Monaco, and can also have stated the fact that he did; the public might not realise the fact that Nauru threatens our security, but might also not believe it. And all these are 'presuppositional'. But without 'the fact that' none of the forms has this feature (though the denial of (A) entails (A'), and the denial of (B) entails (B')). Now 'the fact that p' can be represented by an epsilon term

$$eq(q.q=p)$$

which shows that it is identical with p if p is a fact, for p entails and is entailed by

$$(Eq)(q.q=p)$$

and so also by its equivalent

$$eq(q.q=p).eq(q.q=p)=p.$$

We therefore have an explanation for the supposed behaviour of the first set of examples, for if 'the fact that' is properly expressed as part of their sense, as understood, something like 'presupposition' does take place, although not to the extent of preventing a truth value being assigned when the 'presupposition' does not hold. For, given p, then, for example

The Senator didn't reveal eq(q.q=p)

is equivalent to

The Senator didn't reveal p,

and is true or false in accordance with it. But given
-p then the two are not equivalent, for the latter is
true while which proposition the fact that p is cannot
be determined to settle the truth value of the former.
Nevertheless that fact is still some proposition, and
the former still makes sense, for it is just that then
it is immaterial what truth value we attach to it, not
that it is material we attach no truth value to it.
Naturally, if the Senator revealed nothing or
everything then the former gains a determinate truth
value, but these are extreme cases, which do not
affect the main point.

Strawson, of course, did not concern himself with
this area of application of his theory, any more than
with vagueness or the Liar, fixing primarily on the
reality or otherwise of subjects, rather than the
general truth or otherwise of whole propositions.
Moreover, even with the reality or otherwise of
subjects, he limited its application. In fact,
because of this, Strawson's account suffers a grave
implausibility, right in its home area, for with
regard to existence statements Strawson did not, like
Frege with his lime tree, give a presuppositional
account, so the rationale for Strawson's view would
seem to be broken. Indeed, how are we to understand
existence statements? Moore pointed out that 'tame
tigers exist' was quite unlike 'tame tigers growl'
since the former could only be quantified with 'no'
and 'some', and others have claimed that, in the
singular case, referential tautologies and
contradictions are produced, since if use of a
referring term guarantees it has a referent, it would
seem to be idle to add that that referent exists, and
necessarily false to deny it. So Strawson says [21],
facing Frege's difficulty

An immediate consequence of giving the sense I
propose to 'subject-predicate statement' is that
the existential statements presupposed by subject-

predicate statements will not themselves count as subject-predicate statements; and hence will fall outside the scope of the traditional system as I have recommended that it should be interpreted. For the four forms are to be so interpreted that the question of the truth or falsity of a statement exemplifying one of them does not arise unless there are things (or there is a thing) referred to by the subject term. Consequently, if we tried to assimilate a statement of the pattern 'x's exist' to any of the four forms, or to regard it as a subject-predicate statement at all, we should be faced with the absurd result that the question of whether it was true or false could arise only if it were true; or that, if it were false, the question of whether it was true or false did not arise.

Strawson's solution is to say that existence is a predicate of classes, since to say that the class of x's has members is not to predicate anything of the members themselves. But there is a difficulty even with this:

For no restriction was placed on the range of possible objects of reference. Can we not, then, besides referring to the members of a class, refer to the class itself, and describe it, for example, as having few, many, ten, some, or no members? If so we are faced with...problems. One is that if we treat such a statement as a subject-predicate statement, we seem committed to saying that it presupposes that the class referred to by the subject-term exists.

Strawson's first solution to this difficulty is simply to deny that his theory applies to such subject-predicate statements, but a second option he mentions is the position taken here: classes are given by abstract predicates, as in chapter one, so there are no referential terms which denote them. On this account the predicate of existence is, as before, the standard, second-order, quantificational one '(Ex) x', which automatically allows for Moore's point, since, then, only that expression and its negative are available.

But there are, in detail, three clear forms of expression which relate to the existence of singular subjects. These are, for individuating 'A''

(1) (Ex)A'x
(2) A'exA'x
(3) (Ey)(y=exA'x),

to which we may add a fourth of a quite different kind, namely ''exA'x' has a referent'. But this latter is merely equivalent to ''exA'x' is used', as we have seen, and so says nothing about the object exA'x, only the term used to denote it. Now (1), which contains only an individuating predicate, and not an individual term, would be Strawson's account of the singular case, even if its variant (2), which does contain an individual term, was not available to Strawson at the time of his writing. (3), on the other hand, is the singular existence statement which is necessary and so must be what others have had in mind, making the provision of presuppositions automatic, the existence statement tautologous, and the denial of existence inconsistent. But if (3) says the thing exists, then what does (2) say? That too, unlike (1), is about the thing, but must say something different about it than what (3) says, namely that it exists. We cannot here escape into saying a predicate is its subject, since a referential term is definitely involved, but what does (2) predicate of its referential subject?

Now, of course, individuating property statements like (1) are about their predicate subjects, and (2) is the equivalent individual object form of such a remark, so (2) is about the predicate as much as the thing. Hence the difference between (2) and (3) is that (2) is not a comment just on the existence/non-existence of exA'x, but must include something about the instantiation of A'x. So (2) becomes, I judge, a remark about the object's realism/imaginariness. It is in these terms that we must understand Frege's 'That lime tree is my idea', and statements about creatures being imaginary, generally. If that lime tree is fictional that does not mean it does not exist, merely that it is not a lime tree, i.e. that its name is a misnomer, so that the object does not live up to its name, i.e. is not eponymous. Only in this way are both the object, and the mode of referring to it, the topic of the remark. But something is referred to by 'that lime tree' even in this case, so we must realise there is no place for a presuppositional theory about singular realism/imaginariness statements any more than there is a place for one about singular existence/non-existence statements. In other words, the present account does not need to follow Strawson and say (1) is the only type of existence statement in the area, in order to avoid the referential aspects of (2) and (3).

There is, however, another element in Strawson's account which we do need to follow; it is an element which is doubly valuable because few other writers fix on it, and that is the possible relaxation of the uniqueness requirement [22]. Strawson says we can use 'the king of France' even if there are many kings of France. We have seen what happens when the existence clause is denied; suppose instead that there are kings but several of them - what happens to the epsilon term account then? In fact this is the prime case epsilon terms are designed for, and which reveals their extraordinary power. If (Ex)(Ey)(Kx.Ky.-(x=y)) then 'exKx' refers to some king of France, but not any one in particular, so it expressly allows for the context-dependence of reference Strawson insists upon. Strictly this applies to 'the king of France' and not to 'the one and only king of France', for if the latter, i.e. 'k', is used when there are many kings of France then its reference is 'anyone's guess', i.e. is quite unrestricted. For then -(Ex)(Kx.(y)(Ky D y=x)), and so the referent of 'ex(Kx.(y)(Ky D y=x))' can be selected from the universe at large, not just from amongst the kings. Note again that the indefinition in the non-specific 'exKx' does not mean that such epsilon terms formalise indefinite descriptions like 'a king of France': 'a king of France is bald' is consistent with 'a king of France is not bald', but BexKx contradicts -BexKx - and, as we can now see clearly, it does so whether or not France has any or many kings.

It is useful to see the contrast between the several cases in the live illustration provided by representational pictures. These come in three varieties: we can have non-fictional portraits where an individuating description applies, i.e. A'exA'x; but we can have fictional pictures of two types, the generic type where a non-individuating description applies to many things, i.e. AexAx, and the non-existent type where an individuating or non-individuating description applies to nothing, i.e. - A'exA'x or -AexAx. Now the referent of 'exA'x' is hard to fix, in the first, factual, kind of case, since it is, of course, unavoidably the sitter and we must know already, or search the world for, him or her. In the second kind of case the referent of 'exAx' is more easy to fix, supposing we have taste, i.e. a Scrutonian sense of the appropriate, for if the picture is, say, of a waif or flower-seller then while it may not be an accurate picture of any such individual, it must still be a good picture presenting typical features of many, if it is to be so described, and therefore the search for a referent is more readily rewarded by one simply taking it to be some one waif, or flower seller one is acquainted with, or sets out to select. Indeed the satisfaction and value of such pictures is that they can be so easily used, with a recognisable though personal meaning, by a great mass of people. The third kind of case does not have this mass appeal, and is hardest to understand philosophically, for its object, being a lunacy, must for ever seem strange. However, it is the easiest to find a referent for, in fact, for one doesn't need taste to choose at random from the universe at large. The first thing which comes to hand is then as good as any, even if some might want to take unicorn pictures as poor pictures, say only of rhinoceroses. But such pictures are bad pictures of whatever one takes them to be about, since, if there are no unicorns (-(Ex)Ax), whatever we take the subject of the picture to be is not a unicorn (-AexAx), and so there is no way to get a good likeness whichever way one tries: a fantasy is involved, which defeats the imagination. To enjoy such pictures for what they are one must clearly be aware of the value of physical dissatisfaction: it makes one think.

NOTES

[1] Relevant essays by Quine are 'On What There Is' and 'Meaning and Existential Inference' in From a Logical Point of View, Harper and Row, New York, 1953. See also my 'Singular Subjects', in Dialogue, XVIII, 1979, and 'Internal and External Negations', in Mind, 1979.

[2] C.Lejewski's essay 'Logic and Existence' is in The British Journal for the Philosophy of Science, V, 1954-5, see in particular p108.

[3] L.J.Cohen's reply to Lejewski is in The Diversity of Meaning, Herder and Herder, New York 1962, see p257.

[4] Plantinga's discussion of Idealism and its choice reduction to a form of Realism is in Ch.8 of The Nature of Necessity, Clarendon Press, Oxford 1974.

[5] For the further application of Hilbert's epsilon calculus to these problems see my 'Hilbertian Reference' in Nous 1988.

[6] See Meinong and the Principle of Independence by K.Lambert, Cambridge U.P., 1983, p109.

[7] Meinong's views are in 'On the Theory of Objects' in R.M.Chisholm ed. Realism and the Background of Phenomenology, The Free Press, New York 1960, see p82.

[8] Russell's theory of descriptions is given in 'On Denoting' Mind, XIV, 1905. Russell's further views are in 'The Philosophy of Logical Atomism' in Logic and Knowledge, Allen and Unwin, London, 1956.

[9] J.Hintikka's discussion is in 'Existential Presuppositions and their Elimination', see Models for Modalities Reidel, Dordrecht, 1969, see pp38 - 39 for the quote, Copyright © by D.Reidel Publishing Company, Dordrecht, Holland, 1969.

[10] For more discussion of Buridan's Law, see P.T.Geach's Reference and Generality, Cornell U.P., Ithaca, 1962, p125.

[11] Quine's difficulty with necessity is in Word and Object, M.I.T. Press, Cambridge, Mass., 1960, sec.41, and elsewhere.

[12] Compare A.C. Leisenring's Mathematical Logic and

Hilbert's Epsilon Symbol, Macdonald, London, 1969, pp5, 33.

[13] Hintikka, op. cit. note 9, p32.

[14] Hughes and Cresswell discuss non-identities on p190 of An Introduction to Modal Logic Methuen, London, 1968.

[15] For Frege's essay 'The Thought' see Mind, LXV, 1956, for 'Sense and Reference' see Contemporary Philosophical Logic eds I.M.Copi and J.A.Gould, St Martin's Press, New York 1978.

[16] For J.P.Sartre's views on mental images see Imagination, Michigan U.P., 1972, the following quotes are from pp133,134.

[17] For more on the application of the epsilon calculus to the aesthetics of fictions see my 'Fictions' in the British Journal of Aesthetics, 27.2, 1987.

[18] For S.Kripke's views see 'Naming and Necessity' in D.Davidson and G.Harman eds Semantics of Natural Language, Reidel, Dordrecht, 1972, see pp 258,277,272 especially.

[19] Several aspects of presupposition are discussed in J.D.McCawley's Everything that Linguists have always wanted to know about Logic, Blackwell, Oxford 1981, the point here is from p243, see also, with regard to a later matter, p239.

[20] For the application of supervaluations to Free Logic see Bas van Fraassen's 'Presupposition, Supervaluations and Free Logic' in K.Lambert ed. The Logical Way of Doing Things, Yale U.P., New Haven, 1969; for their application to The Liar, see his 'Truth and Paradoxical Consequence' in R.L.Martin ed. The Paradox of The Liar, Ridgeview, Riseda, 1978; for their application to vagueness see K.Fine's 'Vagueness, Truth and Logic' Synthese 1975, with the following quote from Fine being on p285, copyright © (1975) by D.Reidel Publishing Company, reprinted by permission. On vagueness, see also my 'Consistent Vagueness' in Nous 1988.

[21] For Strawson's account of existence see Introduction to Logical Theory Methuen, London, 1952, Ch.6; the following quotes are from pp190-1.

[22] For Strawson's views on uniqueness see 'On Referring' Mind 1950, p332.

5 Pronouns

In <u>Reference and Generality</u> Geach says [1]:

> Personal reference - i.e. reference corresponding
> to the verb 'refer' as predicated of persons
> rather than of expressions - is of negligible
> importance for logic; and I mention it only to get
> it out of the way. Let me take an example: Smith
> says indignantly to his wife 'The fat old humbug
> we saw yesterday has just been made a full
> professor!'. His wife may know whom he refers to,
> and will consider herself misinformed if and only
> if that person has not been made a full professor.
> But the actual expression 'the fat old humbug we
> saw yesterday' will refer to somebody only if Mr
> and Mrs Smith did meet someone rightly describable
> as a fat old humbug on the day before Smith's
> indignant remark; if this is not so, then Smith's
> actual words will not have conveyed true
> information, even if what Mrs Smith gathered from
> them was true.

But personal reference is not of negligible importance
for logic, since whether there are any fat old humbugs

188

is not a logical matter, so the negative case must be allowed for, requiring (chosen) personal use of referring phrases to be licensed if there is no (causal) impersonal use for them. Prior to the above quote Geach had said about the general question:

> The view that in an assertion of the form 'Some man is P', 'some man' refers to some man seems to make sense because as regards any assertion of this form the question 'Which man?' is in order, and if the assertion is true the question can be answered by naming a man who is P. But we get into difficulties even if we ignore false assertions of this form. Suppose Smith says, as it happens truly: 'Some man has been on top of Mount Everest'. If we now ask Smith 'Which man?' we may mean 'Which man has been on top of Mount Everest?' or 'Which man were you, Smith, referring to?' Either question is in order; and if what Smith says is true the first must have an answer, whether or not Smith knows the answer. But though it is in order to ask whom Smith was referring to, this question need not have an answer; Smith may have learned only that some man has been on top of Mount Everest without learning who has, and then he will not have any definite man in mind.

But it is the second, personal, question which must, without qualification, have an answer, for if Smith says (Ex)(Mx.Px), then who he has in mind is ex(Mx.Px). Prior to hearing that some man has been on top of Mount Everest he might not have had any man in mind, but his hearing just that is all that is necessary to put something in his mind, i.e. make him think of something. Hence the lack of an impersonal referent for 'ex(Mx.Px)' cannot be a possible restriction on its use, and '(Ex)(Mx.Px)' could be false while a name for the object was given. Certainly it would not then be a name for a man who is P, but it could still be a name for a man, or something which is P, and is definitely a name for something. Prior to the last quote, again, Geach had said

> Even if we knew what 'referring' was, how could we say that 'some man' refers just to some man? The

question at once arises: Who can be the man or men
referred to? When I say 'Some men are P', does
the subject-term refer to just such men as the
predicate is true of? But then which man will the
subject-term refer to if a predication of this
sort is false? No way suggests itself for
specifying which men from among all men would then
be referred to; so are we to say that, when 'Some
men are P' is false, all men without exception are
referred to - and 'men' is thus distributed?

But users of '(Ex)(Mx.Px)' thereby refer to something
with 'ex(Mx.Px)', and do so whether or not their
remark is true or false. Certainly 'Ss(Ex)(Mx.Px)'
does not entail '(Ex)(Mx.SsPx)', but the former does
entail 'Ss(Mm.Pm)', where m=ex(Mx.Px), so the speaker
is definitely talking about a particular. Certainly,
again, if there is just one man who is P there will be
an impersonal way of specifying which thing is
referred to, and grounds for the metonymy in saying it
is the term which refers; but even when there is no
'way' still reference occurs, reference given by
personal choice.

Geach is not alone in feeling unable to extract a
pronoun from an indefinite subject: here is Gilbert
Harman [2]:

> Recall that they in
> (25) If any arrows are green, they will hit the
> target
> represents the trace of a variable in
> (27) (Any arrows x)(if x are green, x will hit
> the target).
> Notice that
> (77) If some arrows are green, they will hit
> the target...
> is not equivalent to
> (78) If some arrows are green, some arrows will
> hit the target.
> Furthermore, there seems to be no way to analyse
> they as the trace of a variable bound by some
> arrows. Thus
> (79) (Some arrows x)(if x are green, x will hit
> the target)
> gives a reading of (77) but not the intended

reading on which (77) is equivalent to (25). Nor can we simply confine the scope of some arrows to the antecedent of the conditionals, for the they in the consequent would not fall under its scope:

(80) If (some arrows x)(x are green), x will hit the target.

...one might try to argue that a third kind of pronominalisation is at work here: (77) is equivalent to

(81) If some arrows are green, those arrows will hit the target.

Furthermore, one might take (81) as transformationally derived from

(82) If some arrows are green, those arrows that are green will hit the target.

by deleting that are green.

However the problem with this solution is that the phrase those arrows in (81) would seem itself to be more a kind of pronoun, a variant of they, than a reduced version of those arrows that are green.

Harman thus wants to show that (77) is equivalent to (25) and hence that the case supports an account of pronouns in terms of bound variables, so he tries to argue away the possibility of a 'third kind of pronominalisation'. And, indeed, in Russellian logic, there is no way to extract a pronoun from within the scope of the antecedent of (77),(81) or (82), in order to produce a well-formed expression with the general shape of (80). However, with the common antecedent formalised '$(Ex)(Ax.Gx)$' we can take 'they' in (77), 'those arrows' in (81), and 'those arrows that are green' in (82) to be versions of '$ex(Ax.Gx)$', which is the substantive replacement for the unbound 'x' in (80) - because '$(Ex)(Ax.Gx)$' is

$$Aex(Ax.Gx).Gex(Ax.Gx)$$

and the consequent there now goes on to talk about the same subject. Moreover, it does so whether or not $(Ex)(Ax.Gx)$.

Geach considers a good many cases of this sort, to defend his account of pronouns in terms of bound variables. Thus, again in Reference and Generality, he contrasts

(20):Just one man broke the bank at Monte Carlo, and he has recently died a pauper,

with

(21): Smith broke the bank at Monte Carlo, and he has recently died a pauper,

and says that in the former it is impossible to find any noun or noun phrase for which 'he' goes proxy. Clearly however it is replaceable with 'that man', as Geach admits, so the difficulty is giving a formal account of such an anaphoric phrase. But that is a difficulty only in Russellian logic, since in Hilbert's epsilon calculus, we can symbolise (20) as

$(Ex)(Mx.Bmx.(y)((My.Bmy) D y=x))$.
$Iex(Mx.Bmx.(y)((My.Bmy) D y=x))$,

and the epsilon term expressly does the job of reference which 'he' and 'that man' do, in natural speech. Because of his lack of this facility Geach would want to parse the whole sentence not as a conjunction, but as a quantified conjunction, viz

$(Ex)(Mx.Bmx.(y)((My.Bmy) D y=x).Ix)$

and the two forms are indeed equivalent, as we saw before when discussing Russell. But since Russellian logic lacks the epsilon term the exact thing it cannot do is revealed, namely extract a term from the bound expression to symbolise the personal pronoun.

But in defense of his analysis Geach does not only rely on the Russellian impossibility of analysing 'that man'. He also invokes what he has called 'Buridan's Law', i.e. that if a term in a proposition has a referent it must have that referent regardless of that proposition's truth value. He illustrates this with regard to (21) saying that the referent of 'Smith' there must be settlable independently of whether 'Smith is the man who broke the bank at Monte Carlo' is true. As we saw in another way before, Geach's thesis is plausible if an attributive use of

192

the definite description is then involved, i.e. if the given quasi-identity statement is indeed as it is written, viz

Ms.Bms.(y)((My.Bmy) D y=s).

For in this case we have a contingent statement which gives the identity only through the accidental properties of Smith. But if, instead, it is a referential use of the definite description that is involved, and the right expression is 'Smith is identical with the man who broke the bank at Monte Carlo', then the statement is the proper identity

s=ex(Mx.Bmx.(y)((My.Bmy) D y=x)),

which, if true, is necessarily true, and which, therefore, requires there to be no way to settle the referent of 'Smith' regardless of its truth value, since, expressly, on whether it is true depends the identity of s.

A similar point goes with respect to the reference of 'he' in (20), though now the necessity is assured by the proximity of the pronoun to its antecedent. For while Geach allows it is plausible to suppose, if the first half of (20) is true, that 'he' refers to the man who broke the bank at Monte Carlo, he denies there is any plausible way of giving a referent for 'he' in the reverse case, i.e. if the first half of (20) is false. But 'he' refers to the man who broke the bank at Monte Carlo, both times, since, quite independently of the truth of (20), 'he' is replaceable by

ex(Mx.Bmx.(y)((My.Bmy) D y=x)).

What varies with the truth of the first part of (20) is whether this referring phrase satisfies its contained description, i.e. whether

Mt.Bmt.(y)((My.Bmy) D y=t)

is true when 't' is that referring phrase. But the identity of the entity, and hence the referent of 'he', must be independent of this truth, since this truth is contingent, and identities are necessary.

Geach's attempt to treat all pronouns with quantified antecedents as bound by those antecedents may be illustrated again from <u>Reference and Generality</u> with regard to his 'donkey sentence'

If Smith owns a donkey, he beats it.

As is common in the Russellian tradition, and as we saw with Harman, Geach would identify this conditional with the universal statement

Any donkey Smith owns he beats,

i.e. the quantified conditional

$(x)((Kx.Osx) \supset Bsx)$.

He therefore no more would have a conditional representation for his conditional donkey sentence than he had a conjunctive representation for the conjunctive sentence before. But, in fact, he has no representation for the conditional donkey sentence, since it is distinct from the quantified conditional, its formalization being

$(Ex)(Kx.Osx) \supset Bsex(Kx.Osx)$

i.e.

$(Ka.Osa) \supset Bsa$

when $a=ex(Kx.Osx)$. This latter formalisation shows the conditional is derivable from the quantified conditional, but not vice versa.

But Geach is more concerned at this juncture with the precise function of the 'he' rather than the 'it' in his donkey sentence, pointing out, in particular, that 'If y owns a donkey he beats it' is different from 'If y owns a donkey, Smith beats it', so the 'he' in 'If Smith owns a donkey he beats it' would seem to be not merely a device for avoiding repetition of 'Smith', i.e. not merely a pronoun of laziness. However, it is a pronoun of laziness, each time, like all personal pronouns, since the difference between 'If y owns a donkey, he beats it' and 'If y owns a donkey Smith beats it' does not show the 'he' in 'If Smith owns a donkey he beats it' is not (simply) 'Smith'. The three expressions are

$$(Ex)(Kx.Oyx) \ D \ Byex(Kx.Oyx)$$
$$(Ex)(Kx.Oyx) \ D \ Bsex(Kx.Oyx)$$
$$(Ex)(Kx.Osx) \ D \ Bsex(Kx.Osx),$$

which shows 'he' is certainly not just a device for avoiding the repetition of 's', but that still leaves its function, in the last case, purely a matter of avoiding the repetition of 's', through being a general device for avoiding such repetitions. The point is no different with

If anyone owns a donkey, he beats it

i.e.

$$(Ey)(Ex)(Kx.Oyx) \ D \ Bzex(Kx.Ozx)$$

where $z=ey(Et)(Kt.Oyt)$. So pronouns of laziness are even available with complexly quantified antecedents.

Similar points, we shall now see, go for Geach's argument, in Reference and Generality, against Strawson regarding the derivation of 'he won't live through the day' from 'A man has just drunk a pint of sulphuric acid', though here Russellian logic hasn't even a quantified form which could approximate to such an inference. Also the analysis of personal pronouns helps us to see through Geach's argument, in 'Quine's Syntactical Insights', against 'Socrates owned a dog and it bit him' being a conjunction, for the contradictory of this is 'If Socrates owned a dog, it did not bite him' not 'Socrates did not own a dog which bit him', as Geach supposes. Moreover, Geach starts to see as much, with a final example, from 'Logical Procedures and Expressions': 'A Cambridge philosopher smoked a pipe, and he drank a lot of whiskey'.

On the first score Geach considers Strawson's inference:

A: A man has just drunk a pint of sulphuric acid
B: Nobody who drinks a pint of sulphuric acid lives through the day
A: Very well then, he won't live through the day,

and admits the temptation is to take 'he' as merely a pronoun of laziness picking up the reference of 'a man'. But he thinks that, since one cannot get out of 'a man' a reference to a definite person, therefore 'he' cannot have any reference, since it cannot pick up any definite reference from 'a man'. The flaw in Geach's argument should therefore be quite evident: 'he' does have a reference, but an indefinite one – the same indefinite reference there is in connection with 'a man'. For we can symbolise the premises of the inference not just as '(Ex)(Mx.Kx)' and '(x)((Mx.Kx) D -Lx)', but also as 'Mb.Kb', and '(x)((Mx.Kx) D -Lx)', where b=ex(Mx.Kx), and 'ex(Mx.Kx)' has indeed a reference, although an indefinite one, which can be picked up again in the now-available conclusion '-Lb'.

Geach wants to say that there is no conclusion of this form available from the given premises, only one of the form 'A man has just drunk a pint of sulphuric acid – he won't live through the day', by which he means 'A man, who has just drunk a pint of sulphuric acid, won't live through the day', i.e. '(Ex)(Mx.Kx.-Lx)'. But while this is also available the more particular conclusion is, as well, though not in primitive Russellian logic unenriched with Hilbertian choice functions. Geach thinks that the shorter conclusion is not a conjunct in a conjunctive proposition, and that it can have no truth value, since, on his understanding, 'he' has no reference. But '-Lb' merely has an indeterminate truth value, and may well be a proper conjunct in a conjunctive proposition; for we may form 'Mb.Kb.-Lb', which, note, is still not '(Ex)(Mx.Kx.-Lx)', since that quantified conjunction is 'Mc.Kc.-Lc' with c=ex(Mx.Kx.-Lx).

Geach's difficulty with back-reference across a conjunction is illustrated, of course, in the Monte

196

Carlo case, but that case has a special feature: it involves a uniqueness clause. The general case is illustrated in

Socrates owned a dog, and it bit him,

the formalization of this being

(Ex)(Gx.Osx).Bex(Gx.Osx)s

which is not equivalent, as Geach thinks to

(Ex)(Gx.Osx.Bxs),

precisely because no uniqueness clause is included in the first conjunct. Geach's argument against an unquantified conjunctive form being available, is that its contradictory would in that case have to be

Socrates did not own a dog, or else: Socrates owned a dog, and it did not bite Socrates,

and this disjunction and the previous conjunction, he thinks, could be true, together. The reality, in contrast to this, is rather complex. For the two expressions are indeed contradictories, the second being

-(Ex)(Gx.Osx) v [(Ex)(Gx.Osx).-Bex(Gx.Osx)s].

What makes it seem the conjunction and the disjunction could be true together is the possibility of Socrates owning a second dog, with that second dog not biting him, i.e.

(Ey)(Gy.Osy.-(y=ex(Gx.Osx))).
-Bey(Gy.Osy.-(y=ex(Gx.Osx)))s.

But while this is consistent with the truth of the original conjunction, it does not guarantee the truth of the disjunction, even though it implies

(Ey)(Gy.Osy.-Bys)

i.e.

Socrates owned a dog which did not bite him.

A similar point, of course, arises with respect to

A Cambridge philosopher smoked a pipe, and he drank a lot of whiskey,

which is not, as Geach believes, equivalent to

A Cambridge philosopher, who smoked a pipe, drank a lot of whiskey.

The former is a conjunction

$(Ex)(Px.Sx).Kex(Px.Sx),$

the latter is a quantified conjunction

$(Ex)(Px.Sx.Kx),$

and the former entails the latter, but is not entailed by it. Geach here constructs a case where there are two pipe-smoking Cambridge philosophers X and Y, Y drinking no whiskey, X drinking a lot, and sees that according to which was chosen as 'he', i.e. $ex(Px.Sx)$, the conjunction would be true or false. But since there is a Cambridge philosopher, namely X, who both smoked a pipe and drank a lot of whiskey, Geach confusedly thinks not just the quantified conjunction, but also the conjunction, has a definite truth value in the case, taking that then to be an argument for the identification of the two forms. But, on the contrary, Geach's case exactly illustrates that the conjunction is formally indefinite, and that its epsilon term is not eliminable in favour of a quantifier, for $ex(Px.Sx)$ could be Y, and it is just that indefiniteness which guarantees the reverse of what Geach presumes, namely that the two forms are not identical.

E-TYPES

A number of writers have recognised difficulties in Geach's account of pronouns, and attempted to improve

198

on it. Sommers was the first to do this, in particular pointing out that pronominalisation is not exclusively an intrasentential phenomenon. He says [3]:

> Consider
> A: A man is at the door.   B: Arm him.
> A: A man is at the door.   B: It is not a man but a woman!
> These and similar examples are good evidence that pronominalisation is not exclusively an intrasentential phenomenon. Nevertheless, the bound variable theory persists in the face of such examples. Thus we find Searle parsing 'the king of France exists. Is he bald?' a la Russell as
> (i) $[(Ex)(fx.(y)(fy\ CD\ y=x))].?[Gx]?$
> In a footnote to this suggested translation of (i)...Searle remarks:
>> (i) assumes that quantifiers can sometimes reach across illocutionary force indicators. This seems to be a reasonable assumption since pronouns do it in natural languages: e.g., 'A man came. Did you see him?'
> I have seen Grice assume the same thing in more complicated cases. But I have not seen any explanation of this alleged phenomenon. How does a quantifier bind into a question, an objection, a promise, a command, an entreaty, etc, to absorb it into a single syntactical unit?

Sommers therefore considers here not an inferential context, like that discussed in connection with Strawson in the last section, in which a connected pronominal conclusion is drawn, but straightforward narrative and dialogue contexts in which pronouns refer to entities mentioned in otherwise quite disconnected sentences. The exchanges in dialogue are perhaps the most forceful of these contexts, because there is little plausibility in attributing to separate speakers the non-pronominal quantification forms Geach thought were alone available as formulations. Thus with

A: A philosophy lecturer of my time was a heavy pipe smoker
B: Did he drink alcohol as well?

199

there is no tendency to think that B's question includes a re-formulation of A's remark, i.e. so that it properly reads 'Did a philosophy lecturer in your time, who was a heavy smoker, drink alcohol as well?' Moreover, the change of mood, from assertion to interrogation, quite prevents the question from including the previous statement, as a statement. But the phenomenon would recur, of course, even if B's remark were a statement, say

B: He drank alcohol, I believe,

so it is not the change of mood which essentially prevents the pronoun being construed Geach's way. Equally it is not the change of speaker, for if it were A that made the last remark, we would again have two separate sentences, and no possibility of construing them as such, on a Russellian analysis. But, even then, it is not the change of sentence which is fundamentally preventing a Russellian construal, since once again the phenomenon would recur if A conjoined his two remarks into one. This shows that the core reason no Russellian analysis is available in this case is just the fact that a personal pronoun is involved: we shall see in a moment, more generally, what it is that Russellian logic cannot do in this area, i.e. what exactly defines an E-type pronoun.

Sommers' argument with Geach illustrates many of the features of the present epsilon term analysis. Thus Sommers realises that what is also at stake, in understanding these pronouns, is whether indefinite subjects like 'Some S' involve some kind of reference, and he has argued directly with Geach on this matter. But his formalisation of the pronominal relation goes nowhere near to presenting the full detail available with the Hilbertian one. For pronominalisation Sommers represents initially by indexation, not term substitution, so, e.g.

Tom owned some sheep and Harry vaccinated them

becomes

Tom owned some sheep$_j$, and Harry vaccinated Js,

and hence not all the stated properties of Js are explicit in the symbolisation, making it unclear, amongst other things, whether Tom owned Js, or even whether they are sheep. By contrast, as we have seen, the Hilbertian analysis of the singular remark

Tom owned a sheep and Harry vaccinated it

is

(Sa.Ota).Vha

where a=ex(Sx.Otx), and so the fact that a was asserted to be a sheep, as well as owned by Tom, is shown in the formalisation of the remark, making it clear, also, that these properties are not necessarily actual properties of a. Sommers' plural remark must be similarly analysed

(Sa.Ota).(x)((Sx.Otx) D Vhx),

the plural pronoun 'them' being the indefinite set predicate

eP(x)(Px CD (Sx.Otx)),

so that the remark could also be put

(Sa.Ota).(y)(eP(x)(Px CD (Sx.Otx))y D Vhy).

On this difference between plurals and singulars, there is some confusion elsewhere in Sommers, with his doctrine of the 'wild quantity' of singular terms. Certainly

(Pa CD (Ex)(x=a.Px)).(Pa CD (x)(x=a D Px)),

whereas, for a general predicate 'A', we do not have

(Ex)(Ax.Px) CD (x)(Ax CD Px),

so referential statements about individuals, unlike predicative statements about groups, may be said to have an arbitrary quantity. But attributive statements about individuals still do not have an arbitrary quantity, for if the descriptive predicate

'A'' is individuating then '(Ex)(A'x.Px)' is still distinct from '(x)(A'x D Px)'. The availability of such singular attributive forms, by the way, also means that one can have plural pronouns in connection with single individuals, though these then refer to their role or character, rather than them personally. Thus someone may speak royally of 'we', and address another as 'vous' rather than 'tu', and this also occurs in the third person, for instance using 'they' of an official.

Sommers, besides sketching a general formalisation of pronouns, has also sensed that what are commonly represented as quantified conditionals have a straight conditional expression. But his symbolism is again not accurate enough to distinguish the exact conditional which is equivalent, for example, to

$$(x)((Kx.Osx) \ D \ Bx),$$

i.e.

$$(Kb.Osb) \ D \ Bb,$$

where b=ex(Kx.Osx.-Bx) - the equivalence coming from the fact that the quantified form is also representable as

$$-(Ex)(Kx.Osx.-Bx).$$

This conditional is to be distinguished from

$$(Kc.Osc) \ D \ Bc$$

where c=ex(Kx.Osx), though Sommers conflates the two. The difference between these two types of conditionals was discussed in chapter three.

A fuller discussion of the E-type pronoun phenomenon, though one now lacking any attempt at symbolisation, is given by Evans [4]. Thus Evans is aware that there are two conditionals like

If Mary has any son, she will spoil him

viz. that one, which, following Harman, he would take

to be equivalent to the universal statement

Every son Mary has she will spoil,

i.e.

$(x)(Smx \supset Pmx)$

and another, which he would distinguish by using

If Mary has some son, she will spoil him.

The former alone would allow a Geachian analysis, the latter requires an E-type one, Evans says. Ironically, however, remembering Geach's treatment of Strawson's inference, it is the non-universal conditional which is more 'Geachian', since its epsilon term analysis is

$(Ex)Smx \supset PmexSmx$

showing that from, say 'Sma', with this, we cannot get, as with the universal statement, 'Pma', only '(Ex)(Smx.Pmx)': Andrew might be a son of Mary but we only know then that Mary will spoil one of her sons, not that that son is Andrew.

Evans also tries to allow for Geach's arguments to the effect that indefinite descriptions do not refer. Evans wants to say that the E-type pronoun in, say,

There was a dog. Socrates owned it,

makes reference to the preceding antecedent, but has to limit that reference to mere linguistic cross-reference, to accommodate Geach's views, since neither of them wants to say that that antecedent itself refers to something, and so neither wants to say that the pronoun refers, through the antecedent, to that same thing. The linguistic point helps to remind us to take care with such facts as that the second 'it' in

There was a dog. Socrates owned it. It bit Socrates,

is replaceable, like the first, with 'the dog', making the symbolisation

GexGx.OsexGx.BexGxs,

unlike the 'it' in

There was a dog which Socrates owned. It bit Socrates,

which is replaceable by 'the dog which Socrates owned', making the symbolisation

Gex(Gx.Osx).Osex(Gx.Osx).Bex(Gx.Osx)s.

But each of these pronouns has an extra-linguistic referent, and indeed may have the same extra-linguistic referent, on any occasion of use.

Evans considers a great number of cases of this kind, but after his informal discussion of these he shows he wants something like an epsilon term theoretical analysis, in connection with Geach's example 'A Cambridge philosopher smoked a pipe, and he drank a lot of whiskey'. Supposing, with Geach, that there were two pipe-smoking Cambridge philosophers, X and Y, Evans says that the truth value of the entire remark is indeterminate and depends on which of X and Y we fix on as the referent of 'he'. He therefore distinguishes the sentence from 'A Cambridge philosopher who drank a lot of whiskey smoked a pipe', which does have a determinate truth value; and he gives the former sentence, as above, the same sense as

(Ex)(Px.Sx).Kex(Px.Sx),

rather than the same sense as

(Ex)(Px.Sx.Kx).

But Evans also realises that this makes the truth value of the former user-relative:

...there does not seem to be any great harm in liberalising the account we give of the truth conditions of sentences containing E-type pronouns

204

with a dash of psychologizing, in the interests of a greater realism. For, when the speaker is manifestly <u>talking about</u> something, for example, in narrating an episode, it is acceptable to continue with the use of an E-type pronoun even when the antecedent containing sentence or clause has not provided the basis for a unique specification...

It was with this possibility in mind that I stated the requirement for the appropriate use of an E-type pronoun in terms of having answered, or <u>being prepared to answer upon demand</u> the question 'He? Who?' or 'It? Which?'

In order to effect this liberalisation we should allow the reference of the E-type pronoun to be fixed not only by predicate material explicitly in the antecedent clause, but also by material which the speaker supplies upon demand. This ruling has the effect of making the truth conditions of such remarks somewhat indeterminate; a determinate proposition will have been put forward only when the demand has been made and the material supplied.

This hardly, however, makes for the 'psychologizing' of such remarks, merely the 'personalising' them, and thereby shifting the focus from the words onto their use.

Indeed, Evans only gets to his liberalised account after refining another which was not 'user-friendly', and which had such pronouns as 'he' above, seemingly without human aid, denoting any objects which verify (or that object which verifies) the sentence containing the quantifier antecedent. This made Evans say the second conjunct in Geach's 'Just one man broke the bank at Monte Carlo, and he has recently died a pauper' would lack a truth value if the first conjunct was false, and that likewise the second conjunct in 'A Cambridge philosopher smoked a pipe, and he drank a lot of whiskey' would lack a truth value if the pronoun in it lacked a distinct referent. Also when discussing Geach's 'Socrates did not own a dog or else: Socrates owned a dog, and it did not bite Socrates', he had said that Socrates' owning two dogs would not make this true, but rather truth-value-less, for 'failure of reference' of 'it'. So his previous focus was always on sentences and their predicative truth value, even if, going with his shift towards personalisation, the new focus comes to be more on propositions and their operational truth value. Clearly, on his liberalised, non-linguistic account, Evans can say not just that the term 'the man who broke the bank at Monte Carlo' has a chosen referent, but that <u>the man who broke the bank at Monte Carlo</u> is a chosen object, in the first case if the first conjunct there is false, and likewise in the second and third cases, so he was moving towards not just the Hilbertian epsilon account of terms, but also the Priorian use account of propositions, at this point.

But Evans' original impersonal account was in need of a further refinement. For he came to allow that a pronoun can involve cancellation of explicit predicative material in the antecedent: speaker A may say 'A man jumped out of the crowd and fell in front of the horses', but speaker B may say 'He didn't jump, he was pushed'. This point, which we shall explore in more detail in the next section, unfortunately undermines much of the argument Evans had used, against Geach, for the non-bound nature of E-type pronouns. For one of Evans' arguments against

John owns some sheep and Harry vaccinates them

being formed, as Geach would suppose, by putting a restricted existential quantifier, 'for some sheep x' in front of

John owns x and Harry vaccinates x,

was that, on that account, we should also be able to prefix to this the negative universal quantifier 'for no sheep x', yet

John owns no sheep but Harry vaccinates them

is, he says, ill-formed. But if pronouns may cancel predicative material in the antecedent there is not the needed ungrammaticality with such expressions: for while if John owns no sheep then ex(Sx.Ojx) cannot both be a sheep and owned by John, still Harry might vaccinate it, and indeed, in Evans' actual plural case, when John owns no sheep then <u>necessarily</u> Harry vaccinates all of them, since

$$-(Ex)(Sx.Ojx) D (x)((Sx.Ojx) D Vjx)$$

is a logical truth. In fact, there is no difficulty even with 'Socrates owns every dog, yet it bit him' so long as the 'it' here is 'the dog Socrates does not own', i.e. so that the whole is

$$-(Gd.-Osd).Bds$$

where d=ex(Gx.-Osx). For, as Sommers showed above, an interchange between two people such as

A: A man is at the door.   B: It's not a man but a woman!

makes sense. Hence, also,

There is no man at the door. It's a woman.

makes sense in the mouth of one person. But this is

$$-(Mg.Rg).Wg$$

where g=ex(Mx.Rx). This point against Evans does not interfere with our arguments against Geach's construction of these things, and neither does it interfere with Evans' definition of E-type pronouns in terms of Klima's notion of 'pronouns not in construction with their antecedents' (answering the question about the limits of Russellian logic posed above) - though it does weaken still further any hope of getting a formal analysis through Evans' sort of approach.

It is Hintikka who has previously given the nearest to a formal analysis of E-type pronouns [5]. With Carlson he has explained

If Bill owns a donkey, he beats it

in terms of choosing one of Bill's donkeys, and then, in connection with the consequent, referring pronominally to that very donkey, and saying something about it - so his analysis is very Hilbertian. Moreover, he has noted the link between his 'Game-Theoretic Semantics' and the epsilon calculus, appending a note to that effect to the following passage

> The game-theoretic approach is closely related to the idea of eliminating quantifiers in favour of functions and functionals, and to the basic idea of the so-called 'no counter-example interpretation'. For instance, there is obviously a very close connection between the truth of a statement of the form
> (I) (Ex)(Uy)(Ez)F(x,y,z)
> where the variables are assumed to range over natural numbers, and the statement
> (II) (Ex)(Ef)(Uy)F(x,y,f(y))
> with a function variable 'f'. This function and a number x are precisely what determines 'my' strategy in the game correlated with (I). Hence the force of (II) is in effect to say that there is a winning strategy in the game correlated with (I). If a suitable x and f can in fact be given, the existential quantifiers in (II) can be dropped, leaving us with a quantifier-free statement.

But Hintikka sees his procedure as giving a 'semantics' rather than simply a formal 'object-level' expression for pronouns, and so he does not see that the epsilon calculus bridges that gap, and, as we shall see in the next section, his possible worlds approach, elsewhere, inhibits his method from having full applicability.

Hintikka is, in fact, more influenced by Skolem than by Hilbert. For Skolem allows such an expression as '(Ex)Fx' (if provable) to be replaced by an expression like 'Ff', where 'f' is a certain function, but does not consider the reverse case, where '-(Ex)Fx' is replaceable by '-Ff', with the same 'f'. Hence Hintikka's analysis of the conditional above only works if its antecedent is true, and he is without an analysis in the reverse case. This restricted view also gives Hintikka difficulties with negatives, for while he tries to give a choice analysis of the 'a donkey' above, like Evans he goes so far as to think there can be no analysis of

If Bill owns every donkey, he beats it,

taking it that this is inadmissible. But the epsilon term formalization does not leave

If there is no donkey Bill does not own, still he beats it

without a sense, since we can say, as before

-(Ex)(Kx.-Obx) D Bbex(Kx.-Obx)

in which 'it' is 'the donkey Bill does not own'. The singularity of this conditional is then merely that it is most likely false, if there is no donkey Bill does not own, for the epsilon term, when 'non-denoting' picks its referent idly from the universe at large, making it highly unlikely that Bill beats what is so picked. Note that not only is negation not a barrier to an epsilon term analysis, but complications of other kinds are also no hindrance. Thus Hintikka and Carlson point out that Montague-type grammars would have difficulty with

If Bill owns a donkey that he likes, he beats it,

but this is, of course, no trouble at all here, being

(Ex)(Kx.Obx.Lbx) D Bbex(Kx.Obx.Lbx).

There are still theorists in this area, however, who would prefer a Russellian iota term analysis of such things [6]. Thus Barry Richards agrees that the 'it' in

If John does not own a donkey, he cannot mistreat it

is an E-type occurrence, but thinks there is a difficulty for 'referential semantics' in this case, since he wants to say that the consequent of this conditional can be true, if the antecedent is true,

209

although that would make the 'it' a 'non-referential' singular term. Hence he finds the following traditional analysis plausible

If John does not own a donkey, there is no sole donkey that he owns which is such that he can mistreat it,

i.e.

-(Ex)(Kx.Ojx) D
-(Ex)(Kx.Ojx.(y)((Ky.Ojy) D y=x).Mjx).

But this is to take 'it' in the original as a proform for an attributive phrase, i.e. to be 'a sole one that he owns', and so the analysis has as much plausibility as

-(Ex)(Kx.Ojx) D -(Ex)(Kx.Ojx.Mjx)

for which 'it' is simply 'one that he owns'. But if 'it' is, in truth, 'the donkey he owns', there is no attributive proform, whether including uniqueness or not, in the case, any more than with the disjunction Richards finds no difficulty with, viz.

Either John does not own a donkey, or he keeps it very quiet,

which he analyses as

Either John does not own a donkey, or he keeps the donkey that he owns very quiet,

rather than as

Either John does not own a donkey or he keeps any (sole) donkey he owns very quiet.

So one must take care to read the original disjunction and the original conditional referentially to get their distinctive sense: if the speaker is talking about something, suspecting it is a donkey John owns, he can say with respect to it

Either it is not a donkey John owns, or he keeps

it very quiet,
If it is not a donkey he owns, John cannot
mistreat it,

and if the speaker's suspicions are then recorded in
the name he gives to the object 'the donkey John
owns', these two expressions are formally equivalent
to the non-attributive ones given before.

Clearly it is crucial to getting hold of the
referential sense of E-type pronouns that we should
appreciate Evans' point about cancellation of
predicative material in the antecedent: Richards'
attributive account presumes all such material is
carried through into the proform, expressly by taking
the proform to be for a predicate, not for a term. So
it is important to realise there are cases where
referential terms must cancel their predicative
material, on pain of contradiction, and not just
because of accidental, or playful, misnaming. This
occurs, for instance, with Berry's paradox about the
least number not denotable in English by a noun phrase
with less than 100 letters [7], for if that entity did
indeed satisfy its description there would be an
inconsistency, since the English noun phrase just used
has less than 100 letters.

Formally we can see this as follows. If we
abbreviate 'x is denotable in English by a noun phrase
with less than 100 letters' to 'Nx', we can let 'm' be
'ex(-Nx.(y)(y<x D Ny))'. But that means, taking the
logical symbolisation to be part of English, we must
say that Nm. Hence m does not satisfy its definition,
for it follows that

$$Nm \ v \ (y)(y<m \ D \ Ny)$$

i.e.

$$-(-Nm.(y)(y<m \ D \ Ny)).$$

But, by the epsilon calculus, this is

$$-(Ex)(-Nx.(y)(y<x \ D \ Ny)),$$

hence there is no least number not denotable in

211

English in less than 100 letters. But if there were any numbers not denotable in English in less than 100 letters there would be a least, by the well-ordering theorem. Hence there are no numbers not so denotable, i.e. -(Ex)-Nx, i.e. (x)Nx, i.e. every number is denotable by a noun phrase with less than 100 letters, in English. Now this might itself seem a paradox, but we must remember the choice function behaviour of epsilon terms: if -FexFx then exFx is undetermined, and can be chosen at will. Hence, given the above facts, m is undetermined and can be chosen at will. But 'm' contains less than 100 letters. Hence there is no number which is not denotable in less than 100 letters in English, which is expressly what was needed to be shown. But what must thus hold with Berry's denoting phrase can hold with any other term, and indeed it is just that which distinguishes referential terms from how Russell conceived definite descriptions.

'A-TYPES'

In addition to E-type pronouns there are sometimes said to be 'A-type' ones. Sommers, as we saw in the last section, has argued that 'A man is at the door' can be corrected by saying 'It is not a man but a woman'; he has also argued that 'A ghost made a noise' can be corrected by saying 'It was not a ghost, but the upstairs maid, or a cat'. Evans, again as we saw before, has argued that 'A man jumped out of the crowd and fell in front of the horses' may be corrected with 'He didn't jump, he was pushed'; Strawson has argued that 'A man fell over the edge' may be corrected with 'He didn't fall, he jumped'. Pronouns, therefore, it is well recognised, may cancel predicative material in their antecedent, allowing their descriptive replacements to be used when the description does not apply. Thus Donnellan has argued that 'The man over there with the martini in his glass' is usable to refer to a man who only has water in his glass, and I myself have argued that 'the man in front of me is glued to the ground' can be said of a scarecrow. Clearly these points, in various ways, show that the F need not be F, so they are intuitions of the need for the (same-as-before) epsilon account of pronouns and definite descriptions, recognising, in particular, that -FexFx is possible.

There is a qualification which must be made, however, to the quite liberal use of 'the man over there with martini in his glass' to refer to any man (or, indeed any thing). For exFx may only be -F if -(Ex)Fx, as the Hilbertian relation shows, so one cannot refer with 'the man over there with martini in his glass' to a man over there with water in his glass, if there are men over there with martini in their glasses: the phrase then refers to one of them. This point has been made against Donnellan himself [8], and it has significant implications for our notion of logical possibility, as we shall shortly see, but it does not interfere with the main thrust of Donnellan's point, which was to distinguish referential from attributive uses of definite descriptions: the referential use is still characterised and distinguished by the possibility of misnomers, even if those misnomers must be drawn from fictional names rather than just names at large.

Now Daniel Dennett says [9]:

> There are two opposing views in the philosophical literature...One can be called the Definite Description view and the other, its denial, which takes various forms, can be noncommittally called the Special Reference view.' On the former view, the only distinction to mark is that between believing all F's are G's or some F's are G's on the one hand (general beliefs) and believing just one F is G on the other (specific belief) where such specific beliefs are viewed as adequately captured by Russell's theory of definite descriptions. The latter view, while not denying the existence of that distinction in logical form, insists that even the beliefs the former view calls specific, the beliefs expressed by definite descriptions, are properly general, while there is a further category of truly specific beliefs, which are more strongly about their objects, because they pick out their objects by some sort of direct reference, unmediated by

(the _sense_ of) descriptions of any sort.

But the referential/attributive distinction, and the associated kinds of belief, we can now formalise exactly, by using the distinction between a name and an individuating description: '9 is the number of the planets', for instance, as we saw briefly before, is strictly attributive, and must be symbolised like 'There are 9 planets' i.e.

$$(9x)Px,$$

while '9 is identical with the number of the planets' is properly referential and is to be symbolised

$$9=en(nx)Px.$$

The necessity of the latter expression, and contingency of the former then enables us to avoid the classic puzzle in this area. For if it is necessary that 9 is greater than 4, i.e.

$$L(9 > 4)$$

then there is no doubt we can get

$$L(en(nx)Px > 4),$$

since

$$L(9=en(nx)Px).$$

But without the further assumption 'L(9x)Px', we cannot get

$$L(En)((n > 4).(nx)Px).$$

i.e. that it is necessary that there are more than four planets. Both this unavailable conclusion, and the available one might be roughly transcribed 'the number of the planets is necessarily greater than 4', but we must distinguish between them, taking care to note when 'the number of the planets' is the subject of the proposition, and when, therefore, as a result, the context is transparent. Clearly it is not necessary that there are more than 4 planets, but when

214

'the number of the planets' is used referentially, what it refers to, i.e. 9, necessarily is not less than 4, and transparency is logically guaranteed by the necessity of the identity.

Hughes and Cresswell cannot see this [10], and fall into another trap in the area, for, when trying to defeat the modal law

L(Ex)Fx D (Ex)LFx,

which holds simply because the antecedent 'L(Ex)Fx' is 'LFexFx' which hence entails the consequent '(Ex)LFx', they say:

> Let Fx be 'x is the number of the planets'. Then the antecedent is true, for there must be some number which is the number of the planets (even if there were no planets at all there would still be such a number, viz 0): but the consequent is false, for since it is a contingent matter how many planets there are, there is no number which must be the number of the planets.

Now it is certainly necessary, if p=en(nx)Px, that (En)(n=p), since this follows from p=p, which follows from (n)(n=n), but, equally certainly, there is then an n for which L(n=p), since L(p=p) follows also from p=p. Hence Hughes and Cresswell have no argument if 'n is the number of the planets' is 'n=p'. But, equally, they have no argument if 'n is the number of the planets' is '(nx)Px', for it is indeed contingent how many planets there are, and so -(En)L(nx)Px, but it is also contingent that there is a number of planets, i.e. -L(En)(nx)Px. This latter contingency, however, arises not because there might be no things of the type in question - for zero would indeed be then their number, as Hughes and Cresswell rightly point out - but because there might be no type of thing in question, i.e. 'P' might be being used as a mass noun rather than a count noun. For with a mass noun, an amount of planet, for instance, needs a unit to be specified before a number can be given, so en(nx)Px is quite indeterminate in that case, i.e. is open to arbitrary choice, as is required by - (En)(nx)Px, i.e. -([en(nx)Px]y)Py.

The general point gets us out of other puzzles about transparency in the area [11], for instance the 'Electra Paradox'. Consider

A: Electra knows her brother is Orestes
B: Electra does not know the man in front of her is Orestes
C: The man in front of Electra is identical with her brother.

There is certainly a conflict here, since the contexts are referential and therefore transparent, and we must symbolise them

A': Kc(exHx=s)
B': -Kc(exFx=s)
C': exFx=exHx.

But if in place of B and C we had

D: Electra does not know that Orestes is the man in front of her
E: Her brother is the man in front of Electra

we would have to symbolise these

D': -KcFs
E': FexHx

and even if F were individuating, so that, since FexHx entails FexFx, we could again get from E', C', and hence C, there would be no trouble with A,D, and E being consistent, since from A' and E' we could only get that Kc(exFx=s), which is consistent with D', i.e. -KcFs. That would mean an opacity and 'failure of substitutivity' would arise, but it would arise simply because in D there is properly no term 'the man in front of Electra' to substitute for. Clearly many difficulties to do with opacity in intensional contexts are resolved in this way, through careful attention to whether a description is used predicatively or referentially - though that does not make all opacity so understandable, as we shall later see.

It indeed only makes transparent, i.e. (strong) <u>de re</u> beliefs possible, and does not eliminate opacity entirely, though achieving the former objective is a notable breakthrough, and seeing that the latter, in this type of context, relates to <u>de dicto</u> beliefs is an important re-alignment. But the former point also means we can now symbolise a case of Dennett's

Tom believes of the man shaking hands with him that he is a heavily armed fugitive mass murderer

as

BtAexFx,

and realise this is quite consistent with

Bt-AexFx.

For the possibility of such pairs being true together arises, as above, with cases of mistaken identity, since Electra might well believe that Orestes is not in front of her (Bc-Fs), while believing that there is some man in front of her (Bc(Ex)Fx), and hence while believing that the man in front of her is in front of her (BcFexFx). But if the man in front of her is Orestes (exFx=s), she then believes of Orestes, the man in front of her, both that he is and that he is not in front of her. Dennett dislikes the thought of such contradictory beliefs, since he thinks nothing of interest would follow from their attribution, for there could not then be anything but relations of 'intermittent and unprojectible' interest between the believer and the object of his/her belief in such a case. He says:

One view of <u>de re</u> belief would not suppose that anything at all about Tom's likely behaviour follows from the truth of
(50) Tom believes of the man shaking hands with him that he is a heavily armed fugitive mass murderer.
...I can see no use for such a concept, since nothing of interest would seem to follow from a true attribution of such a belief. Suppose, on this view, that a is believed by me to be F. It

does not follow that a is not also believed by me
to be not-F; and if a is also believed by me to be
G, it does not follow that a is believed by me to
be F and G...The premise of the quest for <u>de re</u>
belief was that there were interesting and
important relations between believers and the
objects of their beliefs - relations we had reason
to capture in our theories - but this termination
of the quest lands us with relations that are only
of intermittent and uprojectible interest. That
being so, there is no longer any motivation I can
see for denying that one believes of the shortest
spy that he is a spy.

But is it not necessary that one believes SexSx, any
more than it is necessarily true that SexSx.
Moreover, not only are beliefs unstructured, so that
BmFa.BmGa does not entail Bm(Fa.Ga), it is also
possible that BmFa.Bm-Fa. For we had both BcFs and
Bc-Fs, with Electra above, and equally we can have
both BtAexFx, and Bt-AexFx: Tom, while he has the
first belief, and although he might fear violence,
needn't react, say in alarm, to the man shaking hands
with him, since he may not recognise that the man
shaking hands with him is indeed the man shaking hands
with him. Certainly, if there is mistaken identity,
Tom <u>may</u> react in alarm but also he may not, so the
highly interesting relation between believers and the
objects of their beliefs which is revealed by the
possibility of contradictions in beliefs is simply
that indeed <u>nothing</u> about behaviour follows then, i.e.
that the behaviour is free, a pure matter of choice or
chance. Note that it doesn't always have to be free,
for if we have BtAexFx and -Bt-AexFx then
straightforward projectible behaviour ensues; but
discovering the source of human freedom in confusion
about the identity of things can hardly be thought to
be not of interest, as Dennett supposes.

It becomes significant, as a result, that Sartre,
for instance, in describing the realisation of his
freedom, was often inclined to say mysterious things
like 'I am what I am not', 'I am not what I am'. He
was then clearly contradicting himself, though the
temptation is still to think he wasn't really being
incoherent, and was instead perhaps just employing a

playful literary figure. But while 'I am not yet what I will be' and 'I no longer am what I was', for instance, are sane and sensible, and might be paradoxically put in Sartre's confusing way, yet they cannot be the meant content of Sartre's sayings, since while they would maybe describe the reform of some character, they would be appropriate only before or after some metamorphosis, not, as Sartre clearly intended, in the midst of some process of riddance and change. Yet in the turmoil of such a change, 'I am not what I am', or the everyday 'I am not myself', surely cannot be true, and if that is the case, Sartre must be being incoherent, and hence, it seems, must properly be rejected by all right and clear thinking men. But not so: for what this suggestion forgets is that Sartre was a Phenomenologist, and hence was far more concerned to convey the experience of freedom than state what was objectively true. If what Sartre was showing us, with such remarks, was that a certain incoherence is a necessary feature of being free, then one cannot reproach him for engaging in his patent inconsistencies. For Sartre's general point was then that, if agent t is free (Ep)Bt(p.-p), and we can in this way state his point quite coherently, even if we can illustrate and demonstrate it in no better fashion than he did. There is nothing inconsistent about 'Bt(q.-q)', or 'Bt-(t=t)', i.e. what may be objectively the case, even though, if such a psychic state is necessary to freedom, what t then believes, i.e. his phenomenological experience, cannot be veracious. We shall see later that Kant supports Sartre in this account of Freedom, indeed it gives Kant his theory of agency, and his rational basis for Ethics. But the phenomenological point, for a start, is just that incoherence (like miraculousness) may be experienced, even though it cannot be an experience of the world, since the world is consistent (banal).

Dennett does not like the thought of the lack of cognition which incoherence brings. Dennett is prepared to give up Russell's Principle, i.e. that it is not possible to make a judgement about an object without knowing what object you are making a judgement about, but he does so, not, as here, by giving up certain knowledge of the character of the object, but by giving up certain knowledge of the existence of the 'object', i.e. by giving up the notion of (strong) <u>de</u> <u>re</u> belief, so that, for him, the classic distinction between <u>de re</u> and <u>de dicto</u> beliefs collapses - all involve merely predicative, i.e. attributive, phrases, and are merely notional. This makes it possible for Dennett to define a notion of belief for which, for a to be believed to be F it must not also be believed to be not-F, and quite generally for the content of beliefs to be structured. He admits, however,

If shunning the strong view, one seeks a view of <u>de re</u> belief as somehow a psychologically distinguished phenomenon, then it cannot be a theory well named, for it will have to be a theory of distinctions within <u>notional</u> attitude psychology. If a is an object <u>in my notional world</u> that I believe to be F it <u>does</u> follow that I do not also believe a to be not-F, and the other implications cited above fall into place as well, but only because notional objects are the 'creatures' of one's beliefs...Having created such creatures, we can then see what real things (if any) they line up with, but not from any position of privileged access in our own cases. There is a very powerful intuition that we can have it both ways: that we can define a sort of <u>aboutness</u> that is <u>both</u> a real relation between a believer and something in the world, and something to which the believer's access is perfect. Evans calls this Russell's Principle...The way out is to give up Russell's principle...and with it the idea of a special sort of <u>de re</u> belief (and other attitudes) intimately and strongly <u>about</u> their objects.

But without such strong beliefs, how can Dennett 'see what real things (if any)' his notional objects 'line up with'? He has denied himself not just 'privileged access' but any access at all to real things. And not only does he make belief too like knowledge, in the process (for, of course, a non-contradictory account must be given of that) Dennett also makes psychology too like engineering: there is no way for 'cognitive science' to design an automated creature with the sort of 'notional worlds' we have, since, in the first place, we do not have 'notional worlds' but only mistaken or rightly taken views of this world (which gives us the possibility of being non-cognitive creatures as well) and one particular type of mistaken view is integral to the understanding of how non-automated we creatures are: the behaviour of someone who is confused about an identity is anyone's guess. As Andrew Woodfield says about the consequences of there being (strong) de re beliefs [12], their existence virtually does away with 'cognitive science':

> One doctrine which will need to be dropped is the Cartesian view that the subject is the best authority on what he or she is thinking...This is because a de re thought also has an external aspect which consists in its being related to a specific object. Because the external relation is not determined subjectively, the subject is not authoritative about that...
> Another interesting consequence is that all versions of the mind-brain identity theory are false. No de re mental state about an object that is external to the person's brain state presupposes the existence of an external object. Any state which did incorporate an environmental object would not be a state of the brain, but would be rather a state of the brain-environment complex...
> A further consequence is that if a lot of our beliefs, desires, perceptions and attitudes are irreducibly de re, then psychologists might as well give up hope of uncovering a system of laws linking these types of states to types of behaviour. There are no such laws to be found.

This all comes out of understanding 'A-type' pronouns, and situations where -FexFx, also the consequent understanding of the separation between reference and any generality. The point about possible cancellation of predicative material in the antecedent is therefore not just needed, as before, to explain 'negative conditionals', and give us a resolution of Berry's Paradox, for it is centrally needed to give us a way into transparent, relational beliefs, making the most significant point we must respect, as a result, the fact that it is a contingent matter whether the shortest spy is the shortest spy, while on Dennett's account of 'opaque, notional beliefs' it is necessary that one believe about the shortest spy that he is the shortest spy.

Now we shall start to look at intensional contexts more fully in the next section, but one aspect of Alethic Modal Logic which is revealed by the contingency of such descriptions is how very different that logic is from Epistemic Logic, and Tense Logic. It might seem that, if the shortest spy had not been the shortest spy, then some other spy logically could have been, and indeed some other spy could be thought to be shortest, and at another time some other spy could in fact be shortest. But if the actual shortest spy had not been shortest, Hilbertian logic requires that no spy would have been shortest, since − SexSx=-(Ex)Sx. This is another way of phrasing the qualification which must be made to Donnellan above. The restriction does not, of course, prevent some other spy being shortest, in some other possible world, so long as this is done by fusing with the spy actually shortest, who would then remain so; nor does it mean that if there is no shortest spy in another possible world there is no one with the name 'the shortest spy' - that merely becomes a misnomer.

One too easily pictures alternative possible worlds as alternative possible times. But one thing which distinguishes worlds from times is that actual-world reference is eliminable, i.e. we can say

    Wap CD p,

whereas temporal reference is never eliminable, i.e. we cannot say, for example

    POp CD p.

Another thing which distinguishes them is that actual identities carry through into all possible worlds, whereas a temporal identity does not necessarily carry through to other times: we have

    Wa(x=y) D Wi(x=y),

but not necessarily

$$PO(x=y) \; D \; Pt(x=y).$$

This difference has further consequences. For instance, if the same contestants Tom, Dick and Harry run several races, then different ones of these may win, say at one time Tom, at another time Dick, giving

Tom=the winner at time t_1
Dick=the winner at time t_2.

And one might think that, in a similar manner, the logical possibilities of what might have been the case at time t_1 could be

Tom=the winner at time t_1 in the actual world a
Dick=the winner at time t_1 in possible world i

so that, as a consequence, since Tom is not and was not Dick, Tom would not be the winner at time t_1 in possible world i. But if 'W'x' is 'x is the winner at time t_1' the fact that

$$Dick=ex[V(W'x,w_i)=1],$$

and

$$Tom=exW'x \; (Tom=ex[V(W'x,w_a)=1]),$$

and

$$-(Tom=Dick),$$

does not mean that

$$V(Tom=Dick,w_i)=0,$$

i.e.

$$V(exW'x=ex[V(W'x,w_i)=1],w_i)=0.$$

Indeed, since we have

$$V((Ex)W'x,w_i)=1$$

and

$$(Ex)[V(W'x,w_i)=1]$$

that means we must have

$$V(W'exW'x,w_i)=1$$

and

$$V(W'ex[V(W'x,w_i)=1],w_i)=1,$$

which together with the individuating nature of 'W'', i.e. the singularity by definition of a winner, means

$$V(exW'x=ex[V(W'x,w_i)=1],w_i)=1,$$

i.e.

$$V(Tom=Dick,w_i)=1.$$

Now we could get a partly corresponding result with respect to time, for if 'N'x' is 'x is the winner', and there is a winner at time t_2, then

$$Pt_2(exN'x=exPt_2N'x)$$

i.e. 'at time t_2 the winner is the winner at time t_2', but, because temporal reference is not eliminable, there would then be no way to identify $exN'x$ with $exPt_1N'x$ outside of a further temporal construction, viz:

$$Pt_1(exN'x=exPt_1N'x),$$

and so the first temporal result would not imply 'at time t_2, the winner at t_1 is the winner at t_2'. But in the other possible world i, Tom, the winner at time t_1 in the actual world a, would be Dick - which gives fresh meaning to the fact that Tom's being Dick is what would have had to occur for those counterfactual circumstances to have been the circumstances that actually obtained. It is further possible, of course, that

$$V(-(Ex)W'x,w_j)=1$$

224

i.e. that there should be no winner in some other counterfactual circumstance, although the actual winner must still be present then, i.e. Tom would still have an identity:

$$V((Ey)(y=exW'x),w_j)=1.$$

This point about the necessity of $(Ey)(y=exW'x)$ and the contingency of $(Ey)W'y$ is lost, in Hintikka's account of logically possible worlds, since, as we saw before, he formalises existence by means of identity, e.g. $(Ex)(x=b)$, and so does not connect contingent existence with an applicable predication. It also means he has difficulty with identities being necessary, which, in the present connection, means he does not see all logically possible worlds as having the same eternal individuals, who merely vary their properties. This infects Saarinen's treatment of intensional identities, as we shall see in the next section, for there we have two sorts of entity, those that exist 'universally' and those that 'exist' in separate possible worlds: clearly individuals (i.e. proper objects given by referring phrases) are eternal, and what varies from one world to the next is the possession and instantiation of properties (given by individuating or non-individuating attributive phrases) - along with how distinct actually distinct individuals would become then. We shall see, in a different way, this same temptation to double the domain of 'objects' with Anscombe and Prior, at the beginning of the next chapter. Of course it is just Davidson's mistake in reifying events, and Frege's mistake in reifying sense: one must not confuse noumenal objects with their phenomenal properties.

IDENTITIES

Saarinen says, in his discussion of intentional identities [13]:

How is cross-identification between different possible worlds carried out? In all the above discussion, we have tacitly assumed that this question is unproblematic or at least irrelevant

225

for our present concerns. However, as has been argued by Hintikka, the problem of cross identification is far from trivial...Indeed, Hintikka has argued that in our conceptual framework we actually cross-identify in TWO essentially different ways. Hintikka has called these two individuation methods the descriptive or physical method and the demonstrative, perspectival or contextual method...
The purpose of the descriptive or physical method of individuation is to pin down from different possible worlds we are considering the SAME CONCRETE PHYSICAL INDIVIDUAL. To use Hintikka's own characterisation, these individuation methods 'can be described briefly by saying that they are just the kind of methods we use in trying to cross-identify between real life and a _roman a clef_...To describe these methods a little bit more fully, one can say that they often rely on the continuity of individuals in space and time'...
Perspectival cross-identification between two alternatives is not on a par with that between the actual world and an alternative. In the latter case CAUSAL considerations play a crucial role. An actual object and an inhabitant of an alternative world are perspectivally cross-identified in case there is a causal relation of an appropriate kind standing between the two.

But even if there were causal relations between different worlds, there would be no causal properties on which identities depended, since identities are necessary. Thinking otherwise yet again derives from Russell's mistaken conflation of referential and attributive constructions. Indeed, Saarinen himself later realises that identities must have merely an intentional origin:

> But how could the duality of the cross-identification methods be built into game-theoretical semantics? So far the problem seems to have been neglected. Individuals are typically introduced when game rules for various quantifiers are applied. The individuals being selected are thereupon named. Now what is the true nature of these names? Even though the point has never been

discussed in greater detail, it is implicit in the literature that these names are used in the semantical games as Kripkean rigid designators; terms which refer to the same individual in each and every possible world. The only explicit statement we are aware of is that of Hintikka and Carlson...'When modal or epistemic concepts are considered, the selection of the worlds as a member of which we are considering a in the output of (G.some) matters. The name 'a' must be required to PICK OUT ONE AND THE SAME INDIVIDUAL IN ALL SUCH WORLDS'...What this means is that in effect the whole problem of trans-world identity is begged; the whole notion of a rigid designator presupposes that a criterion of cross identification is given.

But no criterion, or method, of cross-identification is then presupposed, nor is identity begged, simply an identification is made, when referring terms (which are all 'rigid designators') are used. Hence there is no problem with cross reference in intentional constructions beyond the care needed to identify referential terms. Michael Loux, for instance, made a characteristic error in the following attempt to distinguish de re from de dicto constructions [14]:

Whereas de dicto modality attaches to propositions, an ascription of de re modality specifies the modal status of an object's exemplification of an attribute. Thus we think that the number three necessarily, or essentially exemplifies the property of being prime, but only contingently the property of being fascinating to Quine...We can get at the difference between de dicto and de re modality if we suppose that Kripke is now thinking about the number three and then reflect on
(13) Necessarily the thing Kripke is thinking about is prime
and
(14) The thing Kripke is thinking about is necessarily prime.
(13) involves an ascription of de dicto modality, and (14) an ascription of de re modality. Whereas it is, subject to our supposition about Kripke,

plausible to think that (14) is true, there are compelling reasons for thinking that (13) is false. (13) tells us that a certain proposition, the proposition that the thing Kripke is thinking about is prime, is necessarily true, that it could not have been false. But this is implausible, for surely it could have turned out that Kripke is thinking about something else, say Quine; but had things turned out that way, the proposition that the thing Kripke is thinking about is prime would have been false. (14), however, makes no claim at all about the modal status of a proposition. It simply tells us that the thing Kripke is thinking about has, and has necessarily, the property of being prime; it tells us, that is, that the thing in question could not have existed without being prime. But when we recall that Kripke is, in fact, thinking about the number three, that claim seems true enough.

But while Loux is trying to distinguish the de dicto 'Necessarily there is a thing Kripke is thinking about, and that is prime' from the de re 'Necessarily that is prime', his theory of descriptions is not helping him get the distinction clear. For taking 'Kripke is thinking about x' as '(EF)TkFx', then (13) is identical with (14), and both are de re modalities, on the Hilbertian account of descriptions, since both expressions are then 'LPex(EF)TkFx'. Moreover, if ex(EF)TkFx=3, then 'the thing Kripke is thinking about', stands for the number three, in both expressions. What is not necessarily true is what Loux, using the Russellian account of descriptions, evidently takes (13) to be, namely the de dicto expression above, 'Necessarily, Kripke is thinking about something, and that thing is prime', i.e. 'L((Ey)(EG)TkGy.Pex(EF)TkFx)'. Now the reason 'LPex(EF)TkFx' does not entail this is clearly that it does not entail 'L(Ey)(EG)TkGy', i.e. 'L(EG)TkGex(EF)TkFx', i.e. 'L(EG)TkG3': Kripke is not necessarily thinking about anything, i.e. he is not necessarily thinking about what he is thinking about, i.e. he is not necessarily thinking about the number 3. But while Kripke is not necessarily doing this, given that he is there is no doubt that both (13) and (14) are true. For while Kripke could have been thinking about some other number, which was not prime, and so it might seem that the number he is thinking about need not have been prime, it is the number he would have been thinking about, not the number he is thinking about which would not have that character. In formal terms we have, for some i

$$-Pex(V[(EF)TkFx,w_i]=1)$$

while necessarily

$$Pex(EF)TkFx.$$

Now Geach, who, as we saw before, had no difficulty with the Russellian account of pronouns in conjunctions and conditionals, starts to realise that definite descriptions in intensional contexts cannot be analysed in the Russellian way [15]. In fact he now even starts to suspect that the definite description in

The witch who blighted Bob's mare killed Cob's sow

is not invariably analysable in that way, since Nob's wondering whether that proposition is true would not seem to be his wondering whether it is the case that there is just one witch who blighted Bob's mare, and she killed Cob's sow. Clearly, as before, we must distinguish

$$WnKcex(Ix.Bbx)$$

and

$$Wn(Ex)(Ix.Bbx.(y)((Iy.Bby) D y=x).Kcx).$$

i.e. we must distinguish between de re and de dicto beliefs in the area.

But Geach also worries about cross identification from one propositional attitude context to another, for Russell, again, it seems cannot give the sense of

Hob thinks a witch has blighted Bob's mare, and Nob wonders whether she (the same witch) killed Cob's sow.

But Hilbert has no trouble with this, viz:

Th(Ex)(Ix.Bbx).WnKcex(Ix.Bbx).

Geach tries,

As regards some witch, Hob thinks she has blighted
Bob's mare, and Nob wonders whether she killed
Cob's sow,

i.e.

(Ex)(Ix.ThBbx.WnKcx),

and objects that this would express what the speaker
took to be the real, not the 'intentional' identity of
a witch, and while there is nothing 'intentional'
about 'ex(Ix.Bbx)' in the former expression, apart
from having a reference regardless of whether there
are witches, this is sufficient to allow the former
expression to be an improvement, in Geach's eyes,
since what primarily concerns him here is the fact
that the reporter might ('mistakenly'?) believe that
there are no witches, and so not be committed to
'(Ex)Ix' as in the latter expression. Geach also
tries a further form

As regards somebody, Hob thinks that she is a
witch and has blighted Bob's mare, and Nob wonders
whether she killed Cob's sow,

i.e.

(Ex)(Th(Ix.Bbx).WnKcx),

and objects that that would imply that Hob and Nob had
some one person in mind as a suspected witch, whereas
it might be the case with the first expression that
Hob and Nob just thought there was a witch around and
had not settled on a particular person. But, for one
thing, Nob is not said to wonder whether x is a witch
in this further form, while, for another thing,
Geach's distinction, which he puts as that between
'having some one person in mind' and being 'not
settled on a particular person', is not what is
represented by the difference between that portion of

230

the last expression

$$(Ex)Th(Ix.Bbx)$$

and the corresponding portion of the first expression

$$Th(Ex)(Ix.Bbx).$$

For the latter is

$$Th(Ia.Bba)$$

where $a=ex(Ix.Bbx)$, and so it entails the former. Moreover while the former allows the formation of the 'intentional', or 'thought' object

$$d=exTh(Ix.Bbx)$$

for which

$$Th(Id.Bbd),$$

which makes it what Hob has in mind, there is no settling a priori which object this is without an act of will on someone's part.

The Hilbertian analysis therefore upsets some preconceptions about the nature of 'intentional' objects. Not only are these real objects, but which real objects they are might be quite a surprise. Thus Geach also considers

John wants a stamp,
There is some stamp that John wants,

and tries to roughly define the difference by speaking of 'Just a so-and-so, not necessarily a definite so-and-so' in the first case, as opposed to 'I mean a definite so and so' in the second, but the analyses (following Quine) are

$$Wj(Ex)(Sx.Ojx)$$
$$(Ex)(Sx.WjOjx),$$

so it is the former object, $ex(Sx.Ojx)$, and not the latter, $ex(Sx.WjOjx)$, which is more 'extensionally' identifiable - if (it comes to be that) John has a stamp we can locate the former, but not necessarily the latter, since the one he then has he might not want. Certainly in the former case John has no particular stamp in mind, but that simply means that its definition does not involve reference to his wants, and contrariwise in the second case, having 'a definite so and so' in mind merely relates to the presence of John's wants in its definition, not to its being, in some way, a 'more definite' i.e. less choice-based object.

Edelberg recognises Geach's difficulties [16], and adds another one, for we must not identify

(19) Detective A believes someone murdered Smith, and Detective B believes he murdered Jones,

and

(20) Detective B believes someone murdered Jones, and Detective A believes he murdered Smith,

but, of course, we must equally not identify, in general,

BaSexSx.BbJexSx

and

BbJexJx.BaSexJx.

Edelberg realises that the symbolisation cannot be

(Ex)(BaSx.BbJx)

and

(Ex)(BbJx.BaSx),

since these are symmetrical, but has no way to represent 'Ba(Ex)Sx', and 'Bb(Ex)Jx', as above, i.e. as involving pronouns, 'exSx', 'exJx', which he can go on to use elsewhere. Moreover he thinks of the entities in question as 'thought objects', so it is not clear that he is not thinking instead of

'(Ex)BaSx' and '(Ex)BbJx', and hence of

    BaSexBaSx.BbJexBaSx

and

    BbJexBbJx.BaSexBbJx,

i.e. of statements about objects defined in terms of A's and B's thoughts, and not simply who murdered Smith and Jones. The nearest he comes to the present style of analysis is a 'lazy' one, which involves Russellian definite descriptions with smallest scope, i.e. in this case

    Ba(Ex)Sx.BbJixSx,
    Bb(Ex)Jx.BaSixJx.

But these are not 'lazy' enough, from the present point of view, since, unpacked, they are (taking both 'S' and 'J' to be individuating):

    Ba(Ex)Sx.Bb(Ex)(Sx.Jx)
    Bb(Ex)Jx.Ba(Ex)(Jx.Sx)

and these have both B and A believing someone murdered both Smith and Jones, which need not be: Russell's iota terms do too much work.

A further problem arises, as Edelberg half realises, because while Edelberg's two original statements are generally quite distinct they are not distinct if the murderer of Smith is indeed the murderer of Jones, though Edelberg would want to say that they were distinct even then. Thus in contrast to a case like

    Someone is in the park, and she is eating an apple
    Someone is eating an apple, and she is in the park,

i.e.

    (Ex)Px.AexPx
    (Ex)Ax.PexAx,

where the identity of exPx and exAx makes the two

233

expressions also identical, the actual identity of the murderer of Smith and the murderer of Jones might not seem to make the two expressions identical in Edelberg's main case: if both A and B think someone murdered Smith and someone murdered Jones, and B thinks the man who murdered Smith murdered Jones, then it might seem that (19), i.e.

Ba(Ex)Sx.BbJexSx

was true, while if A thinks Smith and Jones were murdered by two different people, it might seem that (20). i.e.

Bb(Ex)Jx.BaSexJx

was false. But while it might, in the supposed circumstances, be true that

Bb(Ex)Jx.Ba-SexJx

that would not show that it was false that

Bb(Ex)Jx.BaSexJx,

since Ba-SexJx and BaSexJx are quite consistent.

Edelberg confuses the matter by talking about 'intersubjectively extended thought-objects' "the man who shot Smith" and "the man who shot Jones", which 'exist in beliefs', and wonders whether these are distinct, or the same, wondering in particular whether the cross-referential pronouns in (19) and (20) and the like would then have referents, and hence be involved in statements with assessable truth values. He says:

> Suppose we say that in Examples 5-7 there are at most two intersubjectively extended thought-objects which for convenience we can refer to as "the man who shot Smith" and "the man who shot Jones". Are those the same thought-object or not? There are serious problems whichever way we answer. If we say yes, we can account for the truth of (19) in the examples; but we won't be able to account for the falsity of (20) since

there won't be a second thought-object to serve as the semantic referent of the pronoun in (20). If on the other hand we say that these are distinct thought-objects, we will not be able to account for the false use (30) below has in Examples 5 and 6.

> (30) Detective B believes someone murdered Smith **and** Jones, and Detective A believes he is still in Chicago.

For in uttering (30), the speaker could then be speaker-referring only to one of the intersubjectively extended thought-objects, "the man who shot Smith" (who in B's beliefs did murder Smith and Jones, and who in A's beliefs is still in Chicago), or "the man who shot Jones" (who in B's beliefs did murder Smith and Jones, and who in A's beliefs is still in Chicago).

But if there is only one object, i.e. $exJx=exSx$, then we can still account for the 'falsity' of (20), since the pronoun there, i.e. '$exJx$' still has a 'semantic referent', even if $Ba-SexJx$ as well as $BaSexJx$; while if there is not just one object, i.e. $-(exJx=exSx)$, then (30), i.e.

$$Bb(Ex)(Jx.Sx).BaCex(Jx.Sx),$$

may again have a truth value, for although B's belief is then false (since $(Ex)(Jx.Sx)$ entails $exJx=exSx$ when the predicates are individuating) that expressly makes the pronoun '$ex(Jx.Sx)$' have the choice based referent Edelberg, nearly, records. Edelberg thinks, as a result of his difficulty, there should be more choice, i.e. three 'intersubjective thought-objects', now including "the man who shot Smith and Jones", but there may be as many as one fancies so long as one lets the facts settle whether they are identical or distinct. For the fundamental fault with Edelberg's analysis is that, on it, there can never be any settling, outside of beliefs, whether his 'thought objects' are the same or different, since they only 'exist in beliefs'.

Edelberg's original remarks (19) and (20) are certainly not generally identical, but what would make them identical is not some believed or thought identity, but an actual identity in fact, so the crucial point is that we must identify them if exJx=exSx, and this requires recognising the possibility of contradiction in belief contexts. For if exJx=exSx, then (F)(FexJx CD FexSx), so we could not have

BaSexSx.Ba-SexJx,

without the identity producing

BaSexSx.Ba-SexSx.

The full understanding of the case thus again involves understanding the link between transparency and possible contradiction, as we saw with Dennett before. The link was noticed many years ago by Quine [17], for if Tom wants to say that Tully did not denounce Catiline, while Cicero did, and the latter is a transparent use of 'Cicero', then that means Tom wants to say also that Tully did denounce Catiline.

> Surely, therefore, the transparent sense of belief is not to be lightly dismissed. Yet let its urgency not blind us to its oddity. 'Tully', Tom insists, 'did not denounce Catiline. Cicero did'. Surely Tom must be acknowledged to believe, in every sense, that Tully did not denounce Catiline and that Cicero did. But still he must be said also to believe, in the referentially transparent sense, that Tully did denounce Catiline. The oddity of the transparent sense of belief is that it has Tom believing that Tully did and that he did not denounce Catiline. This is not yet a self-contradiction on our part or even Tom's, for a distinction can be reserved between (a) Tom's believing that Tully did and that Tully did not denounce Catiline, and (b) Tom's believing that Tully did and did not denounce Catiline.

Quine thus realised that beliefs might be unstructured, and, in any case, that allowing a contradiction in Tom's beliefs did not involve contradicting ourselves, but he still thought transparency 'odd', and, moreover, had a formidable argument against it - one which we have met, in part, before. For consider

   dp=ex(((x=1).p) v ((x=0).-p)).

Now it seems to be that

   p CD dp=1,

for it is necessary that

   (Ex)((x=1).p) v ((x=0).-p)

and this means that

   ((dp=1).p) v ((dp=0)-p).

Hence

   p D (p.(((dp=1).p) v ((dp=0).-p)))

i.e.

   p D dp=1,

and likewise

   dp=1 D (dp=1.(((dp=1).p) v ((dp=0).-p)))

which seems to mean

   dp=1 D p.

Hence it would seem to follow that

   (p CD q) CD (dp=dq),

and we have a transposition from a material
equivalence to a necessary identity. Now it is well
known that substitution of material equivalents in
propositional attitude contexts does not preserve
truth, hence, if p CD q we need not be able to get

   Tom believes that q

from

Tom believes that p.

But, supposing beliefs are transparent, if dp=dq we should be able to get

Tom believes that dq=1

from

Tom believes that dp=1.

Hence, granting Tom the 'logical acumen' to move to

Tom believes that dr=1

from

Tom believes that r,

and vice versa, it would seem to Quine that transparent belief cannot arise.

Now if Tom's believing that Tully did and that Tully did not denounce Catiline (BtOy.Bt-Oy) does not require Tom's believing that Tully did and did not denounce Catiline (Bt(Oy.-Oy)), there is, in fact, no reason to grant Tom any 'logical acumen': beliefs are unstructured, on Quine's view. But, in any case, the particular assumption Quine is working with must be too strong. For if indeed we did have

L(p CD dp=1)

then, because of the necessity of identity, we would have

(p CD (dp=1)).((dp=1) CD L(dp=1)).(L(dp=1) CD Lp),

and consequently

p CD Lp

i.e. modal collapse. Hence there is a flaw in Quine's argument which would seem to prove that p is logically equivalent to dp=1: it lies, of course, in the second half of the proof above, for while dp=1 D (dp=1.(((dp=1).p) v ((dp=0).-p)))

this does not show

dp=1 D p

without some assumption that dp=1 rules out dp=0, and it is not provable that -(1=0), nor can one otherwise prove that (Ex)(Ey)(-(x=y)) (as we saw with respect to truth values, and the number of entities in the universe, before). Hence Quine has no basis at all for his argument against transparency.

Note that the possibility of fusion between 1 and 0 does not reflect in any way on the incompatibility of, say, (Ex)Fx and -(Ex)Fx. Certainly, as Frege realised, numbers are second order predicates, i.e. 'concepts of concepts', in fact they are kinds of quantifier [18], and one can define, for instance

(0x)Fx CD -(Ex)Fx
(1x)Fx CD (Ex)(Fx.(y)(Fy D y=x)).

But one must not be misled, in this area, by the contrariety of such remarks, i.e. by such facts as, for instance

(0x)Fx D -(1x)Fx

i.e.

-(Ex)Fx D -(Ex)(Fx.(y)(Fy D y=x)).

Given such entailments it does not follow that one cannot have 0=1, for such entailments are not reversible, and, for 0=1 to hold, what needs to be is merely that

(0x)Fx CD (1x)Fx,

i.e.

-(Ex)Fx CD (Ex)(Fx.(y)(Fy D y=x)),

which, consistent with the contrariety of the

239

definitions, only requires there to be some, but not just one, F. Comparable equivalences could hold identifying all the numbers, so long as there are some F, but no definite number of F, e.g. if the universe were Sartre's 'soft, shapeless, dough', undifferentiable into countable objects. That indefinition, moreover, would not make the number of F 'transfinite' or otherwise fixed as greater than any finite number, merely arbitrary, since relative to some unit of measurement.

The crucial link between transparent belief and possible contradiction thus can be maintained against the extant literature, Quine arguing against it that, granting logical acumen it would require believing everything with the same truth value, and Dennett arguing against it that it would sever the link between belief and action. But the former objection we have avoided by not granting (in two senses) Quine's logical acumen; and the latter objection we have welcomed, since it allows for free action, i.e. random, chosen behaviour - a necessary feature of life in general, of course, but especially needed if we are to work with Hilbert's epsilon calculus. Dennett, also had difficulty in distinguishing de re from de dicto beliefs, but we have taken care to avoid that difficulty here, even though, as we saw in chapter one, there is a sense in which all beliefs, indeed all propositional attitudes, are de re.

NOTES

[1] Geach's first three points quoted here are reprinted from pp6-8 of Peter Thomas Geach Reference and Generality: An Examination of Some Medieval and Modern Theories, copyright ©1962 by Cornell University, used by permission of the publisher, Cornell University Press. Later matters discussed relate to pp125-128 of this book, also 'Logical Procedures and Expressions', and 'Quine's Syntactical Insights' in Logic Matters, Blackwell, Oxford, 1972; see also 'Back Reference' in A.Kasher ed. Language in Focus, Reidel, Dordrecht, 1976.

[2] G.Harman's paper is 'Deep Structure as Logical Form' in D.Davidson and G.Harman eds <u>Semantics of Natural Language</u>, Reidel, Dordrecht,. 1972; see p44, for the quote, Copyright © by D.Reidel Publishing Company, Dordrecht, Holland, 1972. See also my 'E-type Pronouns and Epsilon Terms' <u>Canadian Journal of Philosophy</u>, 16.1, 1986.

[3] F.Sommers' work is summarised in <u>The Logic of Natural Language</u>, Clarendon Press, Oxford, 1982, see, for the following quote, p84.

[4] Gareth Evans' work is in 'Pronouns, Quantifiers and Relative Clauses' <u>Canadian Journal of Philosophy</u>, 7.3, 1977, see pp470,500, 513-5, 517 in particular, the later quotation being from pp516-7. See also Evans' 'Pronouns' <u>Linguistic Inquiry</u>, 11, 1980, and <u>The Varieties of Reference</u>, Clarendon Press, Oxford 1982.

[5] J.Hintikka's work is in 'Language Games for Quantifiers' in Logic, <u>Language-Games and Information</u>, Clarendon Press, Oxford 1973, see p77 for the following quote; also see his and L.Carlson's 'Conditionals, Generic Quantifiers and Other Applications of Subgames' in E.Saarinen ed. <u>Game-Theoretical Semantics</u>, Reidel, Dordrecht, 1978, pp191,202.

[6] B.Richards' discussion is in 'Pronouns, Reference and Semantic Laziness' in F.Heny ed. <u>Ambiguities in Intensional Contexts</u>, Reidel, Dordrecht, 1981, see pp224-6.

[7] For a discussion of Berry's Paradox see G.G.Priest's 'The Logical Paradoxes and The Law of the Excluded Middle' in <u>Philosophical Quarterly</u>, 33.131, 1983.

[8] K.Donnellan's paper was 'Reference and Definite Descriptions' in <u>Philosophical Review</u>, LXXV, 1966, it was corrected by M.Devitt in 'Singular Terms' <u>Journal of Philosophy</u>, LXXI, 1974, see also R.Bertolet's 'The Semantic Significance of Donnellan's Distinction', <u>Philosophical Studies</u>, 38, 1980. My paper 'Talking about Something' was published in <u>Analysis</u>, 23, 1963.

[9] D.Dennett's discussion is in 'Beyond Belief' in A. Woodfield ed. <u>Thought and Object</u>, Clarendon Press, Oxford 1982, see p78 for the quote here, and pp86-7 for the later ones.

[10] Hughes and Cresswell's discussion of the number

241

of planets is on p144 of <u>An Introduction to Modal Logic</u> Methuen, London, 1968.

[11] The relation of Donnellan's distinction to the difference between <u>de re</u> and <u>de dicto</u> beliefs is discussed, for instance, in 'Reference, <u>De Re</u> Belief and Rigidity' by D.A.Griffiths, <u>Canadian Journal of Philosophy</u>, LXXXIII, 1986.

[12] Woodfield, op. cit. note 9 pvii, for his views about <u>de re</u> beliefs and psychology.

[13] E.Saarinen's 'Intentional Identity Interpreted' is in his op. cit. note 5, see pp278,287 for the following two quotes, copyright© (1978) D.Reidel Publishing Company, reprinted by permission.

[14] The quote here is reprinted from p31 of <u>The Possible and The Actual: Readings in the Metaphysics of Modality</u>, edited by Michael Loux, copyright © 1979 by Cornell University, used by permission of the publisher, Cornell University Press; see also p44 of this book for a good argument about there being merely 'stipulative' access to possible worlds.

[15] Geach's original paper 'Intentional Identity' was in <u>Journal of Philosophy</u>, LXIV, 1967.

[16] W.Edelberg's 'A New Puzzle About Intentional Identity' was in <u>Journal of Philosophical Logic</u>, 15, 1986, see pp13,16,18 in particular, and for the later quote p19, copyright © (1986) D.Reidel Publishing Company, reprinted by permission; see also my 'Intensional Identities' in <u>Logique et Analyse</u> 1988.

[17] Quine's discussion of transparency and contradiction is in <u>Word and Object</u>, M.I.T Press, Cambridge Mass., 1960, pp148-9.

[18] I take my account of numbers from D.Bostock's <u>Logic and Arithmetic</u>, Clarendon Press, Oxford 1974.

6 Attitudes

OBJECTS

We are now in a position to look in more detail at Prior's theory of propositional attitudes. We saw before how this theory enabled us to resolve difficulties with Truth and the Liar, and how it encapsulated a satisfactory theory of Meaning. We must now look in more detail at the 'predicate logic' of propositional attitudes - an area Prior had more difficulty with.

Prior's propositional idea was that attitude constructions were not to be seen as relational, either to a form of words, or to a reified proposition: they were a <u>sui generis</u> part of speech linking a name (for a person), a verb (of a certain type) and a plain sentence. What other sentences could replace the latter element and save truth was certainly not a matter of material equivalence, nor of strict equivalence, and even provable equivalence, which has emerged as the required relation, Prior was doubtful about. But even if we settle these doubts and realise provable equivalence is the criterion of propositional identity we need get nowhere near to 'relational' attitude constructions in the other

sense, i.e. where an attitude may be <u>about</u> some person
or thing, for we need as well to spell out how there
may be provable identities between terms, to allow the
objects of propositional attitudes to come in. It is
clear, however, that any identity between terms is a
provable identity, for it is provable that x=x, and
so, if x=y, since that means (F)(Fx CD Fy), taking
'Fy' to be 'It is provable that x=y', we see that it
is provable that x=y - that's the proof!

Now, as we saw before, Stalnaker is a little more
forthright than Prior about what constitutes
propositional identity, taking, as here, logical
equivalence to be the determining mark. This means he
recognises 'Cicero is a bachelor' is the same
proposition as 'Cicero is an unmarried man', by
substitution of logical equivalents, but since such
identities as 'Cicero is Tully' are also logically
necessary we can now add to these 'Tully is a
bachelor' and 'Tully is an unmarried man'. This
latter point is to some extent the position Stalnaker
takes, although his understanding of necessary term
identities is limited to those in which only certain
names are used. Indeed, in connection with personal
attitudes, as opposed to impersonal modality, where
Kripke's 'rigid designators' have been supposed to
alone ensure necessity, it is quite generally held
that only certain names allow substitutivity, although
the names which are most commonly taken to break
through 'the web of language' in this other area are
Kaplan's 'vivid names'. Kaplan said about these [1]:

> The notion of a vivid name is intended to go to
> the purely internal aspects of individuation.
> Consider typical cases in which we would be likely
> to say that Ralph knows x or is acquainted with x.
> Then look only at the conglomeration of images,
> names, and partial descriptions which Ralph
> employs to bring x before his mind. Such a
> conglomeration, when suitably arranged and
> regimented, is what I call a vivid name. As with
> pictures, there are degrees of vividness and the
> whole notion is to some degree relative to special
> interests. The crucial feature of this notion is
> that it depends only on Ralph's current mental
> state, and ignores all links whether by

resemblance or genesis with the actual world. If the name is such that on the assumption that there exists some individual x whom it both denotes and resembles we should say that Ralph knows x or is acquainted with x, then the name is vivid.

Such names, therefore, are not linguistic items in themselves, and in fact they relate to the whole of an individual's private mental state, so unfortunately they cannot serve the purpose of ensuring transparency, since there can, as a consequence, be no identities between them: they are like Edelberg's 'thought objects' which can only 'exist in beliefs'. There might be an identity between the objects such vivid names 'denote and resemble', but that would not identify the vivid names any more than identity of Fregean reference would ensure identity of Fregean sense. Moreover, even a believed identity between those objects would not induce propositional identity since one cannot necessarily derive BaSy from BaSx and Ba(x=y). The latter is equivalent to Ba(f)(Fx CD Fy), but even if a could do the instantiation, that would only give us Ba(BaSx CD BaSy), and so not 'BaSx CD BaSy', without some further premise. Clearly one needs a public identity between referring phrases, to get such an equivalence, and vivid names, by design, are not such public referring phrases. Moreover, to understand transparency fully, one needs to realise how extensive such necessary referring-phrase term identities are: these are not confined to names, but terms generally, since what makes them necessary is just that they involve a referring phrase instead of an attributive one. Once that is realised the way propositional attitude constructions may be fully relational becomes clear: they relate to objects in just the way, and to just the extent that non-propositional attitude constructions do.

It is not entirely clear, however, how Prior viewed term identities as bearing on propositional identity and relational attitudes [2]. He says

One of the stock examples that we may as well take from the current discussion in the case of a person Tom believing that Cicero denounced Catiline. This appears to put Tom into a certain relation with Cicero, the relation of believing that he denounced Catiline. But does it? Since Cicero was the same person as Tully, it would seem that if Tom stands in any relation to Cicero he stands in that relation to Tully; but it seems perfectly possible for Tom to believe that Cicero denounced Catiline without believing that Tully did so, since Tom may not know that Cicero and Tully were one and the same individual. We are, however, inclined to say that if Tom believes of Cicero that he denounced Catiline, he _ipso facto_ believes this of Tully; but this is to make a distinction where we suggested there is none – between Tom's believing of Tully that he denounced Catiline, and his simply believing that Tully denounced Catiline (for he might do the former and yet not do the latter).

Thus Prior, following the Russellian tradition, was not straightaway prepared to say that beliefs about Tully were beliefs about Cicero, and tries to separate a _de re_ relational remark, 'believing of Tully', from a _de dicto_ non-relational remark, 'believing that Tully', to ease his difficulties – at the same time as trying, almost contradictorily, to identify these two remarks. Certainly we can distinguish, formally,

$$(Ex)(x=t.BmOx)$$

from

$$Bm(Ex)(x=t.Ox),$$

but these both reduce to 'BmOt', since 'Ft' is the the same as '(Ex)(x=t.Fx)'. On the other hand, even if T' is individuating, we can separate

$$(Ex)(T'x.BmOx)$$

from

$$Bm(Ex)(T'x.Ox),$$

hence we get Prior trying to separate 'individual thoughts' from 'general thoughts' in this area, and then to distinguish two 'general thoughts'

246

For some x, x f's, and Tom believes that x g's,
Tom believes that for some x, x f's and x g's,

in the case where 'x f's' is 'x is called 'Tully'',
and 'x g's' is 'x denounced Catiline'. Unfortunately,
that still leaves Prior with the 'individual thought'
'Tom believes that x g's' to give an account of, and
he does not complete his search for this, considering
Russell's account, and rejecting it, then sketching
Lesniewski's. It should be clear, by now, how an
Hilbertian account will relieve Prior of all his
expressed anxieties about these things.

Moreover it will relieve him of anxieties he hardly
showed he had. Thus he had previously said

> It was said earlier that Othello's ascription of
> infidelity to some particular person, say
> Desdemona, i.e. his believing (or saying) that
> that person is unfaithful, constitutes a relation
> between Othello and that person, although
> 'believing that' on its own does not express a
> relation (it is not a two place predicate but a
> 'predicate at one end and connective at the
> other'). It was also noted that there are cases
> where 'believing that' does not even enter into
> the composition of a relation; namely where what
> is believed is not about anything, and its verbal
> expression does not contain the name of anything.
> These are precisely the cases that we are
> beginning to consider now, and compare more
> closely with the others. It is obvious that if
> Othello believes that no one is unfaithful, this
> does not constitute a relation between Othello and
> anyone at all. This is equally the case, though
> not perhaps so obviously so, if Othello simply
> believes that someone is unfaithful, i.e. that
> someone or other is, without particularizing –
> there is in this case no one to whom Othello
> stands in the relation of believing that she is
> unfaithful, no one of whom he believes this, no x
> such that he believes that x is unfaithful.

But since he is going on to say that one can equally
not form relational beliefs with names like 'Tully'

and 'Cicero' he is in danger of abandoning relational constructions entirely. Indeed in the end he is not even happy with Russell's demonstratives:

> What expressions do meet the Russellian requirements? Russell's own view is that they are generally met by demonstratives, with of course appropriate accompanying gestures. So let's look now at
> 　(15) X says that this individual is bald
> 　(16) X says of this individual that he is bald.
> It must be admitted that these do seem to be logically equivalent - it's very hard to conceive conditions which would verify either of them without ipso facto verifying the other. What seems to disappear when we come to these examples is a certain gap between X's own point of view and the point of view of the reporter...in (15) and (16) the web of language is somehow broken through and X and the reporter have both put their hand on a bit of reality, and the same bit of reality. And that, I think, is just what is supposed to happen with a Russellian name. But does it? I'm not sure. And one reason why I'm not sure is that (15) and (16) retain their peculiarities when the 'this' which occurs in them is not a demonstrative at all, but relative. That is, (15) and (16) stay equivalent when they occur not in isolation, or just eked out by gestures, but when they occur as part of a story, as in (17) and (18):
> 　(17) There lives in Baker Street an individual who is called 'Sherlock Holmes', is a detective, plays the violin, takes cocaine, etc.; and X says that this individual is bald.
> 　(18) There lives in Baker Street an individual who is called 'Sherlock Holmes', is a detective, plays the violin, takes cocaine, etc.; and X says of this individual that he is bald.

Now (17) and (18) are indeed equivalent, like (15) and (16), but the reason that shows Russell's analysis is mistaken is because it shows that not only demonstratives, but also general referring phrases like 'the individual who lives in Baker Street, who is called 'Sherlock Holmes', who is a detective, who plays the violin, and who takes cocaine', i.e. the descriptive replacement for 'this individual' in (17) and (18), also close the gap between X and the reporter, and do so, moreover, whether the story is true or false. The gap is closed so long, and just so long, as they use the same public language. Hence relational constructions are available with definite descriptions, as well as demonstratives, indeed they are, at a remove, with the 'no one' and 'some one' Prior dismissed before.

That is not to decry the regimented usage Prior adopts for distinguishing 'believing of' from 'believing that'. For instance, the first remark about Tom above, namely

For some x, x f's, and Tom believes that x g's,

may be properly re-expressed

Tom believes of some x which f's that it g's,

to make a sensible difference from the 'believes that' form. But when we are not concerned with attributive phrases like 'is called 'Tully'', but referring phrases like 'Tully', 'The individual who...', 'this', the distinction does not mark a sensible difference. That, of course, does not explain why Prior not only wants to dismiss a difference between

Tom believes of Tully that he denounced Catiline

and

Tom believes that Tully denounced Catiline,

but also, at the same time, want to keep one. But remembering Dennett's and Quine's discussions before, it is presumably the resulting contradictoriness of the transparent locution which is making Prior hesitant at this point.

Prior, in <u>Objects of Thought</u>, also voices a number of other difficulties. Thus what is one to do with beliefs about Walter's horse having wings, when Walter has no horse? Again isn't it true, as Miss Anscombe says, that while the name of something 'real' has to

be put into 'X bit...', with 'X worshipped...' this
need not be so? Certainly there is no choice about
the object in the biting case, while in the fictional
cases it is open to question what was believed to have
wings, or what was worshipped. But that still leaves
it something 'real' in both cases: if the Greeks
worshipped Zeus, that means they thought Zeus was a
god, but that doesn't mean Zeus was a god, and if he
wasn't a god then that is what is 'unreal' about him
(or it) - the belief is still about an object, though
an object misdescribed.

We must be careful again, therefore, to be alive to
the distinction between referring and attributive
phrases in these other areas. For a god to exist a
certain attributive predicate must be instantiated,
but for Zeus to exist merely a certain referring name
must be used: it is logically necessary that
$(Ex)(x=z)$, but contingent whether $(Ex)Gx$. If the
Greeks all worshipped Zeus, that means

$$(x)(Hx \supset Wxz)$$

and, since worship involves taking the object to be a
god

$$(y)(x)(Wxy \supset TxGy),$$

where 'TxGy' is 'x thinks y is a god'. But 'TxGz'
does not entail 'Gz', even though it does entail
'$(Et)TxGt$', hence the object of worship is certainly
something real, even if it is not a god. All thoughts
are, in this way, directed at reality, even if they
involve a misconception about it: a believer can only
believe mistakenly that something (the 'object' of his
belief) exists if the 'something' pronominalises an
attribute; there can be no mistake in his belief that
something exists when the 'something' pronominalises a
referring phrase. Thereby, indeed, might be found a
reason both for the tenacity of many religious
beliefs, and for the enduring skepticism about them.
The totem pole or phallus, the earthly father,
biological or priestly, certainly exists, and may be
the 'material object' of some belief, thus giving it a
secure and unshakable basis, but how this object is
conceived in the believer's thoughts is not determined

by this reality, so some property it is taken to have may well not be truly instantiated. There are no objects 'inside' the mind, the only objects are in reality. What there may be 'inside' the mind are certain conceptions of objects - right or wrong conceptions of them.

The difference between 'X bit Zeus' and 'X worshipped Zeus' is therefore not that Zeus must be real in the former but not necessarily in the latter. The difference consists in the fact that x's conception of Zeus is not involved in the former (however much it led up to the act). Given there is this added dimension in the latter, it becomes possible to mark whether X's conception of Zeus is correct: X might worship Zeus and so take him for a god, when Zeus is not a god, or, indeed, when there are no gods, and hence what X worships might not have the character he takes it to have. But that does not mean that what X worships does not have the existence he takes it to have.

A similar point goes with respect to beliefs about Walter's horse, when Walter has no horse. We have now a referring phrase rather than a plain proper name, like Zeus, but the fact that it is articulated is immaterial when it is used as a term, since it secures reference whether or not the object has the inscribed character. Walter's horse, if he has no proper horse, might be his rocking, hobby or clothes horse, or more jokingly, or bizarrely, his hard ridden wife, his fast-driven car, or his big dog, but it is certainly something, and hence there is no trouble with relational beliefs about it, however extreme. Prior asks how Walter's horse can be believed by Sid to have wings, 'if in fact there is just no such animal', but the key word in his question is 'such': what there maybe isn't is something of the kind 'a (sole) horse of Walter's', not something with the name 'Walter's horse'. There is nothing to stop any name, articulated or otherwise, from having a reference: it has to pass no test of appropriateness, if it is a misnomer, so mere sovereign act of will can determine it. Prior, forgetting this, finds it isn't easy to hold together the two propositions he feels drawn towards, namely

When X thinks of Y, aims at Y, worships Y, etc. there is always a Y involved as well as an X,

In some cases, when X thinks of Y etc. there is no Y there at all.

But for there to be 'no Z', 'Z' must be an attributive phrase, so the difficulty is removed simply by adding a 'such' to the 'no Y' in the second proposition and excising the 'a' in the 'a Y' in the first. What there always is when X thinks of Y, is just Y (as well as X) supposing 'Y' is a referring phrase.

Miss Anscombe, as Prior explains, tries to put these distinctions in terms of the distinction between 'intentional objects' and 'material objects'. But this can lead to confusion since the former, as before, are not objects but properties, even when they are individuating properties. Thus Miss Anscombe distinguishes the 'intentional object' of someone's worship as being a god, while its 'material object' is merely a piece of wood, instead of simply saying the person thought the piece of wood was a god; also, in making a similar distinction between the 'intentional object' of someone's aiming and its 'material object', she accepts too readily the description 'a man aims at a stag, but the thing he took for a stag was his father', presumably quite misled by her misappropriation of the word 'object'. The man in question aimed at his father, taking his father to be a stag, but he did not aim at a stag (except <u>per accidens</u>) either as an object in the world, or an object 'in his mind's eye'. What was in his mind was his misconception of his father, but that is not another object.

Miss Anscombe thinks 'intentional objects' may or may not be real: certainly supposed properties may or may not be real. She also thinks 'intentional objects' may be indeterminate: certainly one can think something is a man without thinking it is a man of any particular height, but not hit a man without hitting a man of a particular height. But the former fact merely reflects that

ToMb

does not entail

To(Ey)(Mb.Hby),

even if

(x)(Mx D (Ey)Hxy),

although

Mb.Iob

does entail

(Ey)(Mb.Hby.Iob)

then. Miss Anscombe actually says one can think of a man without thinking of a man of any particular height, but, strictly speaking, that is impossible, since

(Mb.(EF)ToFb) D (Ey)(Mb.Hby.(EF)ToFb).

Now Prior himself was inclined elsewhere, e.g. in Past, Present and Future, to make a distinction amongst objects with as much of a rationale as Miss Anscombe's (or Saarinen's). For in his study of Temporal Logic, and in particular in his construction of the system 'Q', he was inclined to talk about 'necessary beings' and 'contingent beings'. But, yet again, what is necessary is that some used name 'exG'x' identifies an object, i.e. that (Ex)(x=eyG'y), while what may be contingent is whether that object lives up to its name, i.e. has the individuating property inscribed in it, i.e. whether G'exG'x, and so whether (Ex)G'x. The latter may be read 'A single god exists' the former 'The one and only god exists', and the one and only god may exist without, in fact, being a god. So all objects, properly so called, have eternal existence, and what has temporal existence is merely a property.

The point helps us to see, for instance, that there can be no creation ex nihilo, for 'God has brought it about that, for some x, x is a man', i.e. 'Bg(Ex)Mx', which is 'BgMexMx', entails '(Ex)BgMx', i.e. 'For some

253

x, God has brought it about that x is a man'. The reverse, though, does not hold, for '(Ex)BgMx', i.e. 'BgMexBgMx' does not entail 'Bg(Ex)Mx', since God making exBgMx into a man isn't necessarily what brings it about that there are men, i.e. isn't necessarily making exBgMx the first man in existence. Nor does the corresponding thing hold if a predicate is exported: 'Bg(Ex)(Mx.Hxh)' does not entail '(Ex)(Mx.BgHxh)', for the man of a certain height God created may have had the same height before. But the general result shows there is nothing wrong with the Barcan Formula

K(Ex)Fx D (Ex)KFx

and that is so independently of what 'K' may be. Clearly, for instance, 'It will be the case that something is a person that flies' entails 'There is something such that it will be the case that it is a person that flies', even if it does not entail 'Something is a person of whom it will be the case that they fly'.

Prior has doubts about this Barcan formula: he considers, for example, the following case (compare with the discussion of 'L(Ex)Fx D (Ex)LFx' in chapter five):

> Myhill, in discussing the formula [(x)LFx D L(x)Fx], starts from the assumption that not only which objects the universe contains, but also how many of them there are, must be a contingent matter. Suppose there are in fact five - a,b,c,d and e. Then a is necessarily identical with a (everything is necessarily identical with itself), and so is necessarily either identical with a or identical with b or identical with c or identical with d or identical with e (Lp D L(p v q)). Similarly, b is necessarily identical with b and therefore with a or b or c or d or e. They are all, in fact, each for its own reason, necessarily either identical with the 1st or with the 2nd or with the 3rd, etc. If we let this necessary disjunction of identities be F, we have here (x)LFx. But there didn't have to be just 5 individuals, so it didn't have to be true that

everything is either a or b or c or d or e, i.e.
we <u>don't</u> have L(x)Fx; and so we have a counter-
example to the Barcan formula.

But, significantly, Prior, at one place here says 'is
necessarily identical with', while at another place he
says 'is'. Certainly

$$x=eyA'y \ v \ x=eyB'y \ v \ x=eyC'y \ v \ x=eyD'y \ v \ x=eyE'y$$

may be prefaced with '(x)L', but then also with 'L(x)'
- though there is no way to prove, for instance -
(eyA'y=eyB'y). But while

$$A'x \ v \ B'x \ v \ C'x \ v \ D'x \ v \ E'x$$

may not be prefaced with 'L(x)', it also may not be
prefaced with '(x)L'. So in neither case do we have a
counter-example to the Barcan formula.

OPACITY

One source of Frege's idea of opacity is the fact that
this does arise with direct quotation - the quotation
marks in writing separate the words off from the usual
substitution process - and Frege thought a somewhat
similar thing happened in reported speech, which he
called 'indirect quotation'. Frege says, in 'On Sense
and Reference' [3] that while words are used normally
to speak of their referents, when within quotation
marks the words themselves are designated, so such
words there must not be taken as having their ordinary
referents; and, in reported speech, this is again the
case, since there one talks about the sense, for
instance, of another person's words. Frege even
reiterates that it is quite clear to him that in such
reported speech the words do not have their normal
referents, but designate instead their sense. But
while a report on another person's remarks may be
close to quotation of them, it need not be, and in any
case, if James asserts 'That man is mortal' he says
that <u>that man</u> is mortal, so the report is, indeed must
be, as referential as the original remark.

Another source of Frege's idea of opacity came from attachment to 'extensionality' in the form of 'truth functionality', for since, in indirect speech, substitution of material equivalents of the subordinate sentence will not necessarily maintain truth value, it may seem that terms in that indirect speech cannot have their usual referents - especially supposing we think we have already found that the referent of the sentence is its truth value, composed of the referents of its parts. Frege says that he will test this supposition in the case of sentences containing other sentences as parts, but excludes the cases of direct and indirect quotation, the former because the sentences quoted then designate themselves, the latter because the sentences in indirect speech designate thoughts. But the exceptionality of the latter case shows instead simply that the truth-functional thesis is incorrect: the reference of a sentence is not its truth value. For if the truth value of a sentence remains unchanged when an expression is replaced by another with the same 'referent', then, in a sentence containing, in indirect speech, another as part, the referent of that part must be given by logical equivalence, not material equivalence, making the truth value not the referent of that part. Hence the possible failure of substitution of material equivalents to maintain truth does not show the words in that part do not have their usual referents.

But a third, and surely main source of Frege's idea of opacity comes from forgetting the fact that the predicative 'is' is not the 'is' of identity: the predicative 'x is the one and only star which rises in the morning' does not entail the predicative 'x is the one and only star which sets in the evening', although the related referential identity statements are derivable from one another. Frege says that in such expressions as 'The Morning Star is the same as the Evening Star', 'The point of intersection of two medians of a triangle is the same point as the point of intersection of any two medians of that triangle', we have different designations, or 'modes of presentation' of the same object, allowing the statement to 'contain true knowledge'. But there is no true knowledge in those remarks involving 'is the same as', for only if we replace this with 'is' do the statements include such facts as that, with any triangle the point of intersection of two medians is a point, i.e. a point in space. But if what has the sense is the attributive phrase, and what has the reference is the referential phrase, we are, of course, led to a rather different account of 'sense' than that initiated by Frege. For, as was mentioned before, Frege, in the manner of Anscombe and others above, conceived of sense not as the entailments of a predicate, but as a further kind of object, an 'intensional' if not 'extensional' object, which could be referred to by referring phrases when in indirect speech: sense, for Frege, was indirect reference. There is no comparable temptation to reify the notion here, once it is seen that a predicate is in question, and especially when we remember the strictures about sets at the beginning of chapter one. Certainly a concept involves a plural relation to the members of a set, but the fact that it is then a plural relation should be sufficient to disabuse us of the idea that a relation to a single object is what is involved.

But the refusal to follow Frege in his reification of 'intensional entities' must not prevent us from seeing that a sizeable amount in his notion of opacity is indeed attributable just to the half-recognition of the ambiguities produced by referential versus attributive locutions in such contexts. The core of Frege's theory, from which he derives his account of sense, is that the referent of a whole should be dependent on and composed out of the referents of its parts, and so the fact that it seemed that substitution of co-referential terms produced expressions which were not interderivable <u>salva veritate</u>, with indirect speech, was one prime source of the idea that some non-(directly)-referential entity was involved. Indeed an attributive phrase may be involved there, supporting Frege's view that 'sense' is found there, but so also may reference, since the phrase involved may be a properly referential one, allowing, transparently, its replacement by any co-designative term. Even after 100 years, Dummett can still say [4] that when a proper name occurs in indirect speech, replacements of it will leave the truth-value of the whole sentence unaltered so long as they leave the sense of the subordinate clause unaltered, but even after that length of time no one has produced an appropriate replacement for a proper name which allows its (unquoted) occurrence to be opaque. Of course the very concept of opacity prevents this.

Certainly one can also use the additional argument that in (most) indirect speech contexts it is indifferent to the truth value of the whole whether the subordinate clause is true or false, so it may seem the question of term substitution need not be all that is behind the conception of opacity, there being an independent argument for the conclusion that the identity of the subordinate clause is not determined merely by its truth value. But the full working of the epsilon calculus shows that one aspect, at least, of the immateriality of the subordinate truth value is related to the question of reference as well. For through the distinctions in that calculus we have come by a better understanding of the thoughts which Frege saw the identity of the subordinate clauses consisting in. It was partly because assertions were often not involved with such clauses that Frege came to this conclusion, and saw these clauses as loci of aesthetic delight, instead of scientific assessment, and the prime such loci are fictional statements, like 'Odysseus was set ashore at Ithaca while sound asleep', which Frege believed to have no reference, only sense. But we now not only can bring such sources of aesthetic delight into the direct speech area, and realise they have as much reference there as when in the subordinate clauses of indirect speech, we can, as a result, better appreciate what it is that is opaque about them. Certainly without a definite referent they can hardly be asserted, and must remain, as Scruton says 'unasserted', but if such 'non-assertion' is what makes for 'thoughts' it is the choice of the associated referent which generates their opacity - though not now an opacity restricted to indirect speech. Of course there are non-fictional thoughts which are not asserted in indirect speech, along with fictional ones, but Frege's analysis was not fine enough to make that more complete distinction.

Neither was it fine enough to make the distinction we have made before between

A believed that someone shot Smith

i.e.

Ba(Ex)Sx, or BaSexSx

and

A believed of someone that he shot Smith

i.e.

(Ex)BaSx, or BaSexBaSx.

The latter introduces a form of opacity not commonly recognised as such, but opacity nonetheless, since the object is defined in terms of the belief, i.e. 'intensionally', not 'extensionally'. Indeed, as we saw in the last chapter, the mystery with such pairings is how it has come to be thought that the former is more 'intensional'. Russell, who started to make the distinction, would have called the former a 'secondary' context, the latter a 'primary' context, but in terms of their divorce from the belief, in their definitions, the object in the former is more 'primary', i.e. 'extensional'. Of course Russell could not get anywhere near to seeing this since he could not produce anything of the primitive form 'BaSx' let alone either of the more detailed ones above.

None of Frege's arguments is, therefore, a valid defense of opacity, in the sense of non-transparency, in indirect contexts - although there are available valid defenses of something like opacity there in terms of choice, and intensional definition, as we shall see again at the end of this chapter. But the main confusion in Frege was mistaking a predicated description for a referring name, and hence the main culprit after Frege is Russell, whose Theory of Descriptions explicitly conflates these same two things [5]. Russell was certainly aware of one aspect of Frege's confusion, arguing against the distinction between sense (meaning) and reference (denotation), in 'On Denoting', for instance, as follows

> ...consider such a proposition as the following: 'If u is a class which has one member, then that one member is a member of u', or, as we may state it, 'If u is a unit class, <u>the</u> u is a u'. This proposition ought to be <u>always</u> true, since the conclusion is true whenever the hypothesis is true. But 'the u' is a denoting phrase, and it is the denotation, not the meaning, that is said to be a u. Now is u is <u>not</u> a unit class, 'the u' seems to denote nothing; hence our proposition would seem to become nonsense as soon as u is not a unit class.

Indeed Frege, on his presuppositional account, if not his formal account (his 'conventional denotation' account, as Russell calls it) cannot handle what we would symbolise

(E!x)Ux D UexU'x;

but Russell himself was none too clear about the relevant point here, since he goes on

> Now it is plain that such propositions do not become nonsense merely because their hypotheses are false. The King in 'The Tempest' might say, 'If Ferdinand is not drowned, Ferdinand is my only son'. Now 'my only son' is a denoting phrase, which, on the face of it, has a denotation when, and only when, I have exactly one son. But the above statement would nevertheless have remained true if Ferdinand had been in fact drowned. Thus we must either provide a denotation in cases in which it is at first sight absent, or we must abandon the view that the denotation is what is concerned in propositions which contain denoting phrases. The latter is the course I advocate.

So Russell did not recognise that the 'either...or...' here may be inclusive, allowing referring phrases a denotation in all cases, while also allowing that not 'denotation' but 'meaning' might be what 'is concerned' with other phrases. For with 'is' being predicative the King's remark is of the attributive form

-Rf D S'f,

while if 'is' is (misleadingly) short for 'is identical with', the King's remark is of the referential form

-Rf D f=exS'x.

Russell omits the latter type of expression, making all 'denoting phrases', by his own admission, non-denoting.

In terms of the original puzzle with which Russell illustrated his resulting theory of propositional attitudes, on a primary interpretation of

George IV wished to know whether the author of Waverley was Scott,

which Russell took to be

George IV wished to know of a sole author of Waverley whether he was Scott,

this is

(1): (Ex)(A'x.Wg(x=s)),

while on a secondary interpretation it is

George IV wished to know whether a sole author of Waverley was Scott,

i.e.

(2): Wg(Ex)(A'x.(x=s))

i.e. WgA's. Neither, however, gives an analysis of the first form above, which is

(3): Wg(exA'x=s).

But the relations of Russell's pair to

Scott was the author of <u>Waverley</u>,

i.e. A's, i.e. (Ex)(A'x.(x=s)), are very much as he gave them. For with (1) we can get

George IV wished to know if Scott is Scott,

i.e. Wg(s=s), whereas with (2) we cannot get this. From (3), however, we again can, since 'A's' entails 'A'exA'x', making s=exA'x, because of the uniqueness.

The omission of the referential form is a considerable one, nevertheless Russell's mistake was, in one sense, very subtle, for while the secondary form

X says that there is someone who is the sole present king of France, and who is bald,

may indeed be distinguished from the primary form

Someone is the sole present king of France, and X says that he is bald,

since they are, respectively,

Sx(Ez)(K'z.Bz),

and

(Ez)(K'z.SxBz),

if the 'is' in them were replaced by 'is identical with' we would have

Sx(Ez)(z=etK't.Bz)

and

(Ez)(z=etK't.SxBz),

and these two are the same, being both equivalent to

SxBetK't.

A similar point goes with respect to Russell's second puzzle, about negation. For Russell would analyse 'The king of France is bald' as either

(Ex)(K'x.Bx), i.e. (Ex)(x=iyKy.Bx),

or

-(Ex)(K'x.-Bx), i.e. -(Ex)(x=iyKy.-Bx),

with 'The king of France is not bald' being

(Ex)(K'x.-Bx), i.e. (Ex)(x=iyKy.-Bx),

or

-(Ex)(K'x.Bx), i.e. -(Ex)(x=iyKy.Bx),

and thus omitting

BexK'x

and

-BexK'x.

But he would omit these only because he did not properly express 'is identical with the king of France', for, unlike with the iota terms,

(Ex)(x=eyK'y.Bx)

is the same as

-(Ex)(x=eyK'y.-Bx)

both being

BexK'x,

and equally

(Ex)(x=eyK'y.-Bx)

is the same as

$$-(Ex)(x=eyK'y.Bx),$$

both being

$$-BexK'x.$$

This also shows, of course, that there are no scope distinctions with epsilon terms.

The uniqueness of 'K'' in all the above, note, does not mean that only in that case is a referring phrase formulable, so that in other cases there is no distinct third expression, and just two of the primary and secondary forms which Russell gives. For a similar point arises when there is no uniqueness clause in the subject predicate:

$$(Ex)(Kx.Bx)$$

is not the same as

$$BexKx$$

though the latter is the same as

$$(Ex)(x=eyKy.Bx).$$

But Russell's general distinction between quantifiers inside, and quantifiers outside propositional attitude constructions, still remains useful, and following Quine we can again distinguish, for instance, there being a certain sloop that I want to own from my merely wanting to own a sloop, i.e.

$$(Ex)(Sx.WiOix)$$

from

$$Wi(Ex)(Sx.Oix).$$

But we can now go on to identify, and appreciate, not only the sloop we wish was ours, but also what in the world will give us 'relief from slooplessness'. The latter state of beatitude, it is clear, is not a sloop, or indeed any object, but still it derives from the transformation of an object, and is not a pure 'psychic state': for while the former expression is 'Sa.WiOia', where a=ex(Sx.WiOix), which if true guarantees a is already a sloop, the latter expression is 'Wi(Sb.Oib)', where b=ex(Sx.Oix), which if true does not require that b be already a sloop, but equally if true requires that satisfaction comes from, if necessary, making b into a sloop which is mine. If b is already a sloop its transformation comes through gaining possession of it; if b is not a sloop, but, perhaps a pile of lumber or a general mess, its transformation includes, as well, putting some order into it.

However, there are cases where Russell's distinction provides not just two but a lot of distinct expressions, as occurs in the area of Russell's own 'On Denoting' example

I thought your yacht was larger than it is.

For this might be the primary form

(Eh)(Eh')(Hyh.TiHyh'.h'>h)

or the secondary form

(Eh)(Hyh.Ti(Eh')(Hyh'.h'>h)),

but we also have another primary form

(Eh')(TiHyh'.h'>exHyx)

and another secondary form

Ti(Eh')(Hyh'.h'>exHyx).

Moreover, in addition

I thought your yacht is larger than it is

would surely be

Ti(Eh)(Eh')(Hyh.Hyh'.h'>h),

while a further expression Russell mentions is

the size I thought your yacht was is greater   than
the size your yacht is

i.e

exTiHyx > exHyx.

We shall use this latter form of expression, at the
end of this chapter, to resolve some further puzzles
to do with propositional attitudes: I leave it to the
reader,   however,   to   locate which exact   natural
language expressions are formalised by the other
primary and secondary forms catalogued above, for, as
we   have   come to see in this book, and as the above
will amply illustrate, it is not that natural language
expressions   are   systematically   ambiguous   (as   is
suggested by Russell's analysis), but merely that
there is a multiplicity of natural language forms
paralleling the true symbolic ones.

CONTRADICTIONS

As was noted before, there is a direct link between
transparent, de re beliefs, and the possibility of
contradictory   ones.   We have seen this with the
Electra Paradox, and Dennett's discussion of Russell's
Principle, also in connection with Edelberg's puzzle
about Belief. Quine, we saw, tried to use 'logical
acumen'   to   rule   out   transparency,   and   hence
contradiction, at one time; in another place he argues
rather differently. For he allows that his character
Ralph might transparently believe both z(z is a spy)
and z(z is not a spy) of Ortcutt, but exonerates Ralph
from being inconsistent on the fine point that this
does not entail Ralph believes z(z is a spy.z is not a
spy) of Ortcutt. He says [6]:

> Let us sum up our findings concerning the seven
> numbered statements about Ralph.
>   (7) [(Ex)(Ralph believes that x is a spy)]
> is now counted as nonsense,
>   (8) [Ralph believes that (Ex)(x is a spy)]
> as true,
>   (12) [Ralph believes that the man in the brown

hat is a spy]
    (13) [Ralph does not believe that the man seen at the beach is a spy]
as true,
    (14) [Ralph believes that Ortcutt is a spy]
as false, and
    (15) [Ralph believes z(z is a spy) of Ortcutt]
and
    (17) [(Ex)(Ralph believes z(z is a spy) of x)]
as true. Another that is true is:
    (20) Ralph believes that the man seen at the beach is not a spy,
which of course must not be confused with (13).
The kind of exportation which leads from (14) to (15) should doubtless be viewed in general as implicative. Under the terms of our illustrative story, (14) happens to be false; but (20) is true, and it leads by exportation to:
    (21) Ralph believes z(z is not a spy) of the man seen at the beach.
The man at the beach, hence Ortcutt, does not receive reference in (20), because of referential opacity; but he does in (21), so we may conclude from (21) that
    (22) Ralph believes z(z is not a spy) of Ortcutt.
Thus (15) and (22) both count as true. This is not, however, to charge Ralph with contradictory beliefs. Such a charge might reasonably be read into:
    (23) Ralph believes z(z is a spy.z is not a spy) of Ortcutt,
but this merely goes to show that it is undesirable to look upon (15) and (22) as implying (23).

Indeed (15) and (22) do not imply (23), but the unstructured nature of beliefs still should respect the fact that spyhood and non-spyhood are inconsistent, making the former two beliefs already contradictory. Moreover, given that Quine is prepared, in this way, to allow inconsistent beliefs, it is not clear why he does not move straight to a transparent account: there is no advantage in trying to avoid it. On that account (7) makes sense, (8) is unproven, (12) is true, (13) is false, (14) is true, and (15) and (17) (if they mean anything) are equivalent to (14) and (7); also, on this understanding, (20), (21) and (22) are true, while (23) again remains unproven.

There is perhaps one further puzzle with this, besides the question of contradiction: how can Ralph believe Ortcutt is a spy (14), and not believe there are spies (8)? Maybe we cannot rely on people generally to make appropriate inferences, but not being able to deduce there are spies from Ortcutt being a spy might still look a remarkable feat of obtuseness. But it needn't be obtuseness, because what is at stake needn't be someone's slowness at moving to saying 'There are spies' from saying 'Ortcutt is a spy'. Such verbalisations, while sufficient for belief, if sincere, are not necessary for belief, and hence it is some more fundamental behavioural difference which is marked by the two expressions. We see what it is when we realise that belief that there are spies (SexSx) needn't be directed at a known object, and so may become what some might call a nameless dread. Contrariwise, belief that a named person is a spy need not be accompanied by this fear and trembling, in which case we get the behavioural manifestations of the above separation: belief about the known object may or may not lead to a general anxiety and suspicion. Note, of course, that there is one case where belief that there are spies, and belief that Ortcutt is a spy are identical - where, in fact, there is just one spy, Ortcutt, i.e. (y)(Sy CD y=o) - in this case, alone, therefore, there is no reason for any wider uncertainty. There is no difficulty, as a result, with the 'obtuseness' permitted by the present analysis, indeed it illuminates the variety of beliefs, and we can turn to the central question of possible contradictions in such beliefs.

Quine is usually thought to have been against contradictions in beliefs, but, of course, if beliefs are referentially opaque in his supposed way, then it cannot be transparent what Quine's own beliefs are about when he points to the above sentences, especially (15) and (17), and the like. Indeed before the above passage he had almost fallen into contradiction himself, for while he considered that (12) summarized the fact that there was a certain man in a brown hat that Ralph had spotted a number of times, under suspicious circumstances, the comparable fact that there was a grey haired man, seen once at the beach, that Ralph moderately respected as a pillar of the community, Quine summarised as (13). And if these two remarks were indeed what held there would be an even more exacerbated problem with opacity. For if the men are one and the same, then substitution of co-referential descriptive names - or the man's proper name 'Bernard J.Ortcutt' - would induce a contradiction in the reporter's thought, and indeed the laws of logic would rule that pair of propositions out. It is no wonder, if that is the conception, that transparency comes to be thought to be impossible, and that doctrines arise about 'that'-clauses being sealed off from the rest of the sentence so that terms in the part do not properly occur in the whole. It is no wonder, in that case, that it seems improper to 'quantify in', and that belief contexts come to seem quite irredeemably opaque.

But the alternative description of the situation, which merely couples (12) with (20) might seem equally unappealing, and not directly because it leads to contradictory beliefs being attributed now to Ralph. For also at stake, it seems, is the 'disquotational principle' linking direct speech straight to its indirect report: if a normal speaker sincerely assents to 'p' then he believes that p. Clearly it is this principle which is also giving Quine trouble, for he recognises that, if we accept it, and say Ralph believes Bernard to be a spy we shall have to accept conjunctions of the type

w sincerely denies '...'.w believes that...

with the same sentence in both blanks, if we also allow Ralph to say, sincerely, 'Bernard is no spy'. But the disquotational principle merely requires sincere denial of 'p' to entail belief that not-p, so such conjunctions as the above are no more surprising, and no more ruled out, than is sincere assertion and sincere denial of the same thing. A person doing that is maybe confused, maybe illogical, but being

269

illogical is still logically possible. If w sincerely
asserts 'p' then he believes that p, if he sincerely
denies 'p' then he believes that not-p, so, since
sincere assertion and sincere denial are together
possible, so is believing that p and believing that
not-p.

Kripke [7] sees the link between the disquotation
principle and possible contradiction, but uses it to
argue directly against the principle on the ground
that the speaker, in such a situation, need not be
able to deduce that one of his beliefs is in error,
hence there need be no inconsistency in such beliefs:
a speaker, sincerely asserting, for instance, 'Cicero
was bald' and 'Tully was not bald', is not apparently
expressing contradictory beliefs, and hence is not
apparently saying that Cicero was, while Tully was
not, bald. Kripke later argues that a bilingual
person can say 'London is not pretty' and 'Londres est
jolie' without contradicting himself, since he might
think the two names named different things. But
although the actual term relation is a contingent
fact, bilingual use of the two languages embraces it,
just as with 'pretty' and 'jolie', 'bachelor' and
'unmarried man', so Kripke's speaker would not be
bilingual but speaking a 'private language', i.e. just
uttering some sounds. Kripke is also impressed that
even a 'brilliant logician' could not work out such
term identities, but neither could he with the
predicate equivalences, so that only shows that much
of the a priori is not a matter of deduction.
Moreover, Kripke is only too aware that there may be a
posteriori routes to necessary truths, so he has other
starting points from which to realise that brainpower
is not necessary in this area.

Furthermore, as the case drawn from Quine shows,
many of the necessary identities in the a priori are
not to do with proper names, but referential
descriptions. And Kripke has lost all sight of this.
He invented a special class of names which, amongst
other things, would supposedly alone secure
transparency in modal contexts, namely his 'rigid
designators', but much of the thrust of his puzzle
about belief is against the idea that there are any
comparable terms in the general area of propositional

attitudes. At least Kripke realises that names are in the same class as individuating descriptions in this area, even if he denies both their natural mode of operation, for he supposes 'London' to be understood by his 'bilingual' speaker as 'the capital of England' and '<u>Londres</u>' to be understood as 'the capital of <u>Angleterre</u>', but denies that even public use of the identifying descriptions requires Pierre to be contradicting himself: just as Pierre can suppose 'London' and '<u>Londres</u>' do not name the same city, so he can suppose 'England' and '<u>Angleterre</u>' name two different countries, and, in his own eyes, at least, escape inconsistency. But whatever he can do with the names, he cannot consistently suppose of the <u>places</u> that London is not <u>Londres</u>, and that England is not <u>Angleterre</u>: hence if he sincerely says 'the capital of England is not the capital of <u>Angleterre</u>' then he contradicts himself, because of the public meaning such a communication commits him to. So the point against Kripke is not that there is here, with propositional attitudes, as he thinks there is with modality, a special enclave of language which ensures transparency; the point is again that all referential language naturally does this, both here and in modal contexts, without any needed discrimination between names and identifying descriptions.

Kripke's argument against the disquotational principle is therefore an argument about meaning not being a matter of public use. Like a miser, he does not realise that the value of his coins lies entirely in their public purchasing power. It is symptomatic of this that Kripke only rarely takes his troublesome words out of quotes, i.e. stops just mentioning them; but the inhibition, he does not realise, would, if seriously pursued, prevent him from ever specifying what the content of any associated beliefs must be. Thus it is not really possible to say, on Kripke's view, that because a speaker can give sincere assent both to 'Cicero was bald', and 'Tully was not bald', the disquotational principle requires that he believes that Cicero was bald and believes that Tully was not bald, for in the latter part of this we are using 'Cicero' and 'Tully', and so, on Kripke's view, these words would have to refer to whom <u>we</u> meant, not, except by chance, to whom the speaker meant. Nor could Kripke's point be better put by saying, linguistically, that, in accordance with the disquotation principle 'He sincerely says ''Cicero was bald'' entails 'He believes that Cicero was bald', for even then, in order to apply the principle, we would have to use the names, and not just quote them. But having actually used 'Cicero' and 'Tully', remarkably Kripke himself recognises the import of this, since he sees that a direct consequence of the substitutivity principle is that the speaker does have contradictory beliefs, i.e. that what he (Kripke) said when he said that the speaker might believe Cicero was bald and believe Tully was not bald, involves transparent uses of 'Cicero' and 'Tully'. Kripke therefore presumes in his argument what he takes it to disprove, for if saying 'he believes Cicero was bald and believes Tully was not bald' was not attributing contradictory beliefs to the speaker, Kripke would have no argument.

Clearly, as well, it is not the 'brilliant logician' in Kripke which is informing him of this contradiction, but instead the student of Roman history and literature, so it is some lack of self-knowledge, besides a logical confusion, which is hiding from Kripke the relevant facts. That is not to say the question of 'logical acumen' is irrelevant to the discussion, since questions to do with that arose with Quine, as we saw before, and so it is important to see logic's general lack of place in the scheme of these things. Hintikka, for instance, was also concerned with mathematical competence [8]. At one time he held on to a total 'deductive omniscience' in Belief and Knowledge contexts, but more recently he has come to accept that beliefs may be inconsistent – though still only in some cases. He says

> The problem, to give it a label, is <u>the problem of logical omniscience</u>. It seems that the possible-world analysis of knowledge forces us to say that everybody always knows all the logical consequences of what he or she knows and likewise for other propositional attitudes. In other words, the following rule of inference seems inescapable.
> (I) p D q / K_ap D K_aq.
> In other words, whenever the implication (p D q)

272

is logically true, i.e., whenever p logically implies q, whoever knows that p must also know that q. And analogous problems arise for other similar concepts. For instance, the analogous rule of inference for belief seems equally unavoidable. It is the following.

(II) p D q / B_ap D B_aq.

How precisely the problem of logical omniscience comes about will be examined shortly. Meanwhile, it may be appropriate to register our dismay at these apparent consequences of the possible-worlds analysis of propositional attitudes. They are not only bad; they seem to be little short of a complete disaster. For surely, you feel like saying, we all know and believe any number of things whose consequences we have no idea of, Euclid did not know everything that is to be known about elementary geometry, nor did Maxwell know everything there is to be known about electromagnetism. The idealisation involved in the possible-worlds approach to knowledge does not seem excessive. It seems to turn the whole theory into nonsense.

The situation can be corrected, however. In a number of papers...I have in effect shown how to restrict the rules (I)-(II) in an interesting way. The main idea underlying these restrictions is that (I)-(II) are valid only when q can be deduced from p without considering more individuals than are considered in either of them.

Hintikka's separation of the cases rests on whether there is a 'trivial' method of knowing there is an inconsistency; but he therefore presumes remarkable mathematical competence on the part of all believers. For the conclusion cannot be that, if trivial methods for settling whether there is an inconsistency are available, for sure no one will be inconsistent – since a further premise is clearly required to ensure this, namely that believers will apply even those methods correctly. Hence there is really no barrier to realising that deductive omniscience, like mathematical competence, may never be presumed.

In a way, Hintikka always allowed this. For the central feature of Hintikka's original analysis was, of course, the presumed link between propositional attitudes and possible-world semantics. Hintikka formulated the link as

a believes that p =
in all the possible worlds compatible with what a believes, it is the case that p,

i.e. $B_a p$ is true in w iff p is true in every member of $F_B(a,w)$, where w is a certain possible world and $F_B(a,w)$ a set of possible worlds 'alternative' to w. Now this analysis does not in fact rule out the possibility of inconsistent beliefs, since it could be that the set of possible worlds compatible with what a believes is the null set, and so the analysis only requires that if a has contradictory beliefs then he believes anything, since, a fortiori, in every member of a null set of worlds any proposition at all is true. In other words, on Hintikka's original account, a has consistent beliefs only if there are some things he fails to believe, for only then will there be possible worlds compatible with the denial of what he does not believe. This means, certainly, that, whether their beliefs were consistent or not, Hintikka's original believers invariably felt logic as a psychological force: if they had inconsistent beliefs they believed everything, just as an inconsistency entails everything, and if they had consistent beliefs they believed their logical consequences, since these would be automatically drawn in the possible worlds compatible with any initial set of beliefs. But how anybody could be expected to be logical, if they were allowed to be inconsistent, is a mystery. It is a virtue in Hintikka's original account that inconsistent beliefs were allowed, but the natural corollary of this is not that an individual with such beliefs be expected to think clearly: quite the reverse.

How different is the later picture Hintikka draws of the hopeful though confused legatee. This far from mathematically ideal, but no doubt joyous, and so perfect human being asserts that his father was an only child, and also that he has first cousins on his father's side. Moreover he expectantly waits to inherit from both of these supposed relatives. There is no conclusion drawn, however, that this person is a credulous imbecile, accepting every suggestion which is put to him; and no mechanism is sketched of how his brain might get to this conclusion having, in a Kripkean feat of self-self-analysis, realised it was in a confused state, and was basing its views on premises which entailed everything. The range and impact of the confusion are limited as are presumably the consequences which are drawn from any consistent assumptions held. As Hintikka realised, the way to solve the 'problem' of logical omniscience is to admit what he calls 'impossible possible worlds', i.e. worlds which look possible and so are epistemic alternatives, but which are not logically possible. But then the metaphor of 'world' itself starts to look out of place, and what we have instead is simply a series of propositions of the form 'a believes that p', which are ordered or jumbled, as the case may be.

As was mentioned before, in chapter five, section three, the link between freedom and such a jumble was realised by Kant [9].

For the feeling of the sublime involves as its characteristic feature a mental _movement_ combined with the estimate of the object, whereas taste in respect of the beautiful presupposes that the mind is in _restful_ contemplation, and preserves it in this state.

In his third and last critique, Kant describes Sublimity as a mere feeling, which, unlike Beauty, is not an inherent quality of objects but merely a subjective experience deriving from the belief that one is superior to nature. As Kant himself makes explicit, Sublimity thereby links with matters in his second critique, such as Will, Practical Reason, and our Moral Life, rather than (like Beauty) matters in his first critique, such as Understanding, Pure Reason, and Science. Sublimity is, as a result, an unpleasant, tasteless feeling of incomprehension, indeed incoherence, but its positive, and indeed glorious, aspect is a sense of great power, whether with respect to the infinite in Mathematics, or Dynamic Might in Nature. Sartre's words, in place of the presently out of vogue 'sublimity', are 'anguish', and of course 'nausea': the feeling of absurdity and sickness induced by indecision would be a more commonplace description. Sartre says about the anguish of freedom [10]:

> At the very moment when I apprehend my being as horror of the precipice, I am conscious of that horror as not determinant in relation to my possible conduct. In one sense that horror calls for prudent conduct, and is itself a pre-outline of that conduct; in another sense, it posits the final developments of that conduct only as possible, precisely because I do not apprehend it as the cause of these final developments but as need, appeal, etc.

Sartre's two 'senses' here show that he is undecided, i.e. in two minds about whether he will restrain himself or jump. But since he feels horrified, though also not horrified by the precipice - 'fearful but not afraid of an object' according to Kant - the primary form of the experience would seem to be a kind of drunkenness, since it is normally only in such an unstable frame of mind that one can, in parallel with the more readily turned duck-rabbit perceptions, switch such deep feelings off and on, at will. This fluid attitude towards the world naturally gives the participant a remarkable sense of subjective freedom, and great power; but being drunk with power also makes his conduct objectively unpredictable. Kant's mathematical example directly concerns the plain feeling of largeness which can accompany such a feeling of power: we can, and not just at the perceptual level, alter our conception of the size of something, through choice of the unit with which to measure it. Kant, in this way. did not think of the infinite as 'transfinite', i.e. greater than any finite number in a fixed sense, but merely as indefinite, and so capable of being greater than any natural number which is given.

The point is not just important at the level of personal freedom, since, clearly, as Kant realised, the form of social organisation and state which can accommodate such inhuman truths also matters, or, rather, the form of social theory and philosophy which can accept such inhuman truths is affected. For the proper consequence of men being free is, of course, that things in the world will go on being pretty much as they are, but what might change is intellectual comprehension of the rational basis for the study of human behaviour, given this necessarily includes irrationality. Thus in many areas it is already realised, for instance, that the greater majority of people will do average things, and only a minority will be eccentric, since that is what Probability Theory, on the basis of the Laws of Chance, predicts with respect to people's heights, life span, intelligence, etc. But since an individual person's free behaviour is equally a matter of norms and deviances those likelihoods and risks are alone what Moral and Political Theory should establish with respect to our murderous instincts, cruelty, etc. as well as our benevolence, justice, etc. As Sociobiology requires, theory in this area should assess actions for their natural probability, i.e. the measured extent to which they can be expected to arise, and that should be the end of the enterprise.

Such an Obligation Theory, moreover, is not merely programmatic speculation on my part, since the logic of it has already been set out by George Schlesinger [11], and shown to resolve many classic paradoxes in the deontic area. In connection with experienced contradictions I have just one comment to add to it, reiterating and amplifying some of Sartre's views about Moral Dilemmas. For Schlesinger still looks at these as though they took place on a stage in a theatre; he says

> There is no disputing the poignancy of moral dilemmas. Many of the greatest works of literature would not exist without them and there is hardly anything more riveting than the spectacle of a man being torn by conflicting obligations as for instance the demands of the state or of his religion on the one hand and his commitments to his beloved ones or personal ideals on the other. But my admission of the centrality of moral conflicts in the drama of human life does not refute a single word of what I have just said. It is still true that when of two moral

277

obligations one is known to outweigh the other
there is no room even for a moment's hesitation as
it is clear which overrides the other, and when
they are balanced it is unambiguously decided that
neither applies.

But conflicting obligations aren't alternative visual
aspects. Moreover they aren't 'obligations' if
'neither applies'. Something is <u>prima facie</u>
obligatory if its probability is, at least, greater
than a half, and while that allows one can have two
non-obligatory options for action equally balanced in
the sense of each being as likely as not, that case is
purely aesthetic, and can be settled without stress,
perhaps even by tossing a coin. In a proper <u>Moral
Dilemma</u> we have two options equally balanced not so
that each action is as likely as not, but rather so
that each action, each more probable than not, is as
likely as the other. Sartre sketched a famous case of
this kind: a boy had to choose between maintaining his
filial piety, or his patriotic vengeance, and no
system of Ethics, or impartial teacher, could help him
decide. Sartre's advice was 'You are free, therefore
choose, that is to say invent', but that was not
relieving him of a burden, quite the reverse: it was
putting the responsibility on the agent, and thereby
the anguish of the decision. So there is no
requirement that such a choice, even though free, be
inconsequential. There is, however, a requirement
that the possibility of such decisions being
consequential be consequential for Moral Theory, since
such cases are crucial ones, for instance with regard
to Kant's view that, in an ideal world, i.e. 'The
Kingdom of Ends', all obligations would be met. For
if Moral Dilemmas are between competing <u>obligations</u>
then that shows that in no world can all our duties be
done. But, as Kant seems to have realised later in
life, if it wasn't for such tragedies there wouldn't
be forced to be freedom in the world, i.e. in this
world, the already ideal one. So we should learn to
participate in the drunken drama and play-acting which
come with this admission.

There remain some thinkers still trying to construe 'a believes that p' in terms of a relation between a person and some thing: in Davidson's case we get a Realist analysis in terms of extensional things, in Cresswell's case we get an Idealist analysis in terms of intensional entities. Prior's theory can be seen as an improvement on both, indeed Prior himself was aware of these two types of theory when he developed his third, and so a lot of his remarks only need re-reading, in this connection, since they are directly pointed at those other theories. However, now that the meaning of these remarks has been unfolded, it is to be hoped that they will be better understood. Indeed it is not clear, once that has been done, what else needs to be done, except to summarise the matter. Thus Prior was saying back in 1963 [12]:

> The reductionist theory is that the <u>oratio obliqua</u> form is at least indirectly about a form of words, e.g. our
> (2) [James says that man is mortal]
> may be said to mean that James either stands to the form of words 'Man is mortal' in the relation expressed by our
> (1) [James says 'Man is mortal'],
> or stands in that relation to some other form of words which is synonymous with it. The theory which does not reduce but assimilates (2) to (1), is to the effect that (2) expresses a relation, not between James and a form of words, but between James and a more obscure object called a 'proposition', this object being named by the clause introduced by the word 'that'.

One feature of all three types of theory, which we may thus use to distinguish them is their varying understanding of the word 'that': as is evident from Prior, the Realist theory takes it to be a demonstrative either to the exact words which follow or to some other words synonymous with them, the Idealist theory takes it to form a proper name for a new object when united with the clause which follows. Prior's 'Activist' theory maintains that 'that' goes with the preceding verb so 'James says that man is

279

mortal' is to be parsed 'James says that/man is mortal', not 'James says/that man is mortal'.

Davidson himself quotes the Oxford English Dictionary in support of his 'paratactic' theory, for it is there remarked that 'that' arose out of a demonstrative pronoun pointing to the clause it introduces. But if so then it should be replaceable by that clause, without loss of sense, just as 'He is coming' can be replaced by 'John is coming', when the proform 'he' stands for John. Unfortunately for the simplest Realist theory, therefore, as we saw before, 'Bill believed 'Derek was out of the cabinet'' does not make any sense, so 'that' cannot be a demonstrative to a sentence. A similar point is final with regard to the simplest Idealist theory, for if the 'that' in 'that Derek was out of the cabinet' produced a nominalisation of the following sentence, then it would have to be replaceable by 'Derek's being out of the cabinet', while again 'Bill believed Derek's being out of the cabinet' does not make sense. Both objections together show that 'Bill believed p' is not a simple relational expression linking the name 'Bill' with the name or description of some other thing. Moreover, again, the fact that that form is possible strengthens Prior's case considerably, for if 'that' in 'Bill believed that p' is removable simpliciter, then it cannot go with or be related to the following sentence. The proper understanding of 'that', as a result, is it is not a demonstrative to, but a proform for, a sentence, for one can indeed replace

Bill believed Derek was out of the cabinet,

with, for instance,

Bill believed the following: Derek was out of the cabinet,

but the fact that no quotation is involved in either form means that 'the following' does not refer to the following sentence, but merely stands in place of it. It is only because of this that there can be no trouble with The Liar, for if 'this' in 'This is not true' were a proform for the proposition made by the whole sentence, it would have to be an abbreviation for the sentence, not a name for it, and an abbreviation cannot include an abbreviation of itself. Moreover, it is only with proforms for referring phrases that proforms are themselves referential, since, for example, with the predicate proform 'one' in

Jack wanted a donkey, and Jill wanted one too,

replacement gives merely

Jack and Jill each wanted a donkey,

and not, say,

Jack and Jill each wanted the same donkey.

Hence, as Prior said, we must distinguish two senses of 'stand for': it can loosely be used in place of 'refers to', in which case it couples referring phrases with their referents, and proforms for such phrases with their referents; but it is properly used just to couple proforms of different kinds with their appropriate forms, whether those forms are referring phrases, predicative phrases, or whole sentences. The distinction allows there to be both objectual and substitutional quantification with referring phrases, while substitutional quantification alone, for the other two parts of speech.

Of course Davidson does not support the crude Realist theory which simply identifies the following sentence as the object of the supposed attitude relation. Nevertheless his more sophisticated theory has little essential novelty. As Thomas Baldwin says [13]:

> Davidson's original logical form proposal...amounts to the thesis that the following sentences make logically equivalent claims:
> (8) Galileo said the the earth moves.
> (9) An utterance of Galileo's was the same in content as this. The earth moves
> The objections to this thesis are familiar. (i)

The claim made by the use of (8) does not entail that there are any utterances other than Galileo's original one; the claim made by the use of (9) does entail this. (ii) The content of Galileo's statement is rigidly specified in (8), but non-rigidly specified in (9). That is, if what Galileo said was that the earth moves, then by his statement he could not but have said that the earth moves; whereas even if an utterance of Galileo's was the same in content as this utterance - The earth moves - his utterance might not have been the same in content as it (for the content of that utterance might not have been what it is). (iii) Translation of (8) requires translation of the content sentence, whereas in (9), if one translates the second sentence, one changes the referent of the demonstrative, thereby altering the claim made and not merely translating the sentence.
Though familiarity breeds contempt, these objections remain as substantive as ever. They are, of course, much the same as the objections that have often been raised against quotational theories of indirect speech.

Davidson's analysis certainly is novel to the extent that it brings in notions like 'what a sentence means' and 'samesaying', but these ideas are left unanalysed, even in his complete account. Yet how can one ignore the difficulties this lack of analysis creates? For when Davidson parses 'Galileo said that the earth moves' as 'Galileo uttered a sentence that meant in his mouth what 'the earth moves' means now in mine' the first thing he has to avoid, as a consequence, is the suggestion that 'what 'the earth moves' means' is a singular term, also the suggestion that his primitive concept of 'samesaying' is complex. Hence the analysis begs as many questions as it settles. On the other hand, where is the trouble with these things, when they are approached in the right way? For 'what 'the earth moves' means' is indeed not a singular term, and one only needs Prior's substitutional theory of propositional quantification, as before, to properly explain this, moreover samesaying then straightaway gets its required analysis, and we also get, as a bonus, provision for ambiguity and senselessness, which Davidson didn't even contemplate arising. Furthermore, the Priorian approach also relieves Davidson of another immediate difficulty with his analysis: what to do with attitudes which are not connected with explicit speech, for with the meaning-giving form 'Msp' accepted as unanalysable, it comes to be seen that the parallel belief form 'Bap' is equally unanalysable, and involves no mention, only the use of 'p'.

Davidson's whole approach, it is now evident, suffers at the heart from a restricted diet of examples. There is no attempt to explain the meaning-giving form 's means that p' on the same principles as the paratactic analysis, making reference to the O.E.D. of puzzling worth. And if this meaning-giving form were analysed as the indirect speech form it so evidently is, rather than in terms of the T-scheme, then the absurdity of the 'paratactic' analysis would become only too clear: 's means what 'p' means' is not the content of the meaning giving form, since again, that uses 'p', and hence gives it its meaning. Davidson's main example of indirect speech is, as above, a 'saying' example, which verb clearly has a double use, as with the Prior examples given before. But even if we were confused by their similarity, 'James says 'Man is mortal'' and 'James says that man is mortal' would not be the crucial pair which had to be distinguished to get hold of what is going on in indirect speech rather than direct speech. 'Man is mortal' and 'James says that man is mortal' would be a more crucial pair to be distinguished first.

Reported speech certainly often involves a relation to some words uttered by the person spoken about, but while it is not direct quotation, it is too near to it to be a clear paradigm of indirect locutions, since no other indirect speech locution is a report on any sort of speech - indeed, only because of this may the other locutions be used to attribute attitudes to dumb animals. Thus it is not the case, for instance, that belief-reports are reports on spectral 'thoughts' taking place in some non-vocal 'language of thought', which even cats and dogs can master. Maybe they are expectations about what such creatures would say if they could speak, or if they can speak, what they

would say if they were sincere, or, at least, solemn
and sincere, but that does not (generally) reflect on
anything going on now in their vocal cords, or
linguistic control centres - or any other centre - in
their brains. Where a river would probably flow if
there were a flood does not relate to some invisible
wetness presently outside its banks, nor to the
visible wetness presently inside its banks, but to the
river's present relation both to the inside and the
outside of its banks. Likewise what someone would
probably say does not relate to anything he, visibly
or invisibly, is saying, so belief reports are based
on nothing a physiologist or psychologist might in the
future reveal about the creature's brain or speech
apparatus; any speech apparatus merely allows the
true, or false, expression of a belief which is about
the relation the believer has to his inside and the
outside world, most of the evidence for which is hence
available readily, and all of it available publicly,
and independently of what the believer says, if he
says anything.

Cresswell, again, does not go for the crude Idealist
theory which simply has the subordinate clause in
indirect speech referring to an unstructured
intensional entity. Thinking, no doubt, like the
early Wittgenstein, of a <u>tableau vivant</u>, Cresswell
believes meanings are structured, indeed in an almost
grammatical way. Cresswell has in his favour that he
recognises the ambiguity of 'say' and for his main
example focusses on 'believe', but still his meanings
are structured like sentences, making the 'say'
paradigm still clearly dominant in his thought. Thus
his intention is to construct a language of meanings
and hence a kind of second language - which in its
actual finished form could indeed be a language of
very abstract thought. But that language itself could
not be the meaning of ordinary thought, and not just
because of its abstraction. It itself would need to
be used to embody any sense. It seems, generally, to
Idealist theorists that there must be some other world
besides the commonplace one: in the linguistic meaning
area this would be demonstrated on the one hand by
disinterest in the simple Priorian idea that the
meaning of 'p' can be given completely by dropping the
quotes around it, and on the other hand by an

attraction to the construction of some symbol scheme so remote it could hardly be used, only looked at. But as Evans and McDowell said in 1976 [14]:

> It is difficult to emphasise sufficiently the importance of the shift in theoretical perspective which takes place when we see, even as generally as this, the way to state a theory of meaning. We are entirely freed from the idea that there is something ineffable in the native speaker's mastery, or something which we can capture only by getting outside the circle of words and pointing at things. And we are entirely freed from the idea that our semantics must be trivial unless we effect conceptual breakdown and construct a special characteristica universalis in which to state the meanings of words. For we can see how the meanings of expressions in, say, English can be given, if we like, even by themselves without the result being trivial. There is nothing trivial stated by
> (7) Something satisfies 'bald' if and only if it is bald.
> That proposition states an eminently learnable and forgettable relation between an English word and a set of men.

Cresswell [15], although he studied under Prior to try to solve the problem of propositional attitudes, does not consider him in his synoptic article 'The Autonomy of Semantics', and the few mentions of Prior in Structured Meanings do not go into Prior's theory at all deeply, so he measures up to the above Linguistic Idealist, on both the given counts.

Admittedly studying Prior himself is not enough, for Prior does not articulate his theory so far even as to provide the propositional descriptions which were introduced before to formalise 'what 'the earth moves' means'. But Williams considers them at length, even if he tries to formulate them in Russellian iota terms. Cresswell needs such propositional descriptions, since one of his arguments, directly against Prior, is that Prior could not account for expressions like 'what Rob told Bill' in 'Bill believed what Rob told him' - Prior's explicit theory being restricted to complements like 'that p' for 'believes'. Thus Cresswell thinks Prior must have some difficulty with

> Rob told Bill on Monday that Derek was out of the Cabinet
> Bill believed what Rob told him, so
> Bill believed that Derek was out of the Cabinet.

But this is simply

> Trbq
> BbepTrbp, so
> Bbq,

which only needs a uniqueness clause to be added, e.g.

> $(p)(Trbp \supset p=q)$

to be valid. For from the first premise we can get

> $(Ep)Trbp$

and hence

> TrbepTrbp

making

> epTrbp=q,

by the uniqueness clause, and giving the conclusion by substitution in the second premise.

But it is the general provision of epsilon terms which corrects Cresswell's major argument for his approach, and perhaps clarifies the major argument for opacity in indirect speech contexts. For it certainly may seem that someone who believes that 5+7=12 does not thereby believe simply that 12=12, and so it may seem that 5+7=12, which is logically identical with 12=12, cannot be what is believed. Cresswell says

> On the propositional account
> (5) [Veronica believes that 5+7=12]
> is true iff Veronica stands in the appropriate

relation (the believing relation) to the proposition that 5+7=12. Since 5+7 is the same number as 12 then the proposition that 5+7=12 is the same as the proposition that 12=12. so Veronica, on this account, believes that 5+7=12 iff she believes that 12=12.

Indeed the difficulty for what Cresswell here calls the 'propositional' account of propositional attitudes is even more acute, since all necessarily true statements are logically identical, making belief that 5+7=12 indistinguishable from belief, say, that 5+8=13. Cresswell's attempt to escape from the difficulty he calls his 'de re' account, since he wants to say that (5) is true not because Veronica stands in a certain relation to a proposition, but because she stands in another relation to a more numerous set of objects - the meanings of '5','+','7','=', and '12'. Remarkably, at this point, Cresswell simply uses these signs instead of exhibiting his symbolism for their structured meaning, viz.

<<5,7,+>,12,=>,

for he says

On the de re account (5) is true, when it is true, not because Veronica stands in a certain relation to a proposition but rather because Veronica stands in a slightly more complicated relation to a more complicated group of entities. Specifically, she stands in the relation to the (ordered) pair 5 and 7 of believing them to sum to 12. In this solution there is no proposition that 5+7=12; thus, the question whether it is the same proposition as the proposition that 12=12 just does not arise. Obviously, the belief about 5 and 7 that they sum to 12 is different from the belief about 12 that it is identical to 12. Moreover, there is no suggestion that the meaning of '5','7', and '5+7' need be anything other than what the statements of ordinary arithmetic require.

So Veronica is here said to 'stand in the relation to

287

the (ordered) pair 5 and 7 of believing them to sum to
12'. And that nicely isolates a distinct form of
speech. But if this is what needs to be expressed,
how is it to be expressed in the Priorian symbolism,
if in opposition to Cresswell we want to say (5) is
indeed equivalent to

Veronica believes that 12=12?

It is here we must make clear the distinction
between Veronica believing that 5+7=12, (which is
indeed the same as her believing that 12=12, and that
5+8=13), and a quite different thing (which is not
even an event) namely what Veronica believes 5+7 to be
being 12. The expression for the former occurrence is
'Bv(5+7=12)', the expression for the latter identity
is 'exBv(5+7=x)=12', and one difference between the
two is that the former does not rule out 'Bv(5+7=13)',
say, while the latter does rule out 'exBv(5+7=x)=13'.
The former, indeed, entails

(Ex)Bv(5+7=x),

and, with 12=12,

(Ex)(Bv(5+7=x).x=12),

and so, by Hilbert's axiom, it entails

Bv(5+7=exBv(5+7=x)),

and

Bv(5+7=ex(Bv(5+7=x).x=12)).ex(Bv(5+7=x).x=12)=12.

But there is no way to extract from these

exBv(5+7=x)=12,

since there is no telling whether

exBv(5+7=x)=ex(Bv(5+7=x).x=12),

without an additional uniqueness assumption, say that
there is only one thing that Veronica believes 5 plus
7 to be, i.e.

$$(Ex)(y)(Bv(5+7=y) \supset y=x).$$

Hence the crucial thing which the propositional form 'Bv(5+7=12)' hasn't got, which makes it, though a belief, not a '<u>de re</u>' belief, is a means of indicating, for instance, that it is just 12, and not some other number confusedly as well, that Veronica believes 5 plus 7 to be. The <u>de re</u> form 'exBv(5+7=x)=12', which is, again, not a <u>de re</u> belief, though now simply because it is not a belief, is precise in this regard, as well as bringing in an epsilon term for 'what Veronica believes 5 plus 7 to be'. Now this form is certainly the same as 'exBv(12=x)=12', by substitution of identicals in the epsilon term, but the epsilon term in both has a choice of referents, unless the whole is asserted truly, and so the expression allows in a certain kind of opacity. A more general expression, different again from either of the two above, would be

$$exBv(5=x)+exBv(7=x)=12,$$

i.e. 'the sum of what Veronica believes 5 and 7 to be is 12', and, without some further uniqueness assumption, say

$$(Ex)(y)(Bv(5=y) \supset y=x)$$

the precise reference of each epsilon term would be still left open, i.e. be opaque, even upon true assertion, in this case.

Hence we must widen our means of expression if we want to get hold of referentially opaque beliefs: 'BrSo', is not opaque, but 'BrSexBr(o=x)' potentially is, even though a term, and not an attributive phrase is used. But that does not mean we must widen our means of expression to encompass a '<u>characteristica universalis</u>' of the kind that Cresswell constructs: the required expressions and distinctions, as we have seen, are available in ordinary language - so long as we use it.

Wittgenstein said in <u>Remarks on the Foundations of Mathematics</u> [16], way back in 1956 that (I111) mathematical propositions had a function in which believing does not occur, since they were like rules, and one does not believe, for instance, a rule of chess, but merely that a rule of chess runs in a certain way. This was a point both Prior and Stalnaker have made with regard to necessary truths. Wittgenstein also said (I107) that, with internal relations, one can't believe, for instance, that 13x13 yields 196, because it isn't a multiplication of 13 by 13, or it is not a case of something yielded, if 196 comes at the end. This relates to the point just made about a non-linguistic content for mathematical 'beliefs'. But many of Wittgenstein's remarks are about a more general philosophical point: the difficulty Empiricism has with ideals. Wittgenstein says (I107) that we are not willing to use the word 'believe' for the case of a <u>calculation and its result</u>, - or, at least, we are not willing except in the case of a correct calculation. He thereby (I109) draws a line between calculations and experiments, and links the former with a kind of action: accepting a rule. Seeing that 13x13=169, is not believing this, it is - more or less blindly - using a picture, i.e. taking something as a model or paradigm.

NOTES

[1] D.Kaplan's views on vivid names are in 'Quantifying In', see, <u>Words and Objections</u> eds D.Davidson and J.Hintikka, Reidel, Dordrecht, 1969; the given quote being from p229, Copyright c by D.Reidel Publishing Company, Dordrecht, Holland, 1969.

[2] The portions of Prior here discussed are in <u>Objects of Thought</u>, Clarendon Press, Oxford, 1971, Pt.II, Chs 8 and 9, and the appendix, see pp135,134,156-7 respectively for the quotes, © Oxford University Press 1971. Reprinted from <u>Objects of Thought</u> by A.N.Prior, edited by P.T.Geach and A.J.P.Kenny (1971) by permission of Oxford University Press. See also pp136, 125-7 for the later material, and Prior's <u>Past, Present and Future</u> Clarendon Press, Oxford, 1967, p145 for the quote at the end of this section about the Barcan formula.

[3] As translated by M.Black, in <u>Philosophical</u>

Review, 1948, see pp 211,218, and 210 for the relevant details of Frege's views on opacity.

[4] M.Dummett *Frege: Philosophy of Language*, Duckworth, London, 1974, p266.

[5] See *Mind*, XIV, 1905, p484-5 for the following two quotes, and the subsequent puzzles. For Quine's development of the primary/secondary distinction see 'Quantifiers and Propositional Attitudes' *Journal of Philosophy*, LIII, 1956.

[6] For Quine's summary of his views see previous note, p181.

[7] For Kripke's views see 'A Puzzle about Belief' in *Meaning and Use* ed. A.Margalit, Reidel, Dordrecht, 1979, especially pp251,261; see also, for instance, K.Green's 'Is a Logic for Belief Sentences Possible?' *Philosophical Studies* 47, 1985.

[8] For Hintikka's original views see 'Semantics for Propositional Attitudes' in *Philosophical Logic* ed. J.W.Davis et al, Reidel, Dordrecht, 1969. For the following quote, see pp368-9 of 'Impossible Possible Worlds Vindicated' in E.Saarinen ed. *Game Theoretical Semantics*, Reidel, Dordrecht, 1978, Copyright © by D.Reidel Publishing Company, Dordrecht, Holland, 1979. For the 'hopeful legatee', see Hintikka's 'Knowledge, Belief and Logical Consequence' in *The Intentions of Intentionality and Other New Models for Modalities*, Reidel, Dordrecht, 1975.

[9] Kant's third critique, *The Critique of Judgement*, translated by J.C.Meredith was published by the Clarendon Press at Oxford in 1978, see p94 for the quote; see the Introduction for the links with Kant's general philosophy.

[10] J.P.Sartre's *Being and Nothingness*, Methuen, London, 1969, discusses the anguish of freedom on p31.

[11] George Schlesinger's 'The Central Principle of Deontic Logic' is in *Philosophy and Phenomenological Research* XLV, 1985, see for the following quote p522; see also my 'Contradiction and Freedom' in *Philosophy* 1988.

[12] Prior discusses alternatives to his account in 'Oratio Obliqua'; for the given quote, see p115 of the *Proceedings of the Aristotelian Society*, Supplementary Volume, 1963.

[13] For Davidson's views see the references given in Ch2, note 11; T.Baldwin's 'Prior and Davidson on Indirect Speech' is in <u>Philosophical Studies</u> 1982; see p273 for the following quote, copyright © (1982) D.Reidel Publishing Company, reprinted by permission.

[14] G.Evans and J.McDowell discuss meaning on px of their editorial introduction to <u>Truth and Meaning</u>, Oxford U.P., 1976.

[15] For M.J.Cresswell's work see 'The Autonomy of Semantics' in <u>Processes, Beliefs and Questions</u> eds S.Peters and E.Saarinen, Reidel, Dordrecht, 1982, also his <u>Structured Meanings</u>, M.I.T.Press, Cambridge Mass., 1980, see especially p147 on propositional descriptions, and p19 for the following two quotes. See also my 'Prior and Cresswell on Indirect Speech' <u>Australasian Journal of Philosophy</u> 1989.

[16] Blackwell, Oxford, 1956.